A FUNCTIONAL ART

A Functional Art
Reflections of a Hymn Writer

TIMOTHY DUDLEY-SMITH

> In Harvard, where he had once been an undergraduate and where the shades of the Eliots were heavy around him, he confessed that poets would like to possess some kind of 'social utility'...
>
> *Peter Ackroyd on T. S. Eliot, 1984*

OXFORD
UNIVERSITY PRESS

Great Clarendon Street, Oxford, OX2 6DP,
United Kingdom

Oxford University Press is a department of the University of Oxford.
It furthers the University's objective of excellence in research, scholarship,
and education by publishing worldwide. Oxford is a registered trade mark of
Oxford University Press in the UK and in certain other countries

© Oxford University Press 2017

The moral rights of the author have been asserted

First Edition published in 2017

Impression: 1

All rights reserved. No part of this publication may be reproduced, stored in
a retrieval system, or transmitted, in any form or by any means, without the
prior permission in writing of Oxford University Press, or as expressly permitted
by law, by licence or under terms agreed with the appropriate reprographics
rights organization. Enquiries concerning reproduction outside the scope of the
above should be sent to the Rights Department, Oxford University Press, at the
address above

You must not circulate this work in any other form
and you must impose this same condition on any acquirer

Published in the United States of America by Oxford University Press
198 Madison Avenue, New York, NY 10016, United States of America

British Library Cataloguing in Publication Data
Data available

Library of Congress Control Number: 2016961443

ISBN 978–0–19–340871–5

Printed in Great Britain by
Clays Ltd, St Ives plc

Links to third party websites are provided by Oxford in good faith and
for information only. Oxford disclaims any responsibility for the materials
contained in any third party website referenced in this work.

LORD, FOR THE YEARS

LORD, FOR THE YEARS your love has kept and guided,
 urged and inspired us, cheered us on our way,
sought us and saved us, pardoned and provided,
 Lord of the years, we bring our thanks today.

Lord, for that word, the word of life which fires us,
 speaks to our hearts and sets our souls ablaze,
teaches and trains, rebukes us and inspires us,
 Lord of the word, receive your people's praise.

Lord, for our land, in this our generation,
 spirits oppressed by pleasure, wealth and care;
for young and old, for commonwealth and nation,
 Lord of our land, be pleased to hear our prayer.

Lord, for our world; when we disown and doubt him,
 loveless in strength, and comfortless in pain;
hungry and helpless, lost indeed without him,
 Lord of the world, we pray that Christ may reign.

Lord, for ourselves; in living power remake us,
 self on the cross and Christ upon the throne;
past put behind us, for the future take us,
 Lord of our lives, to live for Christ alone.

© Timothy Dudley-Smith in Europe and Africa. © Hope Publishing Company in the United States of America and the rest of the world. Reproduced by permission of Oxford University Press. All rights reserved.

*Collections of hymns
by the same author*

*

Lift Every Heart
collected edition, 1961–83

Songs of Deliverance
A Voice of Singing
Great is the Glory

A House of Praise
collected edition, 1961–2001

A Door for the Word
Praise to the Name
Beyond our Dreaming

A House of Praise, part two
collected edition, 2002–2013

*

with music

A Song was Heard at Christmas
Beneath a Travelling Star
A Calendar of Praise
High Days and Holy Days
The Voice of Faith
Above Every Name
Draw Near to God
A Mirror to the Soul

*To all my friends in the Hymn Society of Great Britain and Ireland
and the Hymn Society in the United States and Canada*

CONTENTS

List of hymn texts   xi
Introduction: Something of Myself   xiii

1. Why Hymns?   1
2. Why New Hymns?   10
3. What Sort of Hymns?   24
4. Good and Not So Good   37
5. Words and Music   55
6. Content and Form   69
7. Meaning and Language   85
8. Rhyme and Metre   107
9. Creativity and Criticism   122
10. What of the Future?   140

Endnotes   151
Bibliography   157
Acknowledgements from Earlier Writing   167
Index   169

LIST OF HYMN TEXTS

In most instances, these can also be sung to tunes other than those suggested below.

1967 'Lord, for the years your love has kept and guided' *Frontispiece*
11 10 11 10 to LORD OF THE YEARS by Michael Baughen
for the centenary of the Scripture Union.

1971 'O Christ the same, through all our story's pages' *page xxi*
11 10 11 10 to LONDONDERRY AIR (Irish traditional)
to mark the opening of the new girls' club of the Cambridge University Mission in Bermondsey, now the Salmon Youth Centre.

1978 'Here within this house of prayer' *page 9*
77 77 77 to DIX by Conrad Kocher
for the Installation of a new Dean of the Cathedral of the Holy and Undivided Trinity, Norwich.

1984 'Give thanks to God on high' *page 23*
66 86 66 to VINEYARD HAVEN by Richard W. Dirksen
to mark the 125th anniversary of Wheaton College, Illinois, whose motto is 'For Christ and his kingdom'.

1992 'Christ is the one who calls' *page 35*
66 66 44 44 to LOVE UNKNOWN by John Ireland
for the Service in St Paul's Cathedral to mark the launch of the 'Springboard' initiative in the Decade of Evangelism.

1996 'Affirm anew the threefold Name' *page 53*
86 86 D (DCM) to ELLACOMBE (German traditional)
for the Lambeth Conference, 1998.

1998 'We bring you, Lord, our prayer and praise' *page 68*
86 86 (CM) to WILTSHIRE by George T. Smart
for the Service in Salisbury Cathedral to mark the fiftieth anniversary of the Universal Declaration of Human Rights.

1999 'Eternal God, before whose face we stand' *page 84*
10 10 10 10 10 10 to UNDE ET MEMORES by W. H. Monk
for a Remembrance Sunday Service in Winchester Cathedral.

2005 'Glory to God, and praise' *page 105*
66 86 D (DSM) to DIADEMATA by G. J. Elvey
for the Tercentenary Service of the Worshipful Company of Fan Makers.

2006 'God who formed the mighty ocean' *page 121*
87 87 D to REX GLORIAE by Henry Smart
or 'Sea Sunday' and the annual 'Harvest of the Sea' Service at All Saints, Brixham.

2012 'We have a dream, who are the heirs' *page 138*
86 86 D (DCM) to COE FEN by Kenneth Naylor
for the bicentenary of Wesley Methodist Church, Cambridge.

A further text will be found within Chapter 7:

1994 'O Lord, whose saving Name' *page 88*
66 66 44 44 to DARWALL'S 148TH by John Darwall
for the rededication of the chapel at Great Ormond Street Hospital for Sick Children.

INTRODUCTION

Something of Myself

There are two things I am confident I can do very well: one is an introduction to any literary work, stating what it is to contain, and how it should be executed in the most perfect manner; the other is a conclusion, shewing from various causes why the execution has not been equal to what the author promised to himself and to the publick.*

Samuel Johnson, 1755

IN MY EARLY STUDENT DAYS, perhaps even while I was still at school, I used to send stories and articles to magazines. Contributors' fees were paid in guineas in those days, and though I got few cheques, I built up quite a collection of rejection slips: professionals in the field used to claim that they could paper the wall of a room with theirs. Most of them went something like this:

The Editor returns this MS with compliments, and regrets that he is unable to make use of it.

This was not how it was done in the days of Queen Victoria. Alexander Macmillan, one of the founders of the firm, wrote to an old friend, a missionary in India who had sent him a manuscript, to explain why his firm could not publish it. He had looked over the collection of papers, 'and read several carefully':

I did not feel they were likely to meet any public I have access to...I conceive of three classes of readers. 1. A general public to be moved by broad, strong representations of truth. 2. A thoughtful class who demand some striking originality, or 3. a learned class who want the pabulum suited to their special digestion. I did not seem to see that you met the popular—you were too meditative, I fancied, for them; I did not feel you were, or aimed to be, so original as to attract the thinking fellows, and as for learned pundits you did not aim at them.[1]

It is a kindly letter, setting out the publisher's fundamental question: who will read this book?

If I now apply that to the book in your hands, I am clear that it is not a history of hymnody: there are plenty of those. It is not a textbook, a handbook or a treatise. It is not a work of scholarship or even originality. I hope simply that what is stated in the subtitle will be found in these pages, namely the reflections arising from more than fifty years as a lover of hymns, a very amateur student, and a writer of them. So much for the subtitle, but the description of hymn writing as 'a functional art' deserves a further word of explanation. It is not a new idea. C. S. Lewis in the 1950s called hymnody 'an extreme case of literature as an applied art'[2] and it may well be that T. S. Eliot was thinking along not dissimilar lines when he confessed, as in the epigraph to this book, that he would like poets to possess some 'social utility'. He went on to search for his in drama: ours exists in the regular worship of the people of God. The phrase itself, however, 'a functional art', I owe to the hymn writer Fred Pratt Green.[3] He was also a poet, enjoying the poet's freedom of self-expression. As a youngster he had been drawn towards training as an architect, and he saw in hymn writing a social function comparable in some ways to architecture. Both are committed to serve the specific needs of a community rather than simply to express a personal vision; and this well describes the nature of a hymn.

Reflections are inevitably personal; but I have kept a series of commonplace books for most of my life which include references to many aspects of hymns and hymnody. What others have found, and written with effect, insight, and authority, has often been behind the reflections in this book, as will be plain from the inordinate number of quotes. I make no apology for these, hoping that readers will find them as thought-provoking, instructive, and entertaining as I have myself. If more of these are drawn from established poets than from hymn writers, this is because more poets have given accounts of their work, or attracted critical biographies. At the risk of appearing pretentious, I have added endnotes to identify sources, so that anyone interested can pursue them.

It will soon be clear who are the authors who most appeal to me. On hymnology, I look to such names such as James Montgomery, Henry Bett, Bernard Manning, Erik Routley or, in our own day, Professor J. R. Watson of Durham and Professor Scotty Gray of Texas, whose ground-breaking *Hermeneutics of Hymnody* was published as these reflections go to press. On poetry, since this book will have something to say on where poetry and hymnody meet, I have a special regard for the later Victorians and their successors, such as Tennyson, Housman, or Walter de la Mare, and more recently for John Betjeman. Eliot and Larkin I often find more appealing in their prose than in their verse. On literature in general, and especially literature as it touches the Christian faith, C. S. Lewis is on a wavelength which is to me both penetrating and accessible, while for the hymn writers themselves, no one can read far into this book without seeing Charles Wesley as incomparable; though this is not to devalue the contributions of others through many centuries, down to the men and women writing hymns today.

Any intending purchaser should also know that these pages make free use of my own writing over many years. If there is sometimes a sense of déjà vu, so that the reader is asking 'Have I not read something like this before?' this may well be because I am drawing very freely on earlier articles, forewords, interviews, and the like which I have contributed from to time. It is a little like the story of Bishop Charles Gore, who was said to have preached the same Easter sermon unchanged year after year, on the grounds that the lapse of twelve months had not altered his fundamental convictions.[4]

Since this Introduction is supposed to offer 'something of myself'—that is, of myself as hymn writer—it is inevitably egocentric, a personal story. I am mindful that this has its pitfalls; William Wordsworth referred to some of them in writing to Edward Moxon, his friend and publisher, just a hundred years before I was born:

...I always feel some apprehension for the destiny of those who in Youth addict themselves to the Composition of Verse. It is a very seducing employment; and though begun in disinterested love of the Muses is too apt to connect itself with self-love...[5]

As if that were not discouragement enough, consider too the following from Joseph Conrad in an 'Author's Note' to his *Tales of Unrest*:

One does one's work first and theorises about it afterwards. It is a very amusing and egotistical occupation, of no use whatever to anyone and just as likely as not to lead to false conclusions.[6]

In the light of those wise words, I shall readily understand if you skip this Introduction. For my purpose, however, it seems simplest to imagine that you, the reader, have been present when I have been asked to talk about hymns at some gathering or other, and the time has come for questions from the floor. They often include the following:

How many hymns have you written?

On the last count, something over 450. If this seems to be rather a lot, that is because I have been doing this for a long time: a few a year for fifty years soon mounts up. Charles Wesley wrote more than nine thousand poetic texts, mostly on Christian themes. It is impossible to be precise in knowing which of these should be counted as a hymn; Frank Baker in the 1960s could write that 'taking the average...Charles Wesley wrote ten lines of verse every day for 50 years, completing an extant poem every other day'.[7] There have been others, of course, hardly less prolific. Charles Smyth quotes a certain Samuel Wilks, Examiner of Indian Correspondence for the East India Company, who for many years composed a hymn every morning, and another every evening, for his household's family prayers. They came to four or five thousand in total, and as far as I know, apart from a private collection of his own, were never published.[8] This is a reminder that quantity counts for very little. Facility easily degenerates into the merely facile.

Have you a favourite among your texts?

I am always tempted to say 'the one I am working on now' or 'the one I wrote most recently'. But I admit to a preference for my many Christmas texts. It has been my practice since the 1960s to write a Christmas hymn or carol for my Christmas card. I think what appeals is the combination of the remembered happiness of what family Christmas meant to me as a child and then as a parent, and the never-failing 'wonder, love, and praise' evoked year upon year by the story of the birth of Jesus. Rowan Williams has written of how

> the rhythm of the Christian year was not just a matter of ecclesiastical convenience but a map of the soul's seasons; to grow up as a Christian involved the passage through darkness and light, hope and fulfilment, over and over again, letting the one story of God's action in Jesus become your own.[9]

This sums up one reason why I await with eagerness the coming of Christmas and seldom grow weary of Christmas hymns. If my own taken in bulk appear repetitive, I find comfort both in the fact that only one or two of them would be sung at any given time; and also in knowing that I am not alone in this. One critic said of A. E. Housman that it sometimes seemed that he had only one poem to write, 'which he writes and rewrites tirelessly, though often times with very brilliant and beautiful variations'.[10] 'Brilliance and beauty' I do not claim, but Christmas continues to evoke a sense of wonder which I am glad to celebrate, year by year, in verse.

What made you become a hymn writer?

It sprang originally from a love of poetry. My father was also my first schoolmaster, and he sometime used to read to his class at the end of the day from the poets which he had found would appeal to boys of ten or twelve. He also read poetry at home, and gave me books of verse. He died when I was eleven, but I remember him well, and have on my shelves not only some of his own collection of anthologies, but Stevenson's *A Child's Garden of Verses* and Housman's *A Shropshire Lad* and *Last Poems*, which I can picture him buying for me in W. H. Smiths in Folkestone on a family holiday. He never wrote poetry, as far as I know, but I wrote juvenile verse as a child and in my early twenties was seeing short lyrics on Christian themes published for the odd guinea or two in the Christian press. But I was not a hymn writer, though I longed to be; I had found in Jesus Christ the Saviour I needed and the Lord I wished to serve and celebrate but I thought hymn writing was for ever a closed book to me since, as a later chapter will confirm, I am all but totally unmusical.

How then did you make the move from Christian poetry to Christian hymns?

The short answer is that it was made for me. In the 1960s a committee was at work preparing the *Anglican Hymn Book*. Most of the members were known to me and one day the chairman, Canon Herbert Taylor, knowing something of my literary interests, asked if I had written any hymns which his committee might see. I explained that I was too lacking in music to write hymns; and that might well have been the end of it. However, he went on to ask 'Have you written any verse, of a kind which might make a hymn?' I told him, after a moment's thought, that I had not long since been reading a review copy of the *New English Bible New Testament* and had been struck with the rendering of Luke 1.46–55, Mary's Song or the Magnificat, one of the set canticles at Evening Prayer. It began 'Tell out, my soul, the greatness of the Lord', and I had seen there the opening of a lyric, and from that first line had written a short poem based on the NEB translation. His committee liked the text, and set it in their book to the tune TIDINGS by William Llewellyn, at that time Director of Music at Charterhouse. The book was promoted at a big clergy conference in Church House, Westminster, in January 1964, where this new hymn was sung for the first time. I was at home, recovering from a burst appendix, but I heard a recording, and thought it a fiasco: the assembled clergy, quite unrehearsed, struggled with unknown words, to an unfamiliar tune. Had I been present I should have cringed; indeed, I did so merely listening at home.

Years later, in a talk, I mentioned this incident, and said that the text had been set 'to a quite unsingable tune'. A modest voice from the back of the room piped up: 'I wrote the tune', and there was the composer, William Llewellyn himself. I apologized in some confusion that I had thoughtlessly used that word, when I ought to have explained that any new tune set to new words is bound to need practice. In their new *Anglican Hymn Book* the editors added a note at the foot of the page, 'This hymn may also be sung to the tune JULIUS or WOODLANDS'; and in fact WOODLANDS, well known and indeed set in the new book to H. Montagu Butler's 'Lift up your hearts', has been the most usual choice of subsequent editors, though TIDINGS is not neglected. Montagu Butler had been headmaster of Harrow. We used to sing his hymn in my school chapel, and I always squirmed slightly at the verse about 'the swamps of subterfuge and shame...the halting tongue that dares not tell the whole', which vividly brought to mind a picture of some young boy's uncomfortable interview in the headmaster's study. The tune WOODLANDS was also written by a schoolmaster, Walter

Greatorex of Gresham's, who encouraged the young W. H. Auden. I was once sent by a friend an Order of Service from a wedding where Greatorex's dates had been confused with mine. Below the words of the hymn my name was printed, followed by the dates '1877–1949': thankfully, a little premature. This was my first accepted hymn text. The editors asked me for another on the under-represented theme of 'home'. I was amazed to discover that, for all my lack of music, I might yet be a hymn writer, and wrote for them 'Lord, who left the highest heaven'; and at the same time I offered them a hymn based on John 14.6, my text for a recent school sermon, 'Christ be my leader'.[11]

Many years later I found myself reflecting on how unwittingly fortunate I had been in that first text. There are several distinct factors which helped it towards acceptance, none of which were remotely present in my mind when I was writing it. First, it escapes 'thee and thou' language, which in 1961 was still by far the most familiar use in hymns. It achieves this because the structure of the hymn, with the apostrophe to one's own soul, does not need these personal pronouns; and the same is true of 'Christ be my leader'. At that time I would have found 'you' and 'your' very difficult to handle, as is shown by the fact that in the *Anglican Hymn Book* my other early text, 'Lord, who left the highest heaven', was published with 'thy' in every verse. Second, again through no forethought of mine, 'Tell out, my soul' is a text 'based on' the Scriptures, and so common to all Christian traditions. Moreover, it offered a version of a Book of Common Prayer canticle at a time when the modernizing of liturgical language was in the air; and the fact that it was on the 'Song of Mary' made it attractive across the denominations, not least in Roman Catholic circles. Finally, though at that time I had never heard of 'gender-inclusive language', I was spared the future problems that would have limited the usefulness of the text had it made reference to 'men' or 'sons' or 'brothers' in a way that was soon to become unacceptable to editors, at first in North America, and then more widely. But of this, back in the 1960s, I was totally unaware. There was, too, one further and highly significant factor in my favour, that the hymn was written at or near the start of the 'hymn explosion' which is discussed in chapter 2; and which meant that editors were actively considering new texts.

Another question which is sometimes put to me is:

Why do you go on writing hymns? Have we not enough already?

It is a very reasonable question, to which there is, of course, more than one answer. In general terms, this also is discussed under 'Why new hymns?' in chapter 2; but in this introductory *apologia* I ought to offer a more personal reply. My calling is to be an ordained minister of Christ's gospel. I discovered this, much to my surprise and even more to the surprise of my family, at the tender age of eleven following my father's death. He had been gravely ill for some time. I vividly remember my poor mother taking me quietly aside and telling me he was not going to get better. Of course I prayed; and you would imagine that on his death I would have abandoned my childish praying as useless. I can only think that, without my earthly father, I felt more keenly the need for a heavenly one. Of course I knew almost nothing of what it meant to be ordained, 'to become a parson' as I then expressed it. I knew very few clergyman and my knowledge of the Bible was limited to Scripture lessons in the classroom on the Kings of Israel and Judah, and a knowledge of the Gospels largely confined to Christmas and Easter. But thanks to Christian Unions at school and university, and particularly to a series of Scripture Union house parties, I came to understand more, to hear and respond to Christ's call to discipleship, and to reaffirm with increasing maturity my sense of vocation.

At Cambridge, studying theology and reading Christian exposition and biography, I longed to think that I might one day use my pen in the service of the gospel. This half-formed dream took shape for me when I was introduced to the early writings of C. S. Lewis. Henry Chadwick, then chaplain of Queens' College, and a family connection, asked me one day if I had read any Lewis, and I replied that I had heard of him, but no more. Henry told me that I must read *The Screwtape Letters* and, holding him naturally in some awe and knowing he would ask me about it when next we met, I bought the book. It was relief to find that it was only a series of very short chapters. I decided I could read one a night without too much trouble, and began to do so. You can probably guess the rest. By the time I fell asleep I was deep into the book, and captivated by Lewis's writing. I bought or borrowed any of his books I could find. The Space Trilogy was then out of print but I read it avidly in the university library during free afternoons, since undergraduates could not borrow novels, and was left breathless with Lewis's gifts as a communicator—a popularizer, in the best sense of the word—of the faith, a baptizer of the imagination. I knew nothing then of his more weighty works of literary scholarship and Narnia was still fifteen years away, but I longed that I too might one day commend the gospel in print, though I could hardly hope for anything approaching the same compelling lucidity, freshness, and precision, the captivating quality of sheer style. I have come to believe those early prayers have in part been answered, though not (as is often the case with prayers) at all as I expected, in a ministry—especially a post-retirement ministry—of hymn writing.

You've spoken of your first three texts. How did you go on from there?

I mentioned the 'hymn explosion' above. In the 1960s, when Michael Baughen and I were both on the staff of the Church Pastoral-Aid Society, he conceived and edited three books. *Youth Praise I* and its successor, *Youth Praise II*, sold between them more than a million copies. They were followed by *Psalm Praise*,[12] for which Michael encouraged me to write new texts. I think most writers will agree that the prospect of publication is a great spur to putting pen to paper. I used to pass my new texts to Michael as editor, and often he would assume the role of composer and write a new tune. We sang his tune DAVOS, I remember, to the text 'I lift my eyes to the quiet hills' in York Minster at his consecration as Bishop of Chester. By 1980 I had something over a hundred texts, mostly unpublished, and was able to put together my first collection.[13] I was never a member of the formally-constituted *Jubilate* group, which came into being just as I was leaving London for Norfolk; but to Michael and other friends among its members I owe the fact that I continued to work at hymn writing in those early years.

In America, it seems the Hope Publishing Company publish your hymns. How did this come about?

In 1980 George Shorney, then in charge of what was (and still is) the family firm, wrote to ask if they could acquire the North American rights for 'Tell out, my soul'. I replied that I had other hymns, and would not want to enter into any agreement just for a single text. On his next visit to England George Shorney was visiting Fred Pratt Green, who had recently become one of his authors and who lived only a few miles from our home in Norfolk. From there, George came to stay with us for a night or two and quickly became a firm friend. It was soon happily arranged that his firm would administer all my copyrights for the United States and Canada. This led to a number of visits to the United States, sometimes including the annual Conference of their flourishing Hymn Society, and to sociable times as a guest of George and Nancy in their home. It is an association which continues today with the next generation of Shorneys, and one which has enriched my life with many friendships.

These days, along with Hope, it seems to be Oxford that publish your hymns. Is that correct?

Thankfully, yes! For a good many years I did my own administration on publications, permissions, and all the consequent correspondence. But I had been in touch with Oxford University Press since the 1970s—perhaps before—when a few of my texts found a place in hymnals they were publishing; and I had tentatively raised the question as to whether one day my hymn writing might come under their experienced care. Decades later, it was the need to make some provision against my death or incapacity, coupled with the increasing complexity of electronic publication, that led me to approach them formally, and so to an agreement. It is an arrangement, as with Hope, in which I feel I have been singularly fortunate, and which again has brought me new friends.

What about tunes? Do you choose the 'suggested tunes' listed in your collections?

Yes and no! As I have mentioned above, I am totally unmusical. This is well known to my friends, some of whom happened to comment in conversation on my tuneless singing. My young wife came at once to my support with, 'I think Timothy sings very nicely.' My friends were too polite to contradict a lady, but I saw them exchange glances which implied complete agreement that love is deaf as well as blind. I therefore looked for help, and found it in the person of Derek Kidner. He was a biblical scholar, a pianist of concert standard, and a writer of style and precision. I did not know him well; but he had served on the committee of the *Anglican Hymn Book* and I knew him to be a lover of hymns. So when I was putting together my early self-published collection I wrote to ask if he would be willing to look over my texts and suggest tunes. I was not really expecting him to agree, but he did so and went on doing so for some twenty-five years. More, he allowed me to raise with him, against each new text, various questions of theology, grammar, syntax, style, and so on, to which he unfailingly replied with concise, sympathetic, and authoritative answers. I have recorded more than once what a debt I owe to his help and encouragement, which gave me confidence to continue. When at last I had to allow him to retire from doing this, I turned instead to two old friends, both retired physicians, Drs Peter Tucker and Jonathan West. They share similar musical gifts but are worshippers in churches of contrasting styles and musical traditions. I am glad to acknowledge here their wise and willing help for many years now, even though the responsibility for 'suggested tunes' has to be mine. I comfort myself with the recollection that leaders of worship and editors of hymnals have their own preferences; conscious of my own limitations, I never stipulate to what tunes my texts must be set.

I think this is the place to mention again William Llewellyn, who has been music editor for six collections of mine where he has both chosen and usually engraved the music, and given me not only his skill but his friendship and hospitality. The first in that series, *Beneath a Travelling Star*, was suggested by Dr Lionel Dakers when we were serving together on the committee for *Common Praise*. He was one of the Directors of *Hymns Ancient & Modern*, so there was no problem about a publisher. Following his death Christine Smith, their publisher, commissioned from me the next five in the series; while the seventh, *A Mirror to the Soul,* was published in 2014 by Tim Ruffer of the Royal School of Church Music. For this present book, I am glad to place on record my particular thanks to the Revd Dr Andrew Pratt, editor of the Hymn Society *Bulletin*, for encouragement to persevere when early drafts were abandoned; and to my daughter, Caroline Gill, herself a poet, for perceptive and painstaking comments and corrections.

To provide an illustration of how hymns continue to serve as 'functional art', there is between each of the following chapters a text of mine, which will serve to show the kind of thing I write. They represent different years—different decades, even—and a variety of metres, but share this in common, that each was written for a particular purpose and in response to a specific request. I feel privileged to have been entrusted with these various commissions. Not much, I think, can be deduced from the dates when they were written. When Philip Larkin was asked by an interviewer in 1964, 'How would you characterize your development as a poet?', he replied, 'I suppose I'm less likely to write a really bad poem now, but possibly equally less likely to write a really good one. If you call that development, then I've developed.'[14] I resonate with him in this, but I would not like anyone to feel, as they read these chapters, that when I refer to established poets, or indeed hymn writers, I seek to class myself among them. This does not mean, however, that we cannot sit at their feet and learn from them.

* * *

When Charles Wesley was in his mid-fifties, some twenty-five years after that momentous Pentecost of his conversion, he published in two volumes his *Short Hymns on Select Passages of the Holy Scriptures*. I venture to borrow from him to end this Introduction the words with which he concludes his Preface, as applicable to all lovers of those hymns, my own included, which are the subject of this book:

Reader, if God ministers grace to thy soul through any of these hymns, give Him the glory, and offer up a prayer for the weak instrument, that, whenever I finish my course, I may depart in peace, having seen in JESUS CHRIST His great salvation.

TDS
Ford, Salisbury,
June 2015

O CHRIST THE SAME

O CHRIST THE SAME, through all our story's pages.
    our loves and hopes, our failures and our fears;
eternal Lord, the King of all the ages,
    unchanging still, amid the passing years:
O living Word, the source of all creation,
    who spread the skies, and set the stars ablaze,
O Christ the same, who wrought our whole salvation,
    we bring our thanks for all our yesterdays.

O Christ the same, the friend of sinners, sharing
    our inmost thoughts, the secrets none can hide,
still as of old upon your body bearing
    the marks of love, in triumph glorified:
O Son of Man, who stooped for us from heaven,
    O Prince of life, in all your saving power,
O Christ the same, to whom our hearts are given,
    we bring our thanks for this the present hour.

O Christ the same, secure within whose keeping
    our lives and loves, our days and years remain,
our work and rest, our waking and our sleeping,
    our calm and storm, our pleasure and our pain:
O Lord of love, for all our joys and sorrows,
    for all our hopes, when earth shall fade and flee,
O Christ the same, beyond our brief tomorrows,
    we bring our thanks for all that is to be.

© Timothy Dudley-Smith in Europe and Africa. © Hope Publishing Company in the United States of America and the rest of the world. Reproduced by permission of Oxford University Press. All rights reserved.

CHAPTER I

Why Hymns?

> When we sing the Praise of God in his Church we are employ'd in that part of worship which of all other is nearest a-kin to Heaven...*
>
> Isaac Watts, 1707

AS AN UNDERGRADUATE at Cambridge, with the war just over, I used to attend the lectures of Charles Raven, Canon of Ely, Master of Christ's College, Regius Professor of Divinity and soon to be Vice-Chancellor. I can see him now in his doctor's gown striding up and down the lecture hall, tall, commanding, and flamboyant. Fifteen years before he had been Chancellor of the new and then still unfinished Liverpool Cathedral. We enjoyed the story of how, one day, Dean Dwelly, famous for his aesthetic sense, was rehearsing for a big Service in the Cathedral. Raven, as a Chaplain to the King, would be in his scarlet cassock. 'You stand there,' the Dean said to Raven. 'You'll make a fine splash of red.' 'My dear fellow,' was Raven's reply, 'I wasn't ordained to be a splash of red!'

In something of the same way, if our hymns could speak to us, I fancy they too would assert themselves. 'We were not written,' I can hear them saying, 'to fill the gap while the preacher moves to the pulpit'; or 'to give the congregation something to occupy them during the choir procession'; or even 'to allow time to take up the collection'. And they would be right to protest. Those are not the true purposes of a hymn. To the question 'Why hymns?' or 'What is a hymn for?' there is one straightforward answer: 'For the praise of God.'

This was indeed Augustine's much-quoted definition of a hymn: 'A song with praise of God'. He goes on to claim that all three of these elements are essential to what he means by a hymn. There must be singing, there must be praise, and it must be 'of God'. This does not mean to my mind, though not all have agreed, that every authentic hymn must be addressed to God. A quick glance at almost any modern hymnbook will show that some hymns are addressed to ourselves ('Hark, my soul! It is the Lord'); some to our fellow-Christians ('Onward, Christian soldiers') or to the world in general ('All people that on earth do dwell'); some to a country, city, or town ('Jerusalem the golden' or 'O little town of Bethlehem'). The last-named even includes a verse addressed to the morning stars. Other hymns seem to have no specific address, but are general exhortations ('Let all the world in every corner sing') or perhaps narrative ('Jesus Christ is risen today' or 'My song is love unknown'): and of course the list goes on. John Ellerton, who wrote the much-loved evening hymn, 'The day thou gavest, Lord, is ended', thought that in a good hymnal there should be 'a preponderance, at least' of hymns which are 'a direct utterance of praise to God'. He adds, 'I would not exclude all others; but there are in most hymnals far too many sets of verses which are nothing more than religious meditations or paraphrases of texts.'[1] I take his point, but some of our best-loved hymns do not address God directly, or only do so in a concluding verse. John Keble's 'New every morning is the love' delays any address to God until verse five: but that did not begin life as a hymn. The great Advent hymn, 'Lo, he comes with clouds descending' waits until the final verse before breaking out with 'Yea, Amen, let all adore thee'; and Isaac Watts' masterpiece, 'When I survey the wondrous cross', from Galatians 6.14, has no address to God at all. I am conscious, reading this, that some of the hymns I have written, and indeed seen included in present-day hymnals, could be described in much this way. In my case, this is due in part to my reluctance to address God as 'you', when it was no longer possible to write 'thee'.

John Ellerton died in 1893; and thirty-two years later Percy Dearmer published *Songs of Praise*. It included three hymns by Ellerton, and a fourth was added in the greatly-enlarged second edition. *Songs of Praise* sought to enrich the church's hymnody by drawing on a wider literary culture, and so contained what to Ellerton would have seemed some very odd choices. There is one of Shakespeare's sonnets; verses by Shelley, well-known as an unbeliever; and poems by Swinburne and the agnostic Thomas Hardy. The saintly George Herbert is in quite a different category, but the book contains a delightful poem from his hand addressed to 'Sweet Day', which he would surely have been astonished to find printed in a hymn book. Nevertheless it is, I think, a fact of experience that a hymn need not be addressed directly to God in order to be a vehicle for his praise, and that this does not contradict but only enlarges Augustine's definition. Psalm 23 might be a case in point, which recounts, in praise of God, the psalmist's own experience in a way which resonates with our own. And do we not find that those hymns most redolent of devotion, and conveying a true sense of the divine, are often *about* God though not *addressed* to him? Think of John Mason's 'How shall I sing that majesty' or Samuel Crossman's 'My song is love unknown', both from the seventeenth century; or Mrs Alexander's 'There is a green hill far away', written in the 1870s and still with the power to touch our hearts.

One further word which we might usefully add to Augustine's definition is 'congregational'. Those in the pews have the Service 'read' to them; the sermon preached to them; perhaps an anthem sung to them; the sacrament administered to them: but in singing together they come into their own. Professor J. R. Watson in his critical and historical study, *The English Hymn*, has described how hymns in public worship 'were important in the Reformation and after, because of the doctrine of the priesthood of all believers, for whom the singing of psalms and hymns was an expression of a universal right to understand and interpret the gospel'.[2] Hymns have of course been written with lesser aims in view. Wartime brings to the fore hymns, often dearly loved and deeply felt, but unsatisfactory for Christian worship. 'I vow to thee, my country' and 'O valiant hearts' trouble Christian sensibilities with lines about 'asking no questions' or 'lesser Calvaries', to look no deeper into their theologies. 'Single-issues' of other kinds can produce a hymnody where the worship of God seems to become only a secondary purpose. I have among other quaint hymn books a very battered pocket edition of *Hymns and Songs for Bands of Hope*. The publisher's blurb says 'Aids to 100% Efficiency in Band of Hope Work'. Temperance is a very proper cause; and the book is careful to say it contains both songs and hymns. The songs are amusingly archaic by modern standards, but in their time no doubt useful in seeking to counter the alcohol abuse which still remains a major social evil:

> O we're a youthful Band of Hope
>   All pledged strong drink to flee,
> Then let our watchword sound afar—
>   'NO DRINK, NO DRINK FOR ME.'
> With heart and voice united,
>   We'll sing our Temperance song,
> Till Britain's curse be done away
>   And drinking customs gone.

But hymns are a different matter; and for all their address to God, and invocation of the Divine, some of what are printed in the book as hymns are not what the word should really mean:

> Guard us with Thy mighty hand,
>   Lead our youthful Temperance Band,
> Guide us, O Celestial King,
>   To our cause great triumphs bring.

The cause is a worthy one, but it is not quite the cause of the gospel. But more disquieting than this is the foisting of a hymn—a real hymn—upon some hapless congregation for some purpose other than divine worship. Gwen Raverat, granddaughter of Charles Darwin, described an instance of just this when writing of her schooldays in *Period Piece*, a memoir of her Cambridge childhood. She writes of her younger self as 'shocked and disgusted' by the regular practice, before an important hockey match, of including in their Evening Prayers a spirited rendering of 'Onward, Christian soldiers', brazenly designed 'to ginger us up for martial prowess next day'.[3]

Although the purpose of a hymn, whatever its form, is to praise God, we can recognize many ways in which the hymns also benefit us, the congregation. At their best, our hymns offer a means to express our personal discipleship; they teach us more about our faith; and they help to unite us as fellow-members of the Body of Christ, where 'member' does not mean someone who happens to be elected or who has paid their subscription, but an organ or a limb. Erik Routley, to my mind the most distinguished hymnologist of his generation, once described hymns as 'songs for unmusical people to sing together'.[4] In one of his earliest books he listed what he saw as three functions of hymnody: 'Codifying doctrine, unifying the body, and glorifying God'.[5] Changing the order, we could restate this as 'praising God, confirming faith, and uniting us in fellowship'. I would want to add that hymns help us to verbalize, actually to utter out loud, what is in our hearts: private thoughts and aspirations for which we cannot always find words, and might otherwise be shy to speak about. Many Christian people whose faith is real and precious to them find difficulty in articulating it. In ordinary conversation, even the name 'Jesus' appears sometimes hard to say. Those who perhaps have had little help or teaching about prayer may often feel deeply a sense of penitence or thankfulness, or a desire to trust God more fully; but somehow lack a way to express this. Hymns, carefully chosen and thoughtfully sung, can offer just such a way. I remember the actress Kathy Staff from the BBC sitcom 'Last of the Summer Wine' being interviewed once on the long-running TV programme, 'Songs of Praise'. She was asked about hymns, and replied to the effect that she valued them because they helped her to give expression to what she wanted to say, but for which she could not always find the words. I am sure she was not alone in this.

The hymns we sing not only express our praise and devotion, but also teach us about what Christians believe; they confirm us in the faith. George Herbert knew this when he included in his poem *The Church Porch* the line 'A verse may find him, who a sermon flies...' and I have heard people claim that they have understood more of their faith from the hymns they have sung than from the sermons they have heard. I do not altogether believe this, however; if true, it shows, surely, a woeful inability to listen since good preaching, to be effective, requires good hearers. Think of your own church, and let your mind's eye run over the pews on a typical Sunday morning. Many, even of the regular worshippers, might be hard put to it to explain such expressions as 'not of works' or 'justification by faith', but know exactly what they mean when singing

> Nothing in my hand I bring,
> Simply to thy cross I cling...

Singing has this penetrating power, summed up by the Scottish patriot Andrew Fletcher of Saltoun, when he famously declared, 'If a man were permitted to make all the ballads, he need not care who should make the laws of a nation.'[6] That was in 1732, but the thought is universal. It was echoed by Dr Johnson, by Shelley, who called poets 'the unacknowledged legislators of the world', and transposed into a Christian context in the 1850s by Dr R. W. Dale of Birmingham, who is quoted as saying, 'Let me write the hymns of a Church, and I care not who writes the theology.'[7]

Three major principles of early education are fulfilled when we sing hymns: *participation*, *repetition*, and *expression*. There is of course value in simply reading or listening to hymns; but to *participate*, to join in the singing, serves to make the words an expression of personal faith and experience, part of the furniture of the mind, and one could even say of the soul. As we participate, the words become familiar because of *repetition*. Without conscious effort, they lodge in the memory, helped both by the tune and by the verse-form. This places a high responsibility on those who write our hymns, and equally on those who choose them for a given congregation and a particular act of worship. If we learn something of our faith from the hymns we sing, it is plainly important that they embody Christian truth, what the Anglican *Declaration of Assent* calls 'the faith uniquely revealed in the Holy Scriptures and set forth in the catholic creeds'. I like to think that T. R. Glover, the Cambridge classical scholar and historian, may have had some of the more surprising lyrics from *Songs of Praise* in mind when he wrote his mischievous pastiche of the 'wilful agnosticism' of the modernist theology of his day:

> We know Thee not, nor guess Thee,
>   O vague beyond our dreams:
> We praise Thee not nor bless Thee,
>   Dim source of all that seems;
>   Unconscious of our witness,
> The music of our heart,
>   O It beyond all Itness
> If aught indeed Thou art.[8]

John Betjeman in his verse autobiography, *Summoned by Bells*, wrote of how in his school chapel he could feel 'safe in the surge of undogmatic hymns'.[9] Yet a hymn with no doctrinal backbone, even if only implicit, cannot do much to teach the truth or confirm faith. By contrast, the right hymn at the right moment can be a pastor's or a preacher's most valuable ally. When Charles Simeon of Cambridge used to hold sermon classes for young clergy on the art of preaching he would borrow a phrase from Richard Baxter a century before, and talk of 'screwing the word of God into the hearers', adding that 'the very hymn...is a turn of the screw'.[10]

A third result of our hymn singing is what Routley called 'unifying the body', or strengthening the fellowship of believers. It is something we do together, and everyone knows that a shared task is one of the key elements in 'team building'. It was a sure instinct, greatly nourished by Charles Wesley's unique talents as a hymn writer, that made singing such an integral part of those first Methodist class-meetings, helping to introduce the members into something more than human friendship. Yet if this corporate and congregational element is of such importance, it is fair to ask why so many of the most powerful hymns use the first person singular, and speak in terms of individual experience—'I' and 'me' and 'my'. There is a paradox here, expressed in Bernard Manning's question, 'When did the men of the eighteenth and nineteenth centuries have most fellowship with one another?' and his reply, 'At those times when they sang the most individual hymns.' He gives some familiar examples (my italics):

> Jesu, Lover of *my* soul
> Rock of Ages, cleft for *me*
> When *I* survey the wondrous cross.[11]

Again, it is J. R. Watson who offers the explanation, namely that in collective singing the 'I' becomes an expression of personal experience which is shared; and though in writing this he is thinking of psalm singing, it is equally true of hymns.[12] As a reviewer of *The English Hymn* pointed out, to make these declarations in unison is at once to submit to a discipline and to be released from inhibition.[13]

Important though they are, these benefits that flow to the congregation from their hymn singing are, so to speak, side-effects. They can never be the main purpose of the hymn, which remains 'the praise of God'. Isaac Watts knew this better than most, and he remains a hero to lovers of hymns. I used to think, mistakenly, that only two copies were known to exist of the first edition of his *Hymns and Spiritual Songs* of 1707. I did not imagine that I would ever have the chance to handle one of these since I had read that one was in the Library of Congress and one in the New York Public Library. But in the summer of 1984 I had a few days in New York as the guest of George Shorney, so I wrote in advance to the library explaining my interest, and asking if it might be possible to see their copy. When the day came, I was very glad I had done so, or I think I should have been turned away. I was on foot and it was over 90 degrees in the streets; it would be an understatement to describe me as 'dishevelled'. However, once in the Public Library I identified myself, filled in the inevitable form, and in due course the book was in my hands. I sat in silence, with a feeling almost of unreality as I remembered the man who wrote it. Before I left I copied out some of the Preface, which went like this:

When we sing the Praise of our God in his Church we are employ'd in that part of worship which of all others is nearest a-kin to Heaven...

I have put those words at the head of this chapter, but the sting is in the tail. Watts continued:

> ...and 'tis pity that this of all others should be perform'd worst upon Earth.

Even I, unmusical as I know myself to be, have been in congregations which illustrate that second point, feelingly expressed by Robert Bridges, most musical of Poets Laureate, in the words: 'It seems a pity that nature shall have arranged that where the people are musical...they would rather listen, and where they are unmusical they would rather sing.'[14]

To the hymn writer, the music is important, but the words even more so; both must reflect all that is contained in Augustine's simple phrase, 'with praise of God'. The poet Philip Larkin, borrowing, probably from Augustus Hare 150 years earlier, refers in one of his books to an old gentleman 'who deleted from his Prayer Book all expressions praising God in the belief that they would be distasteful to that well-bred Person'.[15] Don't be deceived by the gentle humour; the point is a real one; can the praise of creatures like ourselves mean anything to the God revealed to us in Scripture, great beyond our imagining? And even if that were so, is not our worship, which in this context means our hymns and hymn singing, so flawed as to be unacceptable? We certainly know that not all worship is acceptable to him; the prophets made no bones about it. Here is the Lord God's response through Amos to the worshippers of his day:

I hate, I despise your festivals, and I take no delight in your solemn assemblies.... Take away from me the noise of your songs; I will not listen to the melody of your harps.[16]

The reason for this rejection is in the next words: 'But let justice roll down like waters, and righteousness like an ever-flowing stream.' Where there is no social justice, no concern for righteousness, God does not want or receive our worship.

But in happier circumstances there is another side to this coin, found in one of the most remarkable statements in the Gospels. Jesus is resting beside a well on his journey through Samaria. He meets there a woman who has come to draw water for her household and asks her for a drink, an unheard-of request from a Jewish man to a despised Samaritan woman. He engages her in conversation, telling her of the 'living water' that he has come to bring; and then astonishes her by his knowledge of her situation. But let St John tell his own story:

The woman said to him, 'Sir, I see that you are a prophet. Our ancestors worshipped on this mountain, but you say that the place where people must worship is in Jerusalem.' Jesus said to her, 'Woman, believe me, the hour is coming when you will worship the Father neither on this mountain nor in Jerusalem...the hour is coming, and is now here, when the true worshippers will worship the Father in spirit and in truth, for the Father seeks such as these to worship him. God is spirit, and those who worship him must worship in spirit and in truth.'[17]

Familiarity makes it easy to miss just how astonishing this is. William Temple in his *Readings in St John's Gospel*, describes the words 'God is spirit' as 'the most fundamental proposition in all theology';[18] and in the same passage set out above we find the most fundamental mandate for worship. Here are the words again, with my italics: 'for *the Father seeks* such as these to worship him'. We have it therefore on the best authority that God desires—even seeks—the worship of creatures like ourselves. And yet how dare we? It is not only that there is much in our society lacking the justice and righteousness which alone can make human worship truly acceptable; but how dare we offer our flawed and imperfect sacrifice of praise, as all human praise must necessarily be? As a hymn writer I have often asked myself this question. Can this text which I am now struggling with, this text with its compromises, its facile alliteration, its well-worn clichés and what is almost spiritual jargon—can *this* text be a vehicle for the church's worship of the Most High? Must not any offering of ours by vitiated by our unclean hands, by the fallen creatures that we are?

Such thoughts might stifle hymnody for ever, were it not for the grace of God. In the familiar words of the Prayer Book version of Psalm 103.14, 'He knoweth whereof we are made: he remembereth that we are but dust.' And there is a further consolation to be found in the Book of Common Prayer, perhaps where you might least expect it, in Article XXVI of the Thirty-nine Articles of Religion: *Of the Unworthiness of the Ministers, which hinders not the effect of the Sacrament*. It speaks of how 'in the visible Church, the evil be ever mingled with the good' and of how the Sacraments 'be effectual, because of Christ's institution and promise, although they be ministered by evil men'. I comfort myself that here is a principle of wider application, and that for all its faults, God still seeks our worship when it humbly strives to be in spirit and in truth, and therefore we can offer to him the means by which we express such worship, including our incomparable heritage of English hymnody, and the writing, editing, publishing and singing of hymns today. May it not be rather like the four-year-old bringing home to Daddy the 'drawing' she has made in playschool? It is at once worthless, not likely to fetch much at auction, and yet valued for the sake of the giver and the love which prompts the gift. Of course any words or music to be used as a vehicle of praise must be the best that we can manage; but 'spirit and truth' are the essentials, the true devotion of the heart. No one knew this better than John Wesley. Singing was an important part of the worship and fellowship of his early class-meetings. He drew up a set of 'Directions' which included *Sing Lustily*: 'be no more afraid of your Voice now, nor more ashamed of its being heard, than when you sang the songs of Satan'. Next came *Sing Modestly*: 'do not baul', and *In Time*: 'not too slow'; but he concluded with *Sing Spiritually*, 'have an eye to God in every Word you sing'.[19] He wanted his 'Directions' to be obeyed, as is shown by this little incident, recounted in a book published 150 years ago. In an early Methodist assembly one good man sang out of tune, to the offence of Mr Wesley's delicate ear:

'John,' said he, 'you do not sing in tune.' The man stopped, but soon began again. The rebuke was repeated. 'Please, sir, I sing with my heart,' was the sufficient reply. 'Then sing on,' said Mr. W.[20]

* * *

Mandell Creighton, in his day, was a famous Bishop of London. He died in 1901, the same year as Queen Victoria; and his wife then occupied herself writing his *Life* in two substantial volumes. Volume 2 opens with a frontispiece of the bishop in his robes, showing the high-domed forehead and gold-rimmed spectacles of the academic (he had been Professor of Ecclesiastical History at Cambridge) and the bushy beard and side-whiskers of the high Victorian. In the final chapter, his wife gives us in six lines a quiet domestic vignette of the bishop at home in Fulham Palace. With a little imagination, we can picture the scene. It is after dinner, and his family circle are talking together round the fireside. Presently the bishop raises the question, 'What is life given us for?' You would think this a conversation-stopper, to be followed by an awkward silence, but it seems to have been taken up with enthusiasm. It may have been his chaplain, perhaps with much hesitation, who ventured on the reply, 'Life is an opportunity for service.' The bishop 'agreed that there was much in that suggestion' but finally himself gave as his answer, 'Life is an opportunity for loving.'[21] In something of the same way, this chapter has sought to answer the question, 'Why hymns—what are they for?' with the suggestion that hymns provide 'an opportunity for praise'. And this takes us closer to the bishop's reply if we set beside it the words of Psalm 95: 'O come, let us sing to the Lord...Let us come into his presence with thanksgiving'; together with Derek Kidner's comment on those words: 'To come singing into God's presence is not the only way...but it is the way that best expresses love.'[22]

HERE WITHIN THIS HOUSE OF PRAYER

HERE WITHIN THIS HOUSE of prayer
all our Father's love declare;
love that gave us birth, and planned
days and years beneath his hand:
    praise to God whose love and power
    bring us to this present hour!

Here, till earthly praises end,
tell of Christ the sinner's friend;
Christ whose blood for us was shed,
Lamb of God and living bread,
    life divine and truth and way,
    light of everlasting day.

Here may all our faint desire
feel the Spirit's wind and fire,
souls that sleep the sleep of death
stir to life beneath his breath:
    may his power upon us poured
    send us out to serve the Lord!

Here may faith and love increase,
flowing forth in joy and peace
from the Father, Spirit, Son,
undivided, Three-in-One:
    his the glory all our days
    in this house of prayer and praise!

© Timothy Dudley-Smith in Europe and Africa. © Hope Publishing Company in the United States of America and the rest of the world. Reproduced by permission of Oxford University Press. All rights reserved.

CHAPTER 2

Why New Hymns?

> What I, like many other laymen, chiefly desire in church are fewer, better, and shorter hymns; especially fewer.*
>
> C. S. Lewis, 1949

WHEN I WAS JUST BEGINNING to think I might become a hymn writer, I received an entirely unexpected invitation to give a paper to the American hymn society, now the Hymn Society in the United States and Canada, at their 1984 Convocation, thanks to George Shorney, who had just co-published my first hymn collection, *Lift Every Heart*. These annual conferences were usually on the campus of a college or university, and this one was at Elmhurst College, Illinois. One afternoon I wandered quietly into the chapel where a recital was taking place. So as not to be a disturbance, I climbed up to the empty gallery, and sat down to listen. Presently George Shorney silently entered, and tiptoed across to me. 'Would you be willing to take part in a radio phone-in?' he whispered. 'I've never done anything like that before, but if you want me to, I'll have a try. When would it be?' George looked at his watch. 'Our local radio station has been let down by someone who was due to take part. We're on air in about three minutes.' 'How shall we ever get there?', I asked. 'That's no problem,' he told me; 'there's an empty office here with a telephone; we can use that. The producer's on the line, and he'll introduce you, and then just wait for the first listener to call in.'

So I clung to the telephone, trying to marshall my thoughts, and heard the presenter explain that their guest was an English bishop who was interested in writing new hymns. There was then a gap, which seemed an age, before the first caller came on the line. I have never forgotten her. The presenter introduced her: 'This is Gertrude from Chattanooga: what is your question, Gertrude?' And in what seemed to me an archetypal Southern accent, I was confronted with this: 'Why do we have to have these new hymns? I like the old ones.'

I took a deep breath, and assured her that I, too, like the old ones. But I think she spoke for many people when she asked that question. If you ask what is the single characteristic that makes a hymn popular with a congregation, my conclusion can be summed up in the one word 'familiarity', that they know it already. I find just the same thing in myself, that in many areas of life I like what I know. It is a widespread and very human reaction:

For the fact is that hymns carry not only the faith of the Church but also our own personal history. One line of a text, or of music, may open up for us the wounds of grief or the joy of childbirth, the yearning for a better life or the once fervent devotion which is now lukewarm.

In hearing or singing a hymn we can be transported back to our first child's baptism or to the moment when we first felt the hand of God upon us.[1]

Familiar hymns carry resonances deep within our psyche. It would be easy to suppose that they are enough for us. Nevertheless, there are convincing reasons why there should be a place for new hymns. By this, of course, I mean hymns of an acceptable standard; not-so-good hymns are discussed later.

When we say with Gertrude that 'we like the old ones', we are speaking of an immense heritage of Christian hymns, going back to the very beginning. It is sometimes said that Christian hymnody began when Jesus and the eleven disciples were about to leave that upper room where they had just had supper, and make their way to the Garden of Gethsemane. Both Matthew and Mark tell us that they sang a hymn together. The NEB version of this reads, 'after singing the Passover Hymn',[2] which would be one or more of Psalms 113–118 associated with the Passover. But if Jesus and his friends sang together then, surely that could not be the first time? Would not Jesus' teaching sessions with them, their times of fellowship, their meals together around small-burning camp fires under the Galilean stars, sometimes lead to song? What is clear beyond doubt is that *Christian* hymnody, borrowing from the Book of Psalms, goes back to Jesus' own day, and indeed to the Lord himself. He would have been singing with his friends.

It is clear, too, from St Paul's letters that the infant church was a singing church; and so it has continued to be. If you take any hymn book which gives the dates as well as the names of the writers and composers, you cannot help but be struck by how widely they range over the Christian era. There may well be hymns from the fourth century by Augustine or Ambrose, from the seventh by The Venerable Bede or by John of Damascus, and from the twelfth, for example, by Peter Abelard or Bernard of Cluny. We shall find Bunyan, Crossman, and Herbert from the seventeenth century; Cowper, Montgomery, Newton, Watts, and the Wesleys from the eighteenth—and then innumerable Victorians and their successors, right down to the writers alive today. Hymnody is not static but ongoing; there is unbroken continuity in the inheritance of our familiar hymns, but continuity that is open-ended. To add today's hymns to the repertoire is only to do what every previous generation has done. If we treasure our inheritance, we shall want to continue it. You could even say that we had an obligation to do so, that a church which is not helping its people know and value their heritage of hymnody, and be willing to add to it, is neglecting one aspect of its calling.

Of course what we think of as our inheritance changes over the decades, let alone the centuries. The hymns which survive are those whose message still speaks to us across the generations. Part of the difficulty in choosing what to retain and what to discard in a contemporary hymnal is that congregational hymns speak in different ways at different times—and sometimes indeed fall silent, having had their day; it is a nice matter of judgement whether an old text still retains its power. In this, they have something in common with traditional fairy tales. The psychoanalyst Bruno Bettelheim, survivor of Dachau and Buchenwald, has described how such simple yet profound stories can carry different meanings at different times according to the reader, and how the child 'will return to the same tale when he is ready to enlarge on old meanings, or replace them with new ones'.[3] So it can be for us all, child or adult alike, with familiar hymns. It is this which makes our hymnody a living and continuous phenomenon, 'alive—in tattered hymnals, on insecure music-stands, and in the inexact memories of infrequent worshippers everywhere from London to Kuala Lumpur'.[4]

A second answer to 'Why new hymns?' is found in the way that the language of worship has changed. When I was ordained in 1950, every statutory Service was from the Book of Common Prayer, and we thought nothing of its 'thees' and 'thous', its 'pardoneth and absolveth', and the like. When we prayed that those responsible should 'indifferently administer justice'[5] we knew we were not asking for mediocre law courts, but that all should be equal, undifferentiated, before the law. Yet in the course of my lifetime this has all changed. In the Church of England, new 'alternative Services' began to be authorized from the mid-1960s, in a multitude of small temporary booklets called names like 'Series 1' or 'Series 2'. Eventually these new forms of Service came together in a book of more than a thousand pages, *The Alternative Service Book, 1980*, and this in turn was followed twenty years later by *Common Worship*. Other churches during the same period were also busy revising their forms of worship. This has not meant the end of 'thees' and 'thous' and Elizabethan language. The Prayer Book remains in use, and is still one of the authoritative documents defining the teaching of the Church of England. But on any given Sunday, my guess would be that the great majority of Services would be in more contemporary English. There are real gains in this; it serves to some degree to make what is found in church less incomprehensible to the very occasional churchgoer, 'the outsider', as the jargon tends to call him or her. But inevitably there are losses too.

Nor is it only Prayer and Service books where the language has been updated. In my young days 'the Bible' almost always meant the Authorized Version, sometimes called the King James Version. Beside it, but more for the study than the lectern, was the Revised Version of 1898. It is exactly described by its subtitle: *translated out of the original tongues: being the version set forth in* A.D. *1611 compared with the most ancient authorities and revised.* This was followed by at least two major modern individual translations. In 1903 there was published posthumously *The New Testament in Modern Speech* by Richard Weymouth, sometime Headmaster of Mill Hill School, a Baptist scholar who had devoted to it many years of research and study. Ten years later the Scot, James Moffat, published his *The New Testament: A New Translation*, and this was followed by *The Complete Moffat Bible* in 1926. Both, however, retained for some purposes the familiar 'thee' and 'thou'; and neither was authorized for use in the public worship of the Church of England. From 1938–39 onwards, Ronald Knox was at work on his single-handed translation from the Vulgate, frustrated by wartime conditions and the conservatism of the Hierarchy. His final volume appeared in 1949. As far as I know, apart from the slightly eccentric *The New Testament in Basic English* of 1941, this is how matters rested until the *Revised Standard Version* of 1946 and 1952; my first copy was given to me as a leaving present from a parishioner at the end of my curacy in 1953. But now the situation is totally different. Many, if not most, churches read the Scriptures from a modern version; sometimes, indeed, more from a paraphrase than a translation. Good modern translations offer a great gain in intelligibility, though a sad loss to the lodging of Scripture in the memory, since there is no one universal form of words.

But how does this affect our hymnody? It can leave our older hymns 'out of step' in their use of language, compared to all other parts of the Service. This is true not only of the earlier generations of Isaac Watts and the Wesleys; but also, for example, of writers like Robert Bridges, who was still alive when I was born. Unless you know it, and understand where Bridges is coming from, it must seem odd in a Service whose language is recognizably the English of today's speech, to be asked to sing:

> His care he drowneth yonder,
> Lost in the abyss of wonder;
>   To heaven his soul doth steal:
> This life he disesteemeth,
> The day it is that dreameth,
>   That doth from truth his vision seal.[6]

Professor Watson has explained how Bridges was here trying to create 'a formal style, a grand Miltonic discourse that was purposefully not that of ordinary speech' and where 'the language was intentionally elaborate, the syntax difficult'.[7] The inclusion of Bridges' work in all contemporary mainstream hymnals shows that this approach is still valued; but does it not also suggest that there is a strong case for augmenting this heritage, however excellent, with contemporary writing? Indeed, it is just this unease with antiquated language that lies behind the many revisions that have been attempted to familiar hymns. This is not in fact a new idea: many of the hymns we may have been singing all our lives are not exactly what the author wrote. Perhaps the most famous example is Charles Wesley's line 'Hark how all the welkin rings' which we know as 'Hark! The herald angels sing'. The change was first made by George Whitefield in Wesley's lifetime, though whether or not with his approval I have no record. I rather doubt it, however, since a reading of Luke 2.8–14 quickly shows that Wesley's original is more authentic. The message of the angelic host was not 'Glory to the new-born King' but 'Glory to God in the highest...'; and 'Lord of lords and King of kings', from the original version is Paul's description of Almighty God, though also applied in the Book of Revelation to the glorified Saviour.[8] But of course today the trouble lies in the word 'welkin', which from the twelfth century meant 'the vault of heaven'. Shakespeare uses the word in eleven of his plays; but alas, even in Charles Wesley's day it seems to have been 'archaic'. With the best intentions, the editors of the ill-fated 1904 edition of *Hymns Ancient & Modern* restored the original line—but by then it was too late: 'welkin' was past its sell-by date, no longer part of the language.

Another example of an early change for the better is in A. M. Toplady's great hymn 'Rock of Ages' of 1776. Where we sing 'when my eyelids close in death', the original contained the rather spine-chilling 'when my eye-strings break in death'. Indeed, many of our hymns have changed in less dramatic ways over the years; Donald Coggan had a word for this process: he called it 'invisible mending'. Not all older hymns can be so 'mended' with any success; but even so it is very different from an editorial approach that adopts a doctrinaire policy of allowing nothing at all archaic, no language that is not inclusive, or gender-neutral; no 'brothers' without 'sisters'; no generic 'man' to stand for humankind. Indeed, one is sometimes tempted to think that nothing is now allowable unless it is expressed as the present editors would have expressed it, had they been writing the hymn themselves. Again, there will be more to say about this in a later chapter; but it remains one of the reasons why we need *new* hymns, rather than simply living entirely with the old ones; or trying, usually with very limited success, to 'mend' them. John Wesley had firm words on that subject in the preface to his celebrated 1780 *A Collection of Hymns for the Use of the People called Methodists*. He wrote:

Many gentlemen have done my brother and me (though without naming us) the honour to reprint many of our hymns. Now they are perfectly welcome to do so, provided they print them just as they are. But I desire that they would not attempt to mend them—for really they are not able. None of them is able to mend either the sense or the verse. Therefore I must beg of them one of these two favours: either to let them stand just as they are, to take them for better, for worse; or to add the true reading in the margin, or at the bottom of the page, that we may no longer be accountable either for the nonsense or for the doggerel of other men.

John Wesley's concern is not only with expression ('doggerel'), but also with sense or meaning. Hymns sometimes fall out of use, and are then naturally discarded by future editors, because language has changed its meaning: 'bowels', for example, to be found in some older hymns, was once the word for the heart, the seat of emotion and personality. 'Worms' would provide another example. The editors of *An Anthology of Bad Verse* offer two examples (a little suspect since they do not identify authors) of hymns which use the word 'worms' to describe humanity. Bernard Manning, admittedly more than seventy years ago, maintained a robust defence of the word in older hymns of sufficient merit, scorning those who would edit it out, as suggesting 'the faint odour of a literary Keating's Powder: a sort of spiritual insect killer—fatal to worms'.[9] I think, though, that he would not have wanted to retain either of these:

> Earth from afar has heard Thy fame,
> And worms have learnt to lisp Thy name.

Or again,

> O may Thy powerful word
> Inspire the feeble worm
> To rush into Thy kingdom, Lord,
> And take it as by storm.[10]

The structure of a hymn, too, can become unacceptably archaic, employing what now seem infelicitous constructions, which today's writers would try to avoid; and at times their sentiments are no longer those of today's church. It was a right instinct that in 'Thy kingdom come, O God' contemporary editors have changed the original, 'O'er heathen lands afar/Thick darkness broodeth yet', to read 'O'er lands both near and far...'; uninspired, perhaps, but reminding us of the retreat of Christendom and prolonging for a little longer the usefulness of the hymn. The most obvious example is Bishop Heber's 1819 missionary hymn, 'From Greenland's icy mountains', an indispensable addition to the 'Foreign Missions' section of every self-respecting Victorian hymnal. It was still in *Ancient & Modern Revised* in 1950, but today we cannot comfortably sing

> The heathen in his blindness
> Bows down to wood and stone,

when our own societies seem blind to the 'worship' we offer to materialism and consumerism and when 'heathen' has become simply a pejorative term.

Sometimes the trouble is less with what the author meant than with what is now mistakenly read into the words. Few hymn books today would print that verse in the much-loved 'All things bright and beautiful' that speaks of

> The rich man in his castle,
> The poor man at his gate,
> God made them, high and lowly,
> And ordered their estate.

It is read as seeking to sanction invidious class distinctions. But there are two pointers which show that this is not quite fair. The first is to remember the theme of the hymn. We know that it was written by Mrs Alexander (Miss Humphreys, as she was then) to help her class of small children understand the Creed.[11] In the same sequence, her equally famous Christmas hymn, 'Once in royal David's city' was on the clause *'who was conceived by the Holy Ghost, born of the Virgin Mary'*; while 'All things bright and beautiful' was based on *'Maker of heaven and earth'*. With this in mind, it is easy to see that the hymn is about creation, God as *maker*: indeed, the word 'made' comes in every sentence. The second clue lies in the comma in the middle of line three. It throws the emphasis onto the words 'God made them', so that whether we are rich or poor, all are equally God's creation; and this is simply borrowing from Scripture: 'The rich and poor meet together: the Lord is the maker of them all.'[12] Seen in this light, the hymn levels rather than divides them. It is a sad reflection of what scant attention is paid to the meaning that the crucial comma is not always printed, and then the words are sure to mislead. Percy Dearmer did not include them in *Songs of Praise*. He did, however, print 'this appalling verse' in order to castigate it in his companion to the hymnal, *Songs of Praise Discussed*, but he omits the crucial comma and so does the author an injustice. If anything more were needed to demonstrate that the verse is primarily about equality before our Maker, it can be found in the same author's *Verses for Holy Seasons* published two years before, from which she was clearly borrowing:

> The poor man in his straw-roofed cottage,
> The rich man in his lordly hall,
> The old man's voice, the child's first whisper,
> He listens, and He answers all.[13]

I cannot help noticing, too, when the hymn is being sung, that some who might protest if that verse were included, nevertheless sing happily and quite untruthfully of 'the rushes by the water,/We gather every day'. I imagine some of Miss Humphreys' Sunday School children in County Tyrone often did just that, to provide a floor-covering in a labourer's rural home; few in any English congregation do, or have ever done so within living memory.

Let me offer two more considerations in making the case for new hymns. Compare them, first, with other creative enterprises. When people say, 'We surely have enough hymns: our hymn books are bulging with them; why do we need more?' they are expressing what would be ridiculous transposed to other arts. We could not take seriously someone who said 'Surely we have more than enough books—or paintings or poems or symphonies—why do we want new ones?' One reason why we want new ones is that the arts reflect the climate, the ethos, the practice, of their day; and something of this is similarly true of today's hymns. C. S. Lewis, quoted at the head of this chapter, wrote that what he personally desired was 'fewer, better and shorter hymns; especially fewer'. When the cry is that we want our new hymns to be better, I wholeheartedly agree; we all wish we could write better; we all try. Today's hymns are already shorter than many of the older originals; 'Soldiers of Christ, arise', for example, was written in sixteen eight-line verses; while as to 'fewer', that rests for any congregation in the hands of those who order worship, not those who write or publish hymns. It is easy to be impatient with congregations who would cling exclusively to the old, but we need to recognize how quickly all this surge in new hymnody has come about. Much of it has found its way into local church worship, not in a lifetime, but in a single generation. I was once told by a Canadian minister of two of his colleagues discussing their respective congregations, and their attitude to the more militaristic hymns: 'Do your people mind singing of themselves as "Christian soldiers"?', asked one. 'Not at all,' was the reply, 'it is only the word "onward" that they object to.'

Sometimes what appears as reactionary conservatism is not so much resistance to change, as to the unremitting *pace of change*. Nevertheless, a further reason for introducing new hymns (selectively, gradually, giving people a chance to become familiar with a new text) lies in the fact, obvious enough when you think about it, that we only have the old hymns because churchgoers were willing to adopt them when they were new and unfamiliar. I picture to myself such a congregation in the 1860s, coming out of church with something of a grievance. 'I don't much like this new hymn book', someone says to the harassed vicar. 'It may be called *Ancient & Modern*, but there's too much modern for my liking.' His wife agrees with him: 'Who is this Henry Lyte, writing these new-fangled hymns?', she asks, 'Haven't we enough already? What was that first line—"Abide with me"? Why do we have to sing a new hymn that none of us has ever heard of?' They are followed by the oldest parishioner with his fond reminiscence: 'When I was a boy, I was taken to hear Charles Wesley. Now there was a man who really could write *proper* hymns!'

We can find in Thomas Hardy an example of how what we think of as old favourites had once the freshness and power of the new. He writes of Bathsheba, the heroine of *Far from the Madding Crowd*, not long widowed and still semi-convalescent, walking to the village one Friday evening to visit her husband's grave:

Bathsheba heard singing inside the church, and she knew that the singers were practising. She crossed the road, opened the gate, and entered the graveyard...the choir was learning a new hymn. Bathsheba was stirred by emotions which latterly she had assumed to be altogether dead within her. The little attenuated voices of the children brought to her ear in distinct utterance the words they sang without thought or comprehension:

Lead, kindly Light, amid the encircling gloom,
Lead Thou me on.

It was a *new* hymn, written earlier in the century, and Hardy uses the succeeding lines, drifting out of the church, to punctuate a conversation with Gabriel Oak, the man with whom at last Bathsheba will find happiness. The words, the time, her husband's grave, the 'attenuated voices', and the whole occasion unite to stir her heart.[14]

It is easy to think that the familiar hymns which we and indeed our parents may have known since childhood, were somehow 'always there'. But, of course, they were once no more than the germ of an idea in an author's mind, a scribbled note or two, a much-emended draft, and only finally a *new* hymn. Here is a well-known nineteenth-century account of Charles Wesley, prince of hymn writers, still busy in old age working on the hymns that we sing today.

When he was nearly fourscore, he retained something of this eccentricity. He rode every day, (clothed for winter even in summer,) a little horse, grey with age. When he mounted, if a subject struck him, he proceeded to expand, and put it in order. He would write a hymn thus given him, on a card, (kept for the purpose,) with his pencil, in short-hand. Not unfrequently he has come to our house in the City-road, and, having left the poney in the *garden* in front, he would enter, crying out, 'Pen and ink! Pen and ink!' These being supplied, he wrote the hymn he had been composing. When this was done, he would look round on those present, and salute them with much kindness, ask after their health, give out a short hymn, and thus put all in mind of eternity.[15]

'Nearly fourscore' dates this as the 1780s. What Charles Wesley was doing then, writers of every generation have done before and since, not perhaps with the card and pencil, let alone the shorthand and the 'poney', but in their own way. And many would, I believe, echo from experience the sense that a hymn, or at last the starting point of a hymn, is somehow 'given'. There will be more to say about this in a later chapter, but this 'given-ness' is another answer to the question, 'Why new hymns?'

It is an answer that applies very particularly to the generation of hymn writers who have been at work on what today's congregations would call 'new hymns' because it has been their good fortune to be part of the 'hymn explosion' which began about the 1950s. The term 'hymn explosion', though much used at the time, is not the most elegant description. It has been more happily described by Eric Sharpe, writing in the *Bulletin* of the Hymn Society in January 1982 as 'a magnificent hymnic firework display, with some brilliant pyrotechnic effects of occasional breath-taking beauty, including some Roman candles, and inevitably a good proportion of damp squibs!'[16] The article sets the regeneration of hymnody against the secular climate of the day, as does Brian Castle, writing some ten years later. His book, *Sing a New Song to the Lord*,[17] has a chapter on 'The Hymn Explosion' which outlines major changes, even discontinuities, in the secular culture of the time, exemplified perhaps by Bob Dylan in the early 1960s with *The times they are a-changin'*. This wind of change was felt by the church and reflected in this 'hymn explosion', which has been more soberly described as 'an unprecedented flow of hymn writing, a great flowering of hymnody'.[18] But whatever the name, it describes an upsurge in writing and composing, in the publication of hymn books, and in the study of hymnology. I am not sure about the word 'unprecedented' in the description above, since this is by no means the first time such a thing has happened. In the sixty years following his conversion experience of May 1738 Charles Wesley alone wrote nine or ten thousand hymns or poems; while at much the same time the celebrated preacher William Romaine observed in the 1770s a vast variety of new hymnals, 'collection upon collection, and in use, too, new hymns starting up daily—appendix added to appendix—sung in many congregations'.[19] Think too of the output of the remarkable J. M. Neale who died in 1866 at the age of only forty-eight. He was said to have known twenty languages; and when towards the end of his life the first edition of *Hymns Ancient & Modern* was published it drew heavily on his work as translator, as indeed we do today. But those first editors were fortunate to have many contemporaries writing for them whose names still sprinkle the pages of our hymn books. There was John Keble, celebrated as the author of *The Christian Year*; Bishop (formerly Archdeacon) Christopher Wordsworth, nephew of the poet; the honoured John Ellerton; Edward Caswall; F. W. Faber; John Henry Newman, the future Cardinal; and other contemporary contributors very much alive—a hymn explosion indeed!

Today's church, then, is the heir to something not dissimilar, dating from the 1950s well into the following century. When I was a child we sang from the old Standard Edition of *Hymns Ancient & Modern*. Of its 779 hymns, only three authors of texts were alive when I was ten years old, and two of them had died by the time I was thirteen. By contrast, *Common Worship*, the edition of the same hymnal from the year 2000 with 150 fewer hymns, has texts from some forty living authors, contributing between them about one-sixth of the contents. Perhaps we should not be too surprised to find this happening around that time. In an account of creative trends in British advertising, the 1960s have been described as 'witnessing an unparalleled explosion of innovation in almost every sphere of culture':

> ...young creativity supplanted the old, and disrespect for the past supplanted respect. From the Beatles and the Stones to Britten, Tippet, and Maxwell Davies; from Pinter and Joe Orton to Lionel Bart and Joan Littlewood... from *Private Eye* to *That Was The Week That Was*... wherever you looked young creativity burgeoned.[20]

Yet this 'hymn explosion' or 'new flowering' did not come without solid roots in the past, and firm bridges between the old and the new. One of many possible starting points might be as early as 1931 when the enlarged edition of *Songs of Praise* was published, with the young 'Jan Struther' writing in a distinctly twentieth-century style.[21] From there, it all began to gather momentum. With hindsight we can see Albert Bayly as a key figure, not so much in construction as in the subject and content of his writing: 'Locked in the atom', 'power of the turbine', 'the secret process that brings our life to birth'.

Bayly published his first collection, *Rejoice O People*, in 1950. By 1957 Patrick Appleford was on the scene with the twentieth-century Church Light Music Group, though they majored more on music, led by Geoffrey Beaumont, than on words. It was a trend that continued for some time unabated, so that by 1974 Kevin Mayhew was able to edit for Mayhew-McCrimmon *The 20th Century Folk Hymnal, Vol. 1*, a collection of over 100 songs 'of the church folk movement'; to be followed in quick succession by volumes 2, 3, and 4. In 1957, *Christian Praise* introduced to the UK texts by Margaret Clarkson of Canada and Bishop Frank Houghton among other living writers and composers. Sydney Carter, born in 1915 and always associated with *The Lord of the Dance*, was a pioneer in the new *genre* of the worship song with his *Green Print for Song* in 1963, and a few years later a young student, Graham Kendrick, was swapping his electric guitar for an acoustic one, and beginning to write Christian songs in the folk tradition. In Scotland there were gatherings at Dunblane to consult about, and to work together on, a new kind of hymnody, which would introduce the names of Brian Wren, Alan Luff, Alan Gaunt—and, among musicians, Erik Routley and Peter Cutts. Fred Kaan's first collection, *Pilgrim Praise*, belongs to the 1970s, but his congregation at the Pilgrim Church, Plymouth, were singing his hymns well before that, and his first published hymn belongs to 1963. He had spent his teenage years under Nazi occupation in Holland and his hymns reflect his consequent strong social conscience and concern for peace.

It was also in the 1960s that Fred Pratt Green, a Methodist sometimes described as the new Charles Wesley, saw his first hymns published (save for a single much earlier text) in the Ancient & Modern supplement, *100 Hymns for Today*, and the Methodist supplement, *Hymns and Songs*, both dated 1969. In the same year Michael Baughen was preparing *Youth Praise 2,* building on the success of *Youth Praise 1* three years earlier, to meet the needs of church youth groups hungry for a new idiom. Out of this came *Psalm Praise,* and from some of the team who worked on that there followed in 1982 their seminal *Hymns for Today's Church.* So began the Jubilate Group, still active, with Christopher Idle, David Mowbray, and the late Jim Seddon, Michael Perry, and Michael Saward among their text writers; and Noël Tredinnick, David Wilson, and John Barnard among the composers. In 1965, the *Anglican Hymn Book* had introduced some new contemporary hymn writers and composers (I have already recounted how it set me on the road to hymn writing), alongside the best of the old. Bland Tucker and Margaret Clarkson, both Canadians, contributed to the book; as did George Caird and Frank Houghton. At the same time Roman Catholic hymnody was being refreshed by writers such as Brian Foley, James Quinn, and Geoffrey Lacock, and more recently by Bernadette Farrell. Something of the same pattern can be seen during this period in North America, to begin with more in music than in words, though new standards were being set by such as Margaret Clarkson, Carl Daw, Ruth Duck, and Thomas Troeger.

The 1980s proved a fertile decade for women hymn writers, who sometimes felt overlooked in a day when most hymnal committees were largely male. In England, Elizabeth Cosnett was twice the winner of the BBC 'Songs of Praise' competition; Rosalind Brown was beginning to write hymns for her local parish; Emma Turl was at work on psalms and other metrical Bible versions; and June Boyce-Tillman was versifying Celtic texts. All this and more has been chronicled by Janet Wootton, herself a hymn writer, in her comprehensive survey of women's hymn writing.[22] At much the same time, John Bell and the Iona 'Wild Goose' team were breaking new ground with both words and music, springing from their mid-1980s youth ministry in inner-city Glasgow.

The names, many of them my contemporaries, in the paragraphs above tend to be of those personally known to me. But the Index of Authors in any recent hymn book will show that this is only scratching the surface of the new talent that was being discovered on both sides of the Atlantic.

Though this 'flowering' from the 1960s was a distinct phenomenon, it did not appear from nowhere; it was *continuous* with what had gone before, a particularly striking expression of a strand of writing and composing for worship never absent from the church's life. And because this seems to have arisen among different groups and individuals, independent of one another and even in different continents, it can be characterized by the two words: *continuity* and *variety.* It had no single beginning. It was spontaneous, diffuse, and unorganized, and it is difficult to resist the conclusion that it was somehow the gift of the creative Spirit.

Perhaps we should add to *continuity* and *variety* the thought of *collaboration.* When any congregation is asked to sing for the first time a new hymn from a book in their hands, at least nine or ten groups or individuals will have been involved in the different stages leading up to this moment. First of these is *the church* in the widest sense of the word, since it is the church which welcomes or refuses, uses or discards; without the church, there is no hymnody. *The writer,* second on the list, is the servant of the church, working away in the hope of being useful and not simply by way of self-expression, which is why hymn writing can be called ' a functional art'. Third comes *the composer,* whose contribution is plainly crucial; and fourth, *the editor,* of whom there will be more to say. Number five is *the publisher*, who, with the editor or editorial committee, is what in other branches of media is called a 'gate-keeper': acceptance or oblivion are in their hands. Sixth is *the purchaser*, probably the church council, who decide which book will best suit their congregation, and the church treasurer may have something to say on this also. But even when these six lights turn green there is still some way to go. Number seven is *the minister, organist, worship leader, or music committee*, whoever chooses the hymns. Eight, in some churches, will be *the choir* or *music group*, claiming some voice in what they are asked to lead. Nine is *the congregation*, the true owners of their church's hymnody.

And is there a last stage? Perhaps; but probably not, since its name is *posterity*. Our job is to be like the musical King David who, as Paul described him in a sermon, 'served his own generation by the will of God'.[23] The question of how long a text may continue to be useful is not our concern. On the world's stage, Tennyson summed up the matter in a verse entitled 'Fame' which was only published after his death:

> Well, as to Fame, who strides the earth
>   With that long horn she loves to blow,
> I know a little of her worth,
>   And I will tell you what I know—
> This London once was middle sea,
>   These hills were plains within the past,
> They will be plains again, and we,
>   Poor devils, babble 'we shall last'.[24]

Forty years earlier James Montgomery had taken much the same view, writing in the third person, of his own numerous hymn texts:

Tried by the standard which he himself has set up, every one of them would be found wanting... but the judgment he leaves with his readers, to whom he humbly presents these gleanings, under the perfect conviction, that they will be thoroughly sifted, and the chaff burnt up, and the grain, if there be any, gathered into the garner of the true church.[25]

For my part, since my calling is to be a minister of the gospel, I have come to see hymn writing not as a 'tinkling employment', but as a real part of that Christian ministry to which I was ordained. The adjective 'tinkling', with more than a hint of disparagement, is not mine but borrowed from John Berridge, sometime Vicar of Everton, near Cambridge. Many years ago I visited his grave in his own churchyard and reflected on his uncompromising gospel ministry, both in that parish and further afield. You can still see there the lengthy epitaph he composed for himself:

> Here lay the earthly Remains of JOHN BERRIDGE
> late *Vicar of Everton,* and an itinerant Servant
> of JESUS CHRIST who loved his Master and his Work,
> and after running on his Errands many Years was called
> up to wait on him above. Reader art thou born again
> No Salvation without a new Birth.
>
> I was born in Sin Feb. 1716
> Remained ignorant of my fallen State till 1730,
> Lived proudly on Faith & Works for Salvation till 1754

> Admitted to Everton Vicarage 1755
> Fled to JESUS alone for Refuge 1756
> Fell asleep in Christ Jan 22 1793.[26]

Berridge was a tireless preacher and diligent pastor. He was a friend of the young Charles Simeon, though forty years his senior: the one was a Fellow of King's College, Cambridge, the other of Clare. Both suffered calumny, and Berridge was no stranger to the brutal opposition that the Wesleys knew so well. It is against this background that we must read Berridge's 'apology' for turning his mind to hymn writing:

> ...ill-health, some years past, having kept me from travelling. I took up the trade of hymn-making, a handicraft much followed of late, but a business I was not born or bred to, and undertaken chiefly to keep a long sickness from preying on my spirit and to make tedious nights pass over more smoothly. Some tinkling employment was wanted which might amuse and not fatigue me.[27]

Berridge was then sixty-nine; clergy in his day did not 'retire'. To draw a personal comparison, by that age, four years into retirement, I was beginning to see Christian writing, including hymn writing, as a major part of my future ministry. And although Berridge's tongue may have been in his cheek, and self-deprecation part of his character, I take a very different view from that implied in the final sentence of his 'apology'. The Minutes of the Methodist Conference of 1788 might say of Charles Wesley, having in mind his labours, his incessant journeys, his care for the flock and the well-being of the connexion, that 'his least praise was his talent for poetry'; yet, two centuries on, that is not the verdict of a grateful posterity. His was no 'tinkling employment' and nor should it be of any hymn writer. Think of Jane Austen's defence of her craft:

> 'And what are you reading, Miss ———?' 'Oh! it is only a novel!' replies the young lady; while she lays down her book with affected indifference, or momentary shame...only some work in which the greatest powers of the mind are displayed, in which the most thorough knowledge of human nature, the happiest delineation of its varieties, the liveliest effusions of wit and humour are conveyed to the world in the best chosen language.[28]

'Only a hymn?' Only a 'tinkling employment', to find words which may help a congregation to exalt God's Name and receive his word? I submit not.

* * *

So to return to the question, 'Why new hymns?', it seems that they are there already, as a gift to today's church. Perhaps this should not surprise us. Those who have found in God their Deliverer, in Christ their Redeemer, naturally want to sing about it. No hymn lover needs reminding of how song runs through the Bible from beginning to end. The Morning Stars sang at the creation; we have the Song of Moses to celebrate Israel's deliverance at the Red Sea, the Song of Deborah, and the Songs of David, which we know as psalms. In Psalm 40.3 he famously writes of the 'new song' God gave him when he draw him from the desolate pit—a psalm and a 'new song' which meant so much to Charles Wesley in the hour of his conversion. Solomon, David's son, has a whole book of the Old Testament known as 'the Song of Solomon'. He must have been a prolific lyricist and probably a composer as well, since we read that, besides his proverbs, 'his songs were a thousand and five'. In the New Testament we have seen how the

Lord Jesus sang with his disciples before Gethsemane; while Paul in two of his letters wants his infant churches to be singing the praise of God, as he did himself with Silas one midnight in that Philippian prison. Finally, in the Book of Revelation, heaven is filled with the voice of everlasting song, the 'new song' of the age to come, the song of the Lamb.

Of course, our all-too-human 'new song' is a gift we have to winnow carefully if we are to separate the wheat from the chaff and learn to assimilate the best of it with proper sensitivity alongside all we have inherited. Not a great deal, whether words or music, will trouble us for long. Back in 1986, when the new flowering of hymnody was still unproven, the editors of *The New English Hymnal* made their assessment plain. 'The post-war surge in hymnwriting,' says the Preface, 'has not been ignored but we regard much of it as poor in quality and ephemeral in expression.' Perhaps twenty-five years on things now look a little different; I should like to think so. But for those who still find new hymnody difficult to come to terms with, there is comfort in the assurance of T. S. Eliot that eventually it will all find its proper place, through 'the only tribunal that can decide: Time!'[29]

GIVE THANKS TO GOD ON HIGH

GIVE THANKS to God on high
for saints of other days,
whose hope it was to live and die
in love's consuming blaze,
    for Christ and his kingdom,
his glory and his praise.

Their vision long-fulfilled,
our prayer is still the same:
upon their work of faith to build,
their word of truth proclaim,
    for Christ and his kingdom,
and for his holy Name.

New tasks today are ours
who serve a world in pain,
new calls to challenge all our powers
of heart and hand and brain,
    for Christ and his kingdom,
while life and breath remain.

Give thanks to God on high
for all the future sends,
in praise of Christ to live and die
who calls his servants friends,
    for Christ and his kingdom,
whose glory never ends!

© Timothy Dudley-Smith in Europe and Africa. © Hope Publishing Company in the United States of America and the rest of the world. Reproduced by permission of Oxford University Press. All rights reserved.

CHAPTER 3

What Sort of Hymns?

> Let the word of Christ dwell in you richly; teach and admonish in all wisdom; and with gratitude in your hearts sing psalms, hymns and spiritual songs to God.*
>
> St Paul to the Colossians

THE TITLES GIVEN to collections of hymns form a study of their own. Miles Coverdale (d. 1568) chose *Goostly Psalmes and Spiritualle Songes;* William Hunnis (d. 1597) with memorable alliteration has *Seven Sobs of a Sorrowful Soule for Sinne.* Anne Rennew in 1714 called her hymns *Pious and Holy Breathings.* Charles Wesley liked to be more explicit; among his many collections there is one entitled *Hymns on the Occasion of his being Prosecuted in Ireland as a Vagabond* (1749), and another *Preparation for Death, in Several Hymns* (1772). Richard Newman (1819) with becoming modesty chose *Feeble Attempts to Praise God.* Others went for even longer and more descriptive titles, such as John Wesley's celebrated *A Collection of Hymns for the Use of the People called Methodists* of 1780, or Isaac Watts' earlier book of 1719, *The Psalms of David Imitated in the Language of the New Testament, And Apply'd to the Christian State and Worship.* Newton and Cowper's *Olney Hymns* of 1779 is by comparison a model of brevity.

More recently we have come to overwork the word 'praise'. For our generation it began, imaginatively enough, with *Songs of Praise*, a year before I was born. But the present run on the word seems to start with *Congregational Praise* in 1951, followed by *Christian Praise* six years later. *Youth Praise 1 and 2* came in 1966 and 1969, followed by *Psalm Praise* in 1973. Next was *Keswick Praise* (1975), the hymnal of the Lakeland Christian convention, and in the same year the first Supplement to *The English Hymnal*, entitled *English Praise* though not without contributions from the rest of the United Kingdom, Europe, and beyond. Meanwhile the Baptists had rung the changes with their own Supplement, *Praise for Today* (1974, the forerunner of *Baptist Praise and Worship*, 1991), while the Scripture Union published *Jesus Praise* in 1981. *Mission Praise* began in 1983, with an ever-growing family of enlarged editions. And so it went on, from a variety of publishers, with *Junior Praise, Carol Praise, Let's Praise, New English Praise, BBC Songs of Praise,* while from Canadian Presbyterians came *The Book of Praise* (1997), followed a year later by the Anglican Church of Canada's *Common Praise.* Hymns Ancient & Modern borrowed the same title (to match the new *Common Worship* Service Book) for their edition in the year 2000, which was followed by *Sing Praise* in 2010. The wheel came full circle in the year 2000 with the comprehensive and much-valued collection of 976 hymns called simply *Praise!* There cannot be many more variants left to choose from, though I expect any day to find *Pop Praise* or *Rap Praise* or *Bebop Praise*; they may even be with us already.

But for the editorial committee of a new hymnal the title is not usually the first consideration. Some system of arrangement must be found and editors wrestle with the problem. Hymns can be classified in so many different ways. John Wesley in his celebrated 1780 collection arranged his hymns into 'a Little Body of Experimental and Practical Divinity' beginning with a section entitled 'Exhorting and beseeching to return to God' and continuing through 'Praying for Repentance' to 'Believers Rejoicing... Fighting... Suffering', and so on. By contrast, the first editors of *Hymns Ancient & Modern* began with the Church's day (Morning, Evening), and week (Sunday, Monday...), and especially year: Advent, Christmas, Epiphany, Lent, Easter, and on to Trinity Sunday; with later divisions on Occasional Services, followed by 'For the Young... Friendly Societies... Times of Cattle Plague... Processional'. Later editions tend to be variations on this theme, with a large section of 'General Hymns', right down to the 2013 edition, which also includes sections with headings such as 'Wholeness and Healing', 'Creation and the Environment', and 'Justice and Peace'. Other books classify their contents more thematically or in the last resort simply admit defeat and order the texts alphabetically by first line, relying on a comprehensive subject index.

All this does not begin to exhaust the sheer diversity of what we sing. Hymns can be classified as celebratory, rejoicing in the saving acts of God; declaratory, rehearsing some aspect of faith; didactic, opening new windows into truth; hortatory, stirring each other up, as Paul urged Timothy.[1] They can be narrative, telling again some part of 'the old, old story'; meditative, where the music helps us to reflect; petitionary, where we offer God our united prayer or aspiration in song—and these are only examples. Chapter 4 will propose a much simpler classification: Hymns, good and not so good. First, though, consider St Paul's three categories, Hymns, Psalms, and Spiritual Songs. He repeats this description twice in his letters, but with a subtle difference. Here he is writing to the church in Ephesus:

...be filled with the Spirit, as you sing psalms and hymns and spiritual songs among yourselves, singing and making melody to the Lord in your hearts, giving thanks to God the Father at all times and for everything in the name of our Lord Jesus Christ.

Ephesians 5. 18-20

To those at Colossae he says nearly, but not quite, the same:

Let the word of Christ dwell in you richly; teach and admonish in all wisdom; and with gratitude in your hearts sing psalms, hymns and spiritual songs to God. And whatever you do, in word or deed, do everything in the name of the Lord Jesus, giving thanks to God the Father through him.

Colossians 3.16,17

In both letters he divides their musical repertoire into psalms, hymns, and spiritual songs, a classification which fits neatly, if misleadingly, into today's worship. In fact, commentators are by no means agreed as to the distinctions, if any, that Paul had in mind. I think myself he may simply mean 'whatever you are accustomed to sing in worship'. There are considerable similarities in both letters. He wants a strong sense of thankfulness and of fellowship together. He wants them to sing from (or in) the heart, and in the name of the Lord Jesus. But there is a difference, too, relating perhaps to the differing circumstances of these young churches. To Ephesus he places his emphasis on their need for the *Spirit* to inspire their worship, and to the Colossians on the place of the *word* to inform it. In hymnod*y*, as in all Christian living, to have one without the other leads to unbalanced discipleship, but when we link the two passages together, we can say that singing should help the word of Christ to find its way 'richly' into hearts and minds, as the worship is inspired and enabled by the Spirit himself.

We think of Paul more as a preacher than a singer, though we have seen how Luke tells us of Paul and Silas singing hymns in the middle of the night in prison at Philippi. In this, Paul was practising what he preached. When writing to the rather disorderly church at Corinth who needed instruction in how to manage their worship together, he recommended them to do as he did: 'I will sing with the spirit and I will sing with the mind also'; or, in the NEB, 'I will sing hymns as I am inspired to sing, but I will sing intelligently too.'[2] So we are back with the words of Jesus to the Samaritan woman: 'The time... is already here when those who are real worshippers will worship the Father in spirit and in truth.'[3]

Psalms, the first of Paul's divisions, occupy a unique place because they are part of Scripture. We may not be sure how he would distinguish between a hymn and a 'spiritual song'; but the reference to psalms must be mainly to our Book of Psalms, carried over from the worship of the synagogue and sung by the Lord Jesus Christ himself. Those first Christians may also have sung as latter-day psalms what we now recognize as Scripture, since certain passages in our New Testament seem to have been early Christian hymns. The account of Christ's self-emptying in Philippians 2 is an example frequently quoted, and in modern translations this and other passages are sometimes printed as poetry on the page. In our own day, too, verses or short sections of the Bible have often been set to music and included in our hymn books, a practice which helps to fix them in our memories. Nevertheless, the distinctiveness of psalms, in contrast to hymns and songs, lies in their being what the Thirty-nine Articles describe as 'holy Scripture... of whose authority was never any doubt in the Church'. There is something special about singing, or saying, to the glory of God words inspired by the Spirit which were written centuries before Christ, but were on his lips and in his memory. The hymn writer John Ellerton touchingly reminds us that on that dreadful cross Jesus 'sustained his spirit... not with any new utterances of devotion... but with the familiar words of his church's psalmody, the broken fragments of the hymnal of his childhood'.[4] Professor Tom Wright, formerly Bishop of Durham, described the aim of the psalms as the praise of God, 'to celebrate his love and power even in the midst of pain and sorrow, and indeed to bring all human life into his presence'.[5] What more could we ask?

Yet how many churches have lost the psalms from their public worship, finding that when they can no longer muster a choir the traditional Anglican chant cannot be sustained? This is, to my mind, a great loss. Calvin described the Book of Psalms as 'a mirror to the soul', a phrase I borrowed for a collection of my hymns based on psalms:

for not an affection will a man find in himself, an image of which is not reflected in this glass. Nay, all the griefs, sorrows, fears, misgivings, hopes, cares, anxieties, in short, all the troublesome emotions with which the minds of men are wont to be agitated, the Holy Spirit has here pictured to the life.[6]

And alongside this empathy with our 'troublesome emotions', the sense of thankfulness, the spirit of praise, and the expression of joy are all equally part of the book. Indeed, as Derek Kidner has described it, the Psalter, taken on its own terms, is not so much a liturgical library, storing up standard literature for cultic requirements, as a hospitable house, well lived in, where most things can be found and borrowed after some searching, and whose occupants have left on it everywhere the imprint of their experiences and the stamp of their characters.[7]

But in fact the loss of the psalms in any congregation, even the smallest, is not inevitable. Let the people sit comfortably and prayerfully and *say* the psalms. The Prayer Book rubrics clearly expect this as an alternative to singing, and make provision for it. This saying can be varied; now antiphonally, minister and people, men's and women's voices, or two sides of the aisle; now in unison, now shared with a main reader or readers. It will, I think, be found that this often allows closer attention to the words, which yield their meaning and relevance as Holy Scripture in a way which chanting may sometimes have obscured. Indeed, remembering my own difficulties with anything musical, I sometimes wonder whether it was a failure by some congregations to make much sense of chanting that allowed them to take leave of the psalms without apparently any great sense of loss. But psalms demand at least the regard we give to the rest of Scripture.

A sense of this reverence is brought out in a charming if back-handed way in Thomas Hardy's description of John Loveday, the trumpet-major, sharing an evening of rustic music-making:

Bob showed less than his customary liveliness. The miller, wishing to keep up his son's spirits, expressed his regret that, it being Sunday night, they could have no songs to make the evening cheerful; when Mrs Garland proposed that they should sing psalms which, by choosing lively tunes and not thinking of the words, would be almost as good as ballads.[8]

No doubt in part this ingenious compromise arose from an almost superstitious attitude to the words of 'the Good Book'; but also perhaps to a half-sensed awareness that Scripture has the power to strike through 'to the innermost intimacies of man's being', which would lend discomfort to their Sabbath merry-making. It is comparable to that earlier period in Scottish church music when it was not thought proper to use the sacred words of the psalm itself in order to learn a new tune, so that various pieces of doggerel were substituted. Sometimes the verse was related to the nature of the tune, so that the words they invented carried their precentor's instructions:

> All people that OLD HUNDREDTH sing,
>   With cheerful voice this measure take;
> Gar ilka line wi' grandeur ring,
>   Put on the seventh note a shake.

Human nature being what it is, as time went on some of these practice-verses became more and more ribald; and the ruder the rhyme, the better it travelled:

The nearer they came to the edge of the permissible, or passed beyond it, the faster they flew from parish to parish. Thus the same almost unbelievably rude rhymes are found in Orkney, and right down the country to the Mull of Galloway.[9]

The cure had become far worse than the disease.

John Stott, too, provided a detailed summary of what the psalter can contribute to our worship in his commentary on *The Canticles and Selected Psalms*. 'The psalter,' he writes, reveals a God who is both the creator of the world and the redeemer of his people. Moreover, he sustains what he has created and shepherds whom he has redeemed. It is this past and present activity of God, in nature and in grace, which provides the constant theme for the psalmist's praise. Jehovah is not like dead, dumb idols; he is the living God, the Most High God, eternal and omnipresent. He is king. He reigns over the elements and over the nations. He is also a constant refuge, a fortress and a strong tower where his people may find safety. He has entered into a covenant with them, and he is faithful to his covenant. He has given them his law, and expects them to be faithful to it. But, in contrast to God's eternity and greatness, man's life is transitory and his size diminutive. Further, he is sinful, and liable to sickness, persecution and death. He needs to cry to God for the forgiveness of his sins and for deliverance...[10]

The Book of Psalms is one of the church's treasures, a marvellous resource for our private prayers, rooted as it is in the unchanging reality of the human condition, the human soul; but equally for public worship, which it has enriched and sustained since long before the Christian era.

Somewhere between psalms and hymns, in Paul's threefold classification, come metrical psalms. Many congregations sing such hymns regularly, almost unaware that their origin is in the psalter. A typical example might be the various versions of Psalm 23, the shepherd psalm. Think of 'The Lord's my shepherd, I'll not want' from the *Scottish Psalter*, or Joseph Addison's 'The Lord my pasture shall prepare'. We still sing George Herbert's 'The God of love my shepherd is' alongside Sir Henry Baker's 'The King of love my shepherd is'. From our own day we have, for example, Christopher Idle's 'The Lord my shepherd rules my life' or Christopher Walker's 'Because the Lord is my shepherd'; and more recently still Stuart Townend's twentieth-century adaptation of 'The Lord's my shepherd, I'll not want', from the Scottish original of some 400 years ago. Among the metrical psalms we sing today are other familiar texts such as 'Through all the changing scenes of life' on Psalm 34; 'Hail to the Lord's anointed' (Psalm 72); 'O God, our help in ages past' (Psalm 90), or 'Praise, my soul, the King of heaven' (Psalm 103). These hymns, fine as they are, can never be a wholly adequate substitute for the real thing. Rose Macaulay, whose return to faith is chronicled in her *Letters to a Friend*, much valued psalms in general but added: 'Some, one prefers in English, some in Latin; *none* in metrical versions!'[11] It suggests to me just a touch of intellectual pride, and a literary taste too refined for simple versification. But James Montgomery, journalist, editor, and hymn writer 200 years ago in Sheffield, where there are still streets named after him, was of much the same mind:

Of modern imitations of the psalms, it is not necessary to give an opinion here. Without disparagement to the living or the dead... it may be said that the harp of David yet hangs upon the willow, disdaining the touch of any hand less skilful than his own.[12]

Yet we would be the poorer without these metrical versions, and as we have seen, some go back a long way. Martin Luther valued them. He wrote in 1523 to ask a friend's help in turning a psalm into a hymn, adding 'I would like you to avoid new-fangled, fancied words and to use expressions simple and common for people to understand, yet pure and fitting.'[13] In England metrical psalms began to be made familiar by two pairs of writers. A generation or so after Luther's letter, Thomas Sternhold, courtier and Member of Parliament, assisted by John Hopkins, a Suffolk clergyman, had turned the whole psalter into verse. His aim was 'to make sacred ballads for the people' and it is said that in some of them you can hear the rhythm of 'Chevy Chase'. Their work met with some opprobrium and mockery (the asterisks replace an oath unsuitable to repeat):

> Sternhold and Hopkins had great qualms
> When they translated David's psalms,
>   To make the heart right glad:
> But had it been King David's fate
> To hear thee sing and them translate,
>   ***** 'twould set him mad.[14]

Almost every hymn book today retains at least one metrical psalm from this 'old version' as it came to be called. 'All people that on earth do dwell' is based on Psalm 100 to the tune of the OLD HUNREDTH and can grace any occasion. It was sung in Westminster Abbey at the Coronation of Queen Elizabeth II on 2 June, 1953 by a vast and distinguished congregation, so that there was a story current at the time that in an early proof of the Order of Service the word 'dwell' was missing its first letter. These two, Sternhold and Hopkins, held the field for more than a century, until Nahum Tate and Nicholas Brady produced what became known as the 'new version': Tate was Poet Laureate, and Brady also a poet in his own right. Their version, commended by the great and good, was more poetical but less faithful to the original. In James Montgomery's experience, a century or more later, 'Many people preferred the rude simplicity of the one, to the neutral propriety of the other.' However, as befits a Poet Laureate, Tate gave us one narrative hymn still to be found in nearly every hymnal, without which many Christmas celebrations would hardly be complete, 'While shepherds watched their flocks by night'. It has probably also served to introduce every school child to pastiche: 'washed their socks' seems to have a universal charm, combining a satisfying sense of neatness with a delightful spice of naughtiness.

Since the 'old' and the 'new versions', nearly every writer of hymns has tried his or her hand at a metrical psalm and indeed I often have myself, though I prefer to say my text is 'based on' the psalm. 'Inspired by' might be more accurate, but sounds a little pretentious, while 'metrical version' implies (to my mind, at least) something more like a translation of the original. I prefer to follow Isaac Watts, who in his 1719 version of *The Psalms of David* claimed only to imitate rather than translate. In his Preface he declares that he has 'rather expressed myself as I may suppose David would have done, had he lived in the days of Christianity...my grand design in view...to teach my Author to speak like a Christian'. He acknowledges that in this he is not original, since a certain Dr John Patrick had tried much the same a century before, and there have been many since.[15] In 1827, William Wordsworth was asked by the Church of Scotland if he would try his hand at a metrical psalm or 'paraphrase' for their revised collection. He replied:

The interest I take in all that concerns the welfare of the Church of Scotland would have induced me to make an attempt at producing something which might have suited the plan you have explained in a manner & with a care that proves the importance you attach to it, if I could have entertained the least hope of success. But I assure you Sir with frankness and sincerity, that I am unequal to the task...The Sacred writings have a majesty, a beauty, a simplicity, an ardour, a sublimity, that awes and overpowers the spirit of Poetry in uninspired men, at least this is my feeling...Indeed, Sir, I dare not attempt it.[16]

A decade later John Keble was saying much the same sort of thing. He did in fact publish in 1839 *The Psalter in English Verse*, even while declaring in his Preface that:

> It is not without very great misgivings that this Version of the Psalms is published... It was undertaken, in the first instance, with a serious apprehension, which has since grown into a full conviction, that the thing attempted is, strictly speaking, *impossible*...[17]

This is, at least in part, due to the extreme conscientiousness with which Keble sets himself not only to translate the Hebrew into poetical English, but also to work under a number of more or less self-imposed restraints, such as his plan 'to express the effect of each Hebrew clause by a single line'. John Julian, writing 130 years later, was surprised that 'hymnal compilers have strangely neglected this volume', but through today's eyes, that is less surprising. Here is part of Psalm 2:

> 'My King I have anointed still
> On Zion, Mine own holy hill',
> Now let me tell the high decree:—
> The Lord spake out, He spake to Me—
> 'Thou art my Son,' He said, 'to-day
> Begotten: ask, and win Thy way...'

Perhaps this helps to explain why thirty years later we find John Ellerton writing to the revisers of the 1863 SPCK hymnal confidently affirming that 'Metrical psalms are now... generally acknowledged to be a mistake',[18] but time has shown that it was he who was mistaken. They are still in almost every hymn book, and continue to be written and widely sung. The 1970s, for example, saw the publication of *Psalm Praise*; and more recently David Preston and Martin Leckebusch, no doubt among others, have published collections of their own metrical psalms.[19] As is well known, metrical psalms came into their own north of the border, and at times the Scottish churches sang nothing else. 'Martin Browning' neatly parodied some of their characteristic inversions and elisions in a *jeu d'esprit* for the *Bulletin* of the Hymn Society in July 1995:

Meditation from South of the Border on first encountering the Scottish Psalter in use

> The Psalms of David, David's songs
>   In metre sung have I
> According to the vers-i-ons
>   Scots kirk approved by.
>
> Appointed is't, not pointed, book
>   In worship to be used;
> Not so the Psalms of England's folk
>   Which too I have perus'd.
>
> Such syntax 'mong much metrics quaint
>   O seldom see ye may;
> Th' endurance such is of the saints
>   That last these shall for aye.
>
> Thus th'only thing I miss from home
>   Is our Doxologie,
> So glory be 'til kingdom come
>   To th' year sixteen fiftie.[20]

Metrical psalms lead us to the second of St Paul's categories, and since this whole book is about hymns, not much need be said about them here. We have seen that a hymn is 'a [congregational] song with praise of God'; but that is equally true of psalms and 'spiritual songs'. What chiefly distinguishes the hymn is its regular stanzas and repeated music, usually in a recognized metrical form, often aided by rhyme. There are, of course, a good many of them. Over a century ago John Julian in the Preface to the first edition of his *Dictionary of Hymnology* estimated as follows:

> The total number of Christian hymns in the 200 or more languages and dialects in which they have been written or translated is not less than 400,000. When classified into languages the greatest number are to be found in German, English, Latin and Greek, in the order named.

The second edition, only fifteen years later, found much new material to catalogue, but it was only in 2013 that a new (on-line) *Canterbury Dictionary of Hymnology* appeared, a massive project to which Professor J. R. Watson had devoted ten years of his retirement. Before then at least three editors had died in the attempt; and indeed it was only the use of electronic technology that finally achieved what less than twenty-five years before had been deemed 'beyond contemplation, let alone completion'.

What St Paul in his letters calls 'spiritual songs' would not, I think, bear much relation to today's 'worship songs', a genre which has some of its roots in children's 'choruses', but which has largely been introduced into mainstream adult worship comparatively recently. At their best, today's worship songs use words of Scripture, set to easily remembered but not over-obtrusive melodies; or familiar, if not always overtly biblical, texts such as 'Make me a channel of your peace'. At their worst (I am not making this up) we have 'I love Jesus better than ice-cream', 'I'm bananas for the Lord', or texts which include words like 'wanna' or 'gonna', as in 'I'm gonna click, click, click'. I find it difficult to believe that even the most way-out fringe of youth culture is edified by being encouraged to sing, as in a new hymnal which recently came my way, 'Oh, it's great, great, brill, brill, wicked, wicked, skill, skill...', nor indeed 'I wanna be...'. A very widely used UK songbook includes three 'songs' that begin like that. Here is a representative example:

> I wanna sing, wanna sing.
> I wanna sing, wanna sing
> For Jesus, for Jesus, for Jesus,
> Oh I wanna sing for Him.
>
> I wanna clap, wanna clap.
> I wanna clap, wanna clap
> For Jesus, for Jesus, for Jesus,
> Oh, I wanna clap for Him.
>
> I wanna dance, praise, work, love, live...(etc.)[21]

I apologize if that is a hymn you value. There may be circumstances of which I know nothing where it meets the needs of a Christian fellowship. But for myself, I find something degrading in the auto-hypnotic mantra-like quality of such repetition. Even if we ignore the 'etc.—which is just as it appears in the book—the singers will have sung 'I wanna' some sixty times. We can thank God for anyone, of whatever age, who wants to live for Jesus, without feeling we have to endorse such expression. There is, of course, a place for repetition. 'Guide me, O thou great Jehovah' would be the poorer without 'Bread of heaven, Bread of heaven', just as 'Lo, he comes with clouds descending' gains some of its power from that repeated 'deeply wailing'. On Palm Sunday we are pleased to be singing the chorus of praise which punctuates J. M. Neale's 'All glory, laud, and honour'; though even that can become a little wearisome, beginning and ending all seven verses. But those examples differ, it seems to me, in both degree and kind from the repetition embraced by many worship songs, whether in the text or the performance.

In something of the same way, we can distinguish between the use of the personal pronoun 'I' in such hymns as 'When I survey the wondrous cross' or 'I bind unto myself today' and the strong subjectivity that marks its use in many contemporary songs. It is to me something of a danger-signal when in the index of first lines of a new hymnal, a disproportionate number begin with 'I'; and of course such misgivings are intensified if, on inspection—or, even more revealing, in watching a congregation sing them—the experience appears to be more about 'me' than about the Lord.

Because the model for many of these worship songs is drawn from the world of pop music, their shortcomings are sometimes excused on the ground that they are often intended to be ephemeral: they have been described as 'the spiritual equivalent of the paper plate'. This means that they borrow the equipment and seek to create the ambience of pop culture. Indeed, I have heard their real purpose expressed in terms of 'mood creation', which certainly fits well with the almost mesmeric repetition favoured by some worship leaders. Perhaps this is among the major characteristics of worship songs, so that one of their proponents warns that simply using them as replacements for traditional hymns ('stand up—sing once—sit down') is not to exploit their affective potential to the full.[22] 'Affective' here, it seems to me, is not far from 'mood creation', and on the road to manipulation. My dictionary defines 'affective' as 'appertaining to the emotions, opp. to *intellectual*'.

I confess to a sense of dismay when I enter an ancient church and see the chancel largely filled with the drum-kit and amplifiers that seem the essential accompaniment of worship songs. Those who have felt their seductive power in big, professionally staged gatherings or media events occasionally try to import something of what they there experienced into congregations quite unprepared or fitted to receive it. Indeed, one American book, *Why Catholics Can't Sing,* is a long list of passionate variations on this theme. It shows its colours with the subtitle (*The culture of Catholicism and the Triumph of Bad Taste*) and continues through phrases such as 'ego renewal', 'indecent narcissism', 'perpetual adolescence', 'the musical equivalent of the warm bubble-bath', culminating in the release of much pent-up anger in bewailing how 'the incessant glorification of feeling over competence, and trendiness over common sense, pollutes the church's whole musical life'.[23] From a UK perspective much of the book seems a wild exaggeration of anything we commonly experience; but trends have a way of crossing the Atlantic. A. W. Tozer, a highly influential American pastor and author, wrote of how in some Services of this nature 'Christ is courted with a familiarity that reveals a total ignorance of who he is. It is not the reverent intimacy of the adoring saints but the impudent familiarity of the carnal lover.'[24] Nearer home Pete Ward, then of King's College, London, subtitled his book *Selling Worship, How What We Sing has Changed the Church*. This is a serious and even-handed study, but he puts his finger on a particularly troubling issue:

...in contrast to the traditional hymns or more liturgical worship with its extensive use of the psalms, charismatic worship has no reflex which may accommodate those who are grieving or in the darker corners of spiritual experience. As a result, some of the songs and the worship become a problem for some charismatics. Some speak of the tone and language of the worship songs as a cause of spiritual harm in their lives and some drop out of charismatic churches because they feel that their spiritual journey is more complex and ambiguous than what seems to be allowed in the regular worship of the church.[25]

We can recognize something of all this in the frustrated protests of those established congregations who find too many unfamiliar and seemingly trite 'worship songs' taking the place of familiar hymns; songs whose music would not be out of place in TV advertisements. I have heard such people aptly described as 'the unhappy clappy'. They resonate with Jeremiah's words, if not his meaning, when he wrote 'You shall adorn yourselves with jingles'.[26] The congregation's disquiet may not only be about the music but also the quality of the words which they are asked to sing. Indeed, the whole experience of finding an unfamiliar 'worship group' in charge of the singing has been described before:

Music sullies the Divine Service, for in the very sight of God, in the sacred recesses of the sanctuary itself, the singers attempt, with the lewdness of a lascivious singing voice and a singularly foppish manner, to feminise all their spellbound little followers with the girlish way they render the notes and end the phrases.[27]

But that heartfelt invective was written by John of Salisbury, Bishop of Chartres, nearly 900 years ago!

Today things have moved on. It is my hope that we are beginning to see the worship song shed some of its immaturity and grow up. Even its most loyal adherents no longer believe, I understand, that the raw beat of unrelieved percussion has more than an exceptional place in Christian worship. Roger Scruton in his *The Aesthetics of Music* was very negative in his definition: 'Beat is not rhythm, but the last skeleton of rhythm, stripped bare of human life.'[28] Yet John Leach, one of the most ardent enthusiasts of the genre, writing in the 1990s, felt otherwise:

...in renewal songs it is rhythm which is paramount. The tunes may be fatuous and the harmony may consist of one chord change per line up to a maximum of about three, but the rhythm drives the song and makes it a memorable and exciting experience for the worshippers.[29]

This reminds me of the little girl whose aunt took her to the circus. On her return her mother asked how she had enjoyed it. 'Oh mother,' she replied, 'You must go. If you once went, you'd never be satisfied with church again!' Back in 1934 Constant Lambert, then still in his twenties and an avant-garde composer, was saying of the folk songs then in vogue what I hear musicians say today about some worship songs: 'To put it vulgarly,' he wrote, 'the whole trouble with a folk-song is that once you've played it through there is nothing much you can do except play it over again and play it rather louder.'[30]

Some long-suffering congregations would sympathize. Indeed, a major criticism of the worship song centres on its tendency towards performance rather than participation. The worship leader with the microphone, the swaying or toe-tapping backing group, even a kind of cult of celebrity borrowed from the world of show-business, can seem at variance with what Christian worship is really about.

I have to rely on others for any assessment of the music, but I count myself among those who look closely at the words. I confess that I am shocked at times by the slipshod syntax, the false and variable rhyme, the sense that the words have all too often been slapped down on paper in a fit of 'inspiration' and never worked over, considered, or revised. It is Pete Ward again who challenges the claim that such songs are 'all about you, Jesus'. 'This is a crucial insight,' he writes,

but it could be observed that very few of the songs are really about Jesus... rather they are all about the worshipper and their experiences in worship... the songs lay themselves open to the criticism that they have replaced the content of the Christian gospel with human experience. Instead of worshipping Jesus they give the impression that we are worshipping worship.[31]

That is a very sweeping generalization, and there are plenty of exceptions on the other side of the coin. 'In Christ alone', to name a specific text, may well in future years bring the same comfort to those on their last journey as 'Abide with me' has done for earlier generations. But I see in that much-valued text, doctrinal and devotional, as of course in the later work of others in this field, an instance of the general truth that as the worship song grows up, matures, it approaches ever more closely to what we have always thought of as a hymn. David Evans' fine and hugely popular 'Be still, for the presence of the Lord' would be a case in point.

The title of this chapter is 'What Sort of Hymns?'; chapter 4 goes on to look at what makes good hymns—and poor ones also. The answer, it seems to me, in the light of Paul's instructions and of present-day experience, must be to opt for a mixed economy. If I have seemed hard on the worship song, it is partly because, as in Gresham's Law, 'Bad money drives out good'. From what I recognize as a limited, insular, and indeed prejudiced standpoint, I nevertheless grieve for those congregations who are losing touch with our heritage of hymns, in pursuit of the up-to-date and ephemeral. Yet I am glad to set beside these negative assessments the testimony of experience, that many churches whose musical life includes or even centres round such songs exhibit a spirit of praise, a faith expressed in care for the disadvantaged, and a warmth of devotion which deserves respect. In some writing from the United States I have come across the terrible phrase 'worship wars', to describe congregations riven by fundamental disagreements on this issue which, had they been in Ephesus or Colossae, would have brought the sternest reprimand from the Apostle Paul. Even a casual re-reading of the quotes from his letters at the start of this chapter would remind us that worship is not worship at all if it is not 'in the name of the Lord Jesus'—and surely also 'in love and charity with our neighbours'.

CHRIST IS THE ONE WHO CALLS

CHRIST IS THE ONE who calls,
the one who loved and came,
to whom by right it falls
to bear the highest Name:
> and still today
> our hearts are stirred
> to hear his word
> and walk his way.

Christ is the one who seeks,
to whom our souls are known.
The word of love he speaks
can wake a heart of stone;
> for at that sound
> the blind can see,
> the slave is free,
> the lost are found.

Christ is the one who died,
forsaken and betrayed;
who, mocked and crucified,
the price of pardon paid.
> Our dying Lord,
> what grief and loss,
> what bitter cross,
> our souls restored!

Christ is the one who rose
in glory from the grave,
to share his life with those
whom once he died to save.
> He drew death's sting
> and broke its chains,
> who lives and reigns,
> our risen King.

Christ is the one who sends,
his story to declare;
who calls his servants friends
and gives them news to share.
> His truth proclaim
> in all the earth,
> his matchless worth
> and saving Name.

© Timothy Dudley-Smith in Europe and Africa. © Hope Publishing Company in the United States of America and the rest of the world. Reproduced by permission of Oxford University Press. All rights reserved.

CHAPTER 4

Good and Not So Good

> A great many of our hymns are nonsense, sheer nonsense, irritating nonsense if you regard them simply as literature, and yet they undoubtedly awaken the conscience or raise the soul to God. It is a great puzzle, the badness of most really effective and stirring hymns.*
>
> Archbishop Edward White Benson, 1894

IN APRIL 1892 the President of Magdalen College, Oxford, visited Tennyson at Farringford, his home on the Isle of Wight. The President, Herbert Warren, was an old friend, and with Tennyson's son Hallam he made notes of their talk together. Benjamin Jowett, Master of Balliol, had admired the short 'hymn' in Tennyson's dialect drama, *The Promise of May*, and had asked him to write another.

'Will you write the hymn?' Warren enquired, to be met with this reply:

A good hymn is the most difficult thing in the world to write. In a good hymn you have to be commonplace and poetical. The moment you cease to be commonplace and put in any expression at all out of the common, it ceases to be a hymn...What will people come to in a hundred years? do you think they will give up all religious forms and go and sit in silence in the Churches listening to the organ?[1]

As I write this, 120 years on, that does not seem to be the case. Hymns may perhaps be sung less often than in Tennyson's day since there are fewer church Services but they continue to be sung in very considerable numbers. If you were brought up to go to church on Sundays, and in the course of the Service you sing four hymns, and if you do this up to the psalmist's three score years and ten, then you will sing something like 13,000 hymns in the course of a lifetime. If you go to an evening Service or a mid-week meeting, it must be even more. But 13,000 hymns at three minutes each is equivalent to doing nothing else but sing hymns, eight hours a day, for nearly three months of your life. Hymns are bound to leave their mark on you, for good or ill, 'second only to the Bible in terms of their influence'.[2] In short, hymns matter; what we are singing is clearly important; we need hymns of *quality*, orthodoxy, and substance.

But the word 'quality' will mean very different things to different people. Warren Lewis, brother to C. S. Lewis, reflected on this in his diary for 15 August, 1946:

The horrid undertaking of having my hair cut this morning; for some time we had the shop to ourselves, and poor Victor unburdened himself to me. Amongst other things he spoke of the great spiritual comfort the hymns bring him in Church on Sundays, quoting couplets which almost made me blush they seemed so banal. But it was a valuable experience, showing how rash it is to dogmatize about what 'everyone' feels about this or that part of the Service. I should like no hymns at all: Victor would, if I had my thoughtless way, be deprived of his nourishment for the week, or at least a good part of it.³

Paul, in the two letters already quoted, and Jesus himself by the well in Samaria, spoke of Christian worship 'in spirit and in truth'. By 'in spirit', I take it that real worship should be a spiritual experience to which our liturgies, readings, prayers—and singing—have given us access. Our hymns are to 'enable' or 'empower' our worship and so become vehicles of spiritual praise, praise from the heart. This means that we are not primarily looking for hymns whose influence is confined to the mind or intellect, even the theological mind; nor hymns that are mainly social statements, however worthy in their own terms; to me these lack something essential to a 'good' hymn. The same is true of hymns which offer an experience which is primarily emotional, or even primarily ecclesiastical. I think it was William Temple who said that you could make out a strong case that in the long run 'religion' had done more harm than good; and for a hymn to be merely about religion falls short, surely, of the need for worship 'in spirit'. Charles Simeon, the Cambridge divine of two centuries ago, used to sum up the aim of all preaching in three phrases: to humble the sinner, to exalt the Saviour, and to promote holiness.⁴ If the words of a hymn cannot contribute in some way to even one of these, it may have merits literary, intellectual, theological, social, ecclesiastical, religious even—but regretfully one might have to class it as less than a good hymn.

Alongside 'in spirit' lies the second requirement, 'in truth'. This includes two distinct senses, in terms of being both true to the Scriptures—the truth of revelation—and also to our own experience, what we have discovered in our tentative steps towards a spiritual life. Worship 'in truth' must surely include something of the vision of God, and of that personal relationship of grace with the Christ revealed to us in Scripture.

Together with these essentials, we can list other very desirable qualities. A good hymn should be inclusive enough to unite a congregation in more than the mere act of singing. Bruce Hindmarsh writes of how John Newton's initial exclamation, 'Amazing grace!... invites immediate congregational consent and release of emotional energy.'⁵ It is much helped in this by the American folk-tune, so that to 'inclusive' we can add 'singable' as a key attribute of a good hymn. A ready 'singability' means that worshippers can identify themselves in what the hymn is expressing, rather than concentrating on the correct performance of it; a more contemporary word for it might be 'user-friendly'. Thomas Cranmer, preparing the 1549 edition of what was to become our Book of Common Prayer, had the humility to recognize that though unmatched as a master of liturgical prose, he was no hymn writer: 'Mine English verses,' he wrote, 'want the grace and facility that I could wish they had.' C. S. Lewis, in quoting this, describes it as 'a statement which in his age shows more loyalty to poetry than a wilderness of sonnets'.⁶ 'Colourful' is another attribute of some of our best-loved hymns; not an essential, but valued when it is achieved. Think of the richness of texture in a hymn like 'Be thou my vision'; or, in Chesterton's trademark style, the vivid images of his 'Judge eternal, throned in splendour': the fire of judgement, the healing wings, the city and the homesteads, and the impassioned 'cleave our darkness with thy sword'. Another, even less definable, quality is *warmth*; the warmth of family, of shared humanity and our common pilgrimage, of comfort as well as challenge, of the sense that in the end all shall be well. 'It is not enough' to quote Ellerton again, 'that [hymns] *suggest* devotion, they must be capable of *expressing* it.'⁷

No one will have read this far without realizing that Charles Wesley is one of my hymn-writing heroes. I owe this, at least in part, to Bernard Manning's small but influential book of 'five informal papers' entitled *The Hymns of Wesley and Watts*. Manning was Senior Tutor and sometime Bursar at Jesus College, Cambridge between the wars, as well as a university lecturer in history. Speaking to the University Methodist Society in November 1932, he summed up Charles Wesley's achievement:

It is Wesley's glory that he united these three strains—dogma, experience, mysticism—in verse so simple that it could be understood, and so smooth that it could be used, by plain men.[8]

'Smoothness' here, I take it, is partly what Sir Philip Sidney calls 'the sweet slyding, fit for a verse'[9] of poetry in the English tongue, and partly the metrical precision, so unobtrusive as to seem inevitable, in managing stress and fitting text to tune. A century before Manning, the hymn writer James Montgomery had set down his own analysis of the qualities which make Charles Wesley unsurpassed as a writer of English hymns; and Wesley's work is still indispensable to our worship, as the index of contributors to almost any current mainstream hymnal will demonstrate. Here is Montgomery on Wesley, in the Introductory Essay to his *The Christian Psalmist*:

Christian experience furnishes him with everlasting and inexhaustible themes; and it must be confessed, that he celebrated them with an affluence of diction, and a splendour of colouring, rarely surpassed. At the same time, he has invested them with a power of truth, and endeared them both to the imagination and the affections, with a pathos which makes feeling conviction, and leaves the understanding little to do but acquiesce in the decisions of the heart.[10]

Most of the following chapters will touch on different aspects of the question, 'What makes a good hymn?', so by way of contrast consider now what mars a hymn (apart from technical faults), or 'What makes a less-than-good hymn?'

* * *

It is easier to think of such hymns than to describe them. Tolstoy famously begins *Anna Karenina* with the observation that 'All happy families resemble one another, but each unhappy family is unhappy in its own way.' I would be hard put to it to describe in just what way all good hymns resemble one another, though as we have seen, certain qualities may be shared; but it is certainly true that poor hymns fail in a variety of different ways. I must ask to be excused from citing all but the most glaring examples, since what might by some standards be classed as a not-so-good hymn may be precious to some reader of these words, and that deserves respect.

It seems to me a pity to make hymns a cause, or even a celebration, of division; this is the opposite of the unifying quality of good hymns. I admit that Charles Wesley seems to have done this, in his hymns protesting against any doctrine of limited atonement. The universality he so insistently emphasizes (not, of course, *universalism*, the doctrine that all will find salvation regardless of faith or life) is designed to affirm an understanding of election dear to him, but fervently denied not only by opponents of the Wesleys, but by some who began as their followers. Here is a classic example, which I believe to be not only a worthy hymn but a great one. Yet it remains a dangerous precedent to employ hymnody as an arm of controversy. These are three verses out of seventeen, with the capitalization and italics of emphasis just as Charles set it down:

> Father, whose *Everlasting Love*
> Thy only Son for Sinners gave,
> Whose Grace to *All* did *freely* move,
> And sent Him down a *World to save;*
>
> Thy *Undistinguishing* Regard
> Was cast on *Adam's* fallen Race:
> *For All* Thou hast in CHRIST prepar'd
> *Sufficient, Sovereign, Saving* Grace.
>
> Arise, O GOD, maintain thy Cause!
> The Fulness of the Gentiles call:
> Lift up the Standard of thy Cross,
> And All shall own Thou dieds't for All.[11]

Regardless of the circumstances which gave rise to them, these are surely verses which all Christians can rejoice to sing.

Theological controversy is one thing; ecclesiastical partisanship is something different. I always enjoy the story which David Edwards tells in his *Christian England* of how George Whitefield was once preaching from a balcony in Philadelphia. Looking skywards, he cried out, 'Father Abraham, whom have you in heaven? Any Episcopalians?... Presbyterians?... Independents or Seceders?... Have you any Methodists?' To which the answer from heaven came, according to Whitefield, 'We don't know those names here.'[12] Something of the same should, I feel, be true of our hymnody. When we sing 'Lead, kindly light' it should not matter if we are singing the work of an Anglican or a Roman Catholic: what matters is the Christian faith expressed in the content. In actual fact we are told the hymn was written aboard ship in June 1833, when Newman was Vicar of St Mary's, Oxford; he would remain an Anglican for a further twelve years. As a poet, so Owen Chadwick tells us, Newman's aim in the 1830s was to use his poetry to create 'a semi-political engine' in the church controversies of the time.[13] This is a wholly legitimate aim for poetry (think of the younger days of William Wordsworth, for example) but surely beyond the proper bounds of hymnody.

Yet sometimes hymns, which at their best unite all believers, have been enlisted to exalt mere denominationalism; though I would be glad to think this is largely a fairly fringe activity, and a thing of the past. Here are the Baptists:

> John was a baptist preacher,
> When he baptiz'd the Lamb,
> Then Jesus was a baptist,
> And thus the baptists came;
> If you would follow Jesus,
> As Christians ought to do,
> You'd come and be immersed
> And be a baptist too.[14]

The American hymnologist W. J. Reynolds, himself a Baptist from whom—to his credit— I quote this, describes it as from some early 'quaint hymns of folk tradition'. Then there are the Methodists:

> My father says it is the best,
> *There's a meeting here tonight;*

> To live and die a Methodist,
>   *There's a meeting here tonight.*
>
> I'm a Methodist bred and a Methodist born,
>   *There's a meeting here tonight;*
> And when I'm dead there's a Methodist gone,
>   *There's a meeting here tonight.*[15]

This is from the repertoire of the Fisk Jubilee Singers of the 1890s. They began as a student choir from the pioneer African-American Fisk University, and went on to achieve celebrity touring with a concert programme, mainly of 'spirituals', the old slave songs. The Roman Catholics could also sing of their distinctiveness:

> I am a faithful Catholic,
>   I love my holy Faith;
> I will be true to Holy Church
>   And steadfast until death.
>
> I shun the haunts of those who seek
>   To ensnare poor catholic youth;
> No Church I own, no Schools I know
>   But those that teach the Truth.[16]

Incidentally but irresistibly, I add from Cardinal Wiseman's hymn, 'Long live the Pope', the first and perhaps the only mention in hymnody of the electric telegraph:

> For like the sparks of unseen fire,
> That speak along the magic wire,
> From home to home, from heart to heart,
> The words of countless children dart:
>   *'God bless our Pope, the great, the good.'*

The hymn can still be found in the 1998 hymn book of the London Oratory—but, alas, omitting this verse so redolent of the Victorian age.[17]

Nor is the Church of England immune from this sort of thing. Indeed, Ian Bradley tells us in his study of Victorian hymns, *Abide with Me*, that John Mason Neale, author of 'Good King Wenceslas' and prolific contributor to the original edition of *Hymns Ancient & Modern*, made his first venture into hymnody with these verses 'to free our poor children from the yoke of Watts':

> I am a little Catholic,
> And Christian is my name,
> And I believe in Holy Church
> In every age the same.
>
> And I believe the English Church
> To be a part of her,
> The Holy Church throughout the world
> That cannot fail or err.[18]

Lest there should be any doubt that he did not believe this could be said of the free churches, consider the following, also from his pen; it would be charitable to suppose he did not intend it as a hymn:

> The good old Church of England!
>   With her priests through all the land,
> And her twenty thousand churches,
>   How nobly does she stand!
> Dissenters are like mushrooms,
>   That flourish but a day;
> Twelve hundred years, through smiles and tears,
>   She hath lasted on alway!

J. R. Watson rightly describes this as 'callow nonsense', and adds that such a verse is impossible to read with a straight face after Noël Coward's 'The stately homes of England'.[19] We find it amusing only because it is so brazenly offensive, telling us more about the writer's views than about his subject.

Again, what are we to say of Dean Plumptre's 'Thy hand, O God, has guided/Thy flock from age to age'? This was first published under the heading 'Church Defence', and has been sung in Anglican churches for over a century. I remember at school tunelessly belting out the extended final lines, and I have often sung it since. But how does it appear to other than Anglican eyes? To a fair-minded Methodist it seems assertive, and excessive in its claims:

> The 'One church' and 'one faith' is presumably the Church of England and its particular form of belief, which stands (as if in close and special relationship) linguistically in parallel to 'one Lord'... there is little doubt that for many singers at this time 'the church' would have meant the Established Church with the Queen at its head.[20]

To be sure, as Professor Watson says, the text does not absolutely require to be read in this way; but I recall how in ecumenical discussions in the 1960s and 1970s there was a telling phrase, 'Anglican arrogance', describing that 'effortless superiority' which appeared none the less real for being unintended and unconscious. Perhaps, indeed, that is most clearly experienced not in a literal reading of the text, but in the triumphalism that marks the singing of it to Basil Harwood's stirring tune. John Betjeman, by contrast, has his tongue firmly in his cheek:

> His Kingdom stretch from See to See
> Till all the world is C of E.[21]

When it was claimed for the *English Hymnal* of 1906 that 'No other book has ever done so much for the High Church cause',[22] that was a legitimate expression of personal opinion. But the *aim* of the original editors, so the Preface tells us, was far more than merely partisan: it was designed to be 'a collection of the best hymns in the English language', something, I suppose, to which all hymn book editors aspire, though not all commend their work with such uncompromising confidence and panache. The only cause that hymns and hymn books can fittingly serve is the glory of God and the good of his universal church.

It would be tedious to try to catalogue the diversity of technical failings that mark a not-so-good hymn. Instead, let us join Edward White Benson, Archbishop of Canterbury towards the end of Queen Victoria's reign, in the days when Addington Palace, Croydon, was the Archbishop's rural retreat. Benson is entertaining Sir Edmund Gosse in January 1894, and Gosse wrote an account of their conversation. Picture the Archbishop, late in the afternoon of that winter's day, 'talking very loud', striding up and down the drawing room 'so that I was obliged to pursue him among the chairs and round the tables'. Gosse had been asked whether he enjoyed John Keble's *The Christian Year* and confessed that he did not, finding his verse 'frigid and tame'. The Archbishop strongly disagreed:

> I delight in Keble. He is the common ground on which poetry and religion meet. Now, a great deal, the majority, of our religious verse is not poetry at all. A great many of our hymns are nonsense, sheer nonsense, irritating nonsense, if you regard them simply as literature, and yet they undoubtedly awaken the conscience or raise the soul to God. It is a great puzzle, the badness of most really effective and stirring hymns.[23]

It would be good to know what 'effective and stirring hymns' Archbishop Benson had in mind. Perhaps 'The church's one foundation', which had made a great impression at the first Lambeth Conference only six years earlier? Or the quintessentially Anglican 'Thy hand, O God, has guided/Thy flock from age to age', discussed above, which is stirring enough when sung to THORNBURY? It had first appeared even more recently, in the 1889 supplement to *Hymns Ancient & Modern*.

Alas, we shall never know just what hymns the Archbishop was thinking of, but his experience that even not-so-good hymns can be stirring and effective is not uncommon. His son and biographer, A. C. Benson, certainly contributed to that experience with the words he wrote, at the request of King Edward VII, to Edward Elgar's Pomp and Circumstance March No. 1, 'Land of hope and glory'. Arthur Benson was an inveterate diarist; his journal runs to some 180 volumes in the library of Magdalene College, Cambridge, where he was Master, and he confided to it his own feelings about hymn singing. When staying at his mother's house, after his father's death, so David Newsome, his editor, tells us,

> he would smoke after dinner; read or join in whatever the others were minded to do until evening prayers or compline. This ritual was a great trial for Arthur. He hated kneeling upright on the floor; he felt foolish singing hymns in a domestic setting, (hymns 'bearing the same relation to poetry and music that onions and toasted cheese do to claret and peaches'); and he regarded compline as 'the one perfect symbol of *all* that is unreal and fantastic in religion'.[24]

It is a little surprising to find, therefore, that he was himself a hymn writer. Before Cambridge, he taught at Eton in the shadow of Windsor Castle, and was counted by the Queen as among her personal friends. He had a fatal propensity to *write*. At one stage he was producing his books of light essays so fast that his publisher could not keep up with him. David Newsome writes:

> The medium that came most easily to him was verse. Even he had to admit that he amazed himself at the rapidity with which he could produce an ode, a lyric, a sonnet practically to order...[25]

In fairness I should add that David Newsome recounts elsewhere that John Henry Newman, a prolific writer with lasting hymns to his name, once similarly observed that 'the medium that came most easily to him was actually the poetic'.[26] But Newman had a strong vein of real poetry which it is not easy to find in Benson. He made up for this, however, with a confidence in his ability that matched his social standing.

On one occasion word came from the Queen at Windsor, requesting special hymns for the Confirmation of Prince Leopold of Battenburg.[27] A confirmation hymn is seldom easy to write; add to that a request for *hymns* rather than a single text and that the confirmation was of royalty, and it sounds a formidable assignment. Arthur Benson clearly did not find it so. His diary records how he wrote two immediately: 'I wrote them on the train from London to Horsted Keynes.'[28] On reading this, I felt I had to see these hymns, but they could not be traced in the archives at Windsor. However, the University Library at Cambridge had one of the fifty privately printed copies of Benson's *Hymns and Carols,* containing confirmation hymns for Prince Leopold and the Princess Patricia of Connaught.[29] They proved to be what I ought to have expected: orthodox, metrically regular, derivative, conventional, suitable—but dull. And perhaps this sums up the great majority of not-so-good hymns in any collection.

'Suitable', 'dull', 'worthy' even, are verdicts which often apply to texts written with a particular and circumscribed occasion in mind; an experience shared, it seems, by Poets Laureate. In Victorian times the occasion may have been Saints Days in the church's calendar. Christopher Wordsworth, Bishop of Lincoln and nephew of the poet, wrote one such couplet:

> Let us emulate the names
> Of St. Philip and St, James...

to which his children gleefully added another of their own:

> Let us try to be as good
> As St Simon and St Jude.[30]

A further couplet of this nature, said to have been recalled by Archbishop Donald Coggan, was published in the *Church Times* in 1995:

> O blessed Saint Bartholomew,
> We wish that more of thee we knew.

This kind of banal, even laughable, facility represents a trap which I have sought to evade—not always successfully, perhaps—in my own hymns celebrating some of the apostles, evangelists, and saints of the New Testament. When responding to requests for specific occasions, anniversaries, and the like, I make it clear first that I can never promise to deliver, only to try, and second that my aim is generally to write for the particular instance as a special case of something more universal. Those who are aware that 'Lord, for the years' was written for the centenary of the Scripture Union can find that reflected in the text. But it was written in such a way that it might find a wider usefulness, and in this I was following fairly universal precedent. Charles Wesley's well-known hymn, 'Ye servants of God, your master proclaim' was one of four hymns written 'to be sung in a tumult' during the troubled times of civic unrest around the Jacobite rebellion of 1745. Bishop Heber's 'From Greenland's icy mountains', once the archetypal hymn of foreign missions, was originally written to support a special nation-wide collection in aid of the Society for the Propagation of the Gospel at Whitsuntide, 1819. S. J. Stone's stirring battle-cry, 'The church's one foundation' is still regularly sung today, but owes its conception to its young author's indignation at the long-forgotten 'Colenso Controversy' when Bishop Colenso of Natal questioned the historical accuracy of parts of the Bible. This explains the slightly hysterical language of the original third verse, now never printed:

> The Church shall never perish!
>   Her dear Lord, to defend,
> To guide, sustain, and cherish,
>   Is with her to the end;
> Though there be those who hate her,
>   And false souls in her pale,
> Against or foe or traitor
>   She ever shall prevail.

Nevertheless, the hymn as a whole has more than stood the test of time, as indeed has another hymn of the period, 'Onward, Christian soldiers', also written with a particular purpose in mind. The words were jotted down in some haste, so the story goes, by Sabine Baring-Gould for a Children's Festival at Horbury Brig, Yorkshire, including a Whitsunday procession with cross and banners. There still remains some confusion about exactly when it was written, since it was printed above his initials in the *Church Times* of 15 October, 1864, a date which differs from the author's own recollection set out in a letter some fifty years later:

The hymn, 'Onward, Christian Soldiers' was written on Whitsun Eve, 1865. It had been resolved that the Brig Children should come up to the parish church on Whitsun Tuesday; and Mr Fred Knowles came to me at the Vicarage and asked what they were to sing on the long walk...I said I would write a processional. 'You must be sharp about it', said Mr. Knowles 'for this is Saturday and there will shortly be no printing done.' So I set to work and knocked off the hymn in about ten minutes. We got it printed, and practised on Sunday afternoon at School, and it was sung to a tune by Haydn on the Tuesday. I sent it to the *Church Times* and it was therein printed and published.[31]

By the time of this letter Baring-Gould was well into his eighties, and can be forgiven if his memory was unreliable; but to confuse the issue further the date given in the letter, 1865, is not very legible, and it has been suggested that it should be read as 1864. Perhaps to give the marching children a little more time, Baring-Gould wrote six eight-line verses in his 'ten minutes', with a chorus after each. *Hymns Ancient & Modern* of 1868 omitted the fourth verse, and it has rarely been sung since. It is said to form a link between the third and fifth verses, but this is hardly needed since the chorus comes between; and it is generally felt that the last two lines fall below an acceptable standard:

> What the Saints established
> That I hold for true,
> What the Saints believed
> That believe I too.
> Long as earth endureth
> Men that faith will hold,
> Kingdoms, nations, empires,
> In destruction rolled.

These examples are enough to show that not all hymns written 'to order', so to speak, lack inspiration, but how many must there be that, with good reason, have not survived? Some of those that continued to find a limited usefulness, as with many hymns for Saints Days, are enough to show that the bar was not set very high. This was expressed, a little unkindly, in the entry on Dean Plumptre in the *Dictionary of National Biography*:

'Several of Plumptre's hymns have been admitted into popular collections, and satisfy their not very exacting requirements.' The new *Oxford Dictionary of National Biography* is less dismissive.

The problem of not-so-good hymns, those that seem dated, pedestrian, and uninspiring, is felt particularly, perhaps, by those who are poets themselves, or at least lovers of literature, and who judge the hymns by standards different from those of the ordinary worshipper. Ruskin famously described Victorian hymnody as it appeared to him, consisting

> partly of the expression of what the singers never in their lives felt, or attempted to feel: and partly in the address of prayers to God, which nothing could more disagreeably astonish them than His attending to.[32]

Robert Bridges, in a letter of 1902, described with savage precision his feelings about the church, its clergy, and its hymns. He would not be Poet Laureate for another eleven years, but had already published his own *Yattendon Hymnal* in the village where he was choirmaster:

> I took Elizabeth in to Exeter the other day to be confirmed...I did not admire the ceremony. The Service was ruined by the introduction of some of the most maudlin and washy hymns with their tunes out of HAM [*Hymns Ancient & Modern*]. I was earnestly praying the Preserver of Souls that my dear little girl might be safe-guarded thro' life from the unholy spirit that all the parsons seemed to be invoking, and that she might have the Spirit of Wisdom, and understanding, and the Spirit of Might, instead of that Spirit of bosh and ignorance, and weakness—which sounded in the air and was apparent in nearly all the faces of the clergy.[33]

I think we can discern in that the discontent not only of the man of letters, but of the musician. Those whose preferred musical taste runs to something more classical than the hymn tune (perhaps especially some of the Victorian hymn tunes?) seem to find in that an additional reason for being discontented with the hymns they are asked to sing. This is very clear in Bridges' comments on John Julian's massive *Dictionary of Hymnology* which appeared at about this time. In a footnote to his 'A Practical Discourse on Some Principles of Hymn-Singing', contributed to the very first number of the *Journal of Theological Studies*, October 1899, and subsequently more than once reprinted, he unburdens himself, using his idiosyncratic spelling:

> When one turns the pages of thatt most depressing of all books ever compiled by the groaning creatur, Julian's hymn-dictionary, and sees the thousands of carefully tabulated English hymns, by far the greater number not only pitiable as efforts of human intelligence, but absolutely worthless as vocal material for melodic treatment, one wishes that all this effort had been directed to supply a real want...[34]

I am an admirer of Bridges, but I confess that I find this elitist, arrogant, and blinkered. He had not learnt the lesson that Warren Lewis took away from his conversation with Victor, his barber. To regard the words of hymns primarily as 'vocal material for melodic treatment' shows a serious misunderstanding of the part played by hymns in worship, and indeed in much spiritual experience.

More serious than Bridges' misgivings about 'melodic treatment,' is the knife-edge between usefulness and unworthiness which is found in much Christian creativity. It can be seen in low-budget housing-estate church building, in some of the book illustration of children's Bible stories, in 'devotional' art and painted statues—and in hymns. Rowan Williams wrestled with this in his Foreword to the commemorative volume celebrating the centenary of *The English Hymnal:*

> Too often, the arts in church, music in particular, refuse to aim too high, on the no doubt laudable principles that there is less distance to fall if you get it wrong and less risk of confusing faith with taste. It is the time-honoured defence of terrible plaster statues and inane choruses, and it is very far from being completely wrong.... To be wary of identifying genuinely religious art with what we regard as aesthetically right is a proper caution against excluding the 'extremism' that arises from encounter with a strange and disturbing God. Yet it is just this which ought to make us equally cautious about deliberately lowering our sights and settling for stock responses.[35]

In this consideration of not-so-good hymns there are two factors which diminish, or even destroy, the usefulness of a hymn text for today's editors, which seem to have been quite unknown to their predecessors: *archaisms* and *inclusive language*. Archaisms, apart from extreme cases such as 'welkin', were hardly an issue when the language of hymns echoed that of the Authorized Version or the Prayer Book. Writers, editors, and worshippers alike felt that a certain flavour of antiquity was appropriate for congregational song. Owen Barfield indeed felt that 'the verse form... remains one of the most constant empirical distinctions between poetry and the prosaic'[36] and could be seen as a kind of archaism. If 'welkin' is an extreme case, a bridge too far, another might be J. M. Neale's translation of 'Jerusalem the golden', which includes the couplet:

> They stand, those halls of Sion,
> Conjubilant with song...

The OED cites 'conjubilant' as 'rare', and quotes Neale's verse as their only example of its use. It was included in the first edition of *Hymns Ancient & Modern*, but then changed to 'all jubilant' (an example of 'invisible mending') until in their 2000 edition, *Common Praise,* Neale's original was restored. In general, however, although those earlier writers and editors were not troubled by language which would have seemed antiquated in any but a religious context, they could not avoid the pitfalls which attend the changing meaning of words, as in an example quoted earlier, the Wesleys' free use of 'bowels' as a metaphor for the heart. Commonplace and correct in their day, it would be liable to misunderstanding if retained unaltered in our own. To take another example, this time from Bible translation, William Tyndale in 1530 could write of how Pharaoh's 'jolly captains' were drowned in the Red Sea, when 'jolly' meant 'high-hearted, gallant, bold or defiant'.[37] Today, however, some consider unacceptable anything that dates a hymn text to an earlier day, even to the period in which it was written. 'Thee' and 'thou' and words like 'beholdeth' are ruthlessly pruned away, and syntax reconstructed in a less 'archaic' idiom. William Kethe wrote in the sixteenth century:

> The Lord, ye know, is God indeed;
> Without our aid he did us make;
> We are his folk, he doth us feed,
> And for his sheep he doth us take.

That has been sung in churches, chapels, and cathedrals for four hundred years. But recent revisers would have us sing:

> Know that the Lord is God indeed,
> He formed us all without our aid;
> We are the flock he loves to feed,
> The sheep who by his hand are made.

It is a personal opinion, but I find it hard to think that the revision justifies the loss of both the original character, and the traditional familiarity, of the text as William Kethe wrote it.

I recognize that 'thee' and 'thou' are not part of our contemporary speech. I respect the motives of those who would try to make our worship more accessible to the newcomer. But where older hymns are concerned I feel the attempt is usually misguided, and seldom a success. In the *English Hymnal*, 1900, for example, a glance at the first twenty-five hymns shows that sixteen of them include 'thee and thou' language, and a few others use 'ye'. It would be easy to suppose these could be 'modernized' by some judicious 'invisible mending'. 'You' could replace, both 'thee' and 'thou', and 'yours' take the place of 'thine'. But even where this can be done, it is at best a new patch on an old garment. Who would want to sing 'Guide me, O you great Jehovah...'? The process soon runs into even deeper trouble, when one of these words forms part of a rhyming pair.

This is very different from suggesting that today's hymn writers should use 'thees and thous', even though I did just that in a few of my earliest texts, and it felt very natural to do so. But that was in the 1960s and the tradition has changed for ever in the past fifty years or so. Indeed, the pendulum may now have swung to the other extreme. I think of a text rejected by an editor who would have liked to include it, solely because it contained the word 'defiled' which he was unwilling to print and I was unprepared to change: it is a word which appears more than a hundred times in today's New International Version of the Bible.

For the writer, archaisms in new texts are not hard to avoid. More difficult is the question of *inclusive language*, that is the need to use language which gives neither gender preferential treatment; and, in practice, no longer regards the masculine as the norm: 'Man' can no longer embrace 'Woman', nor God be adequately described as 'He'. These exemplify for hymnody the two main divisions of inclusive language: language of *persons* and language of *deity*. It requires no great leap of understanding to see that today's language increasingly avoids using the shorthand term 'brothers', as Paul does in his letters, to mean 'brothers of both sexes'. The word itself can still be used, of course. We can refer to the twelve apostles as 'a band of brothers'. But it has become unacceptable to use the generic 'man', as English has done since time immemorial, to mean human beings. Taken literally, 'man' can be understood as excluding half the human race: hence the term 'inclusive language'.

People, folk, mortals, humans, humankind are seen as inclusive; 'man' and 'men' are not. I confess that when I first met this, it seemed to me like cloud-cuckoo land; for ours is, I think, the first generation to take account of this. I recall, back in 1988, sitting-in on the preliminary meeting of a new hymnal committee in America where various guidelines were being laid down for the projected book. These included, almost without discussion, the adoption of inclusive language of persons in all contemporary texts. An anguished cry came from the veteran Canadian hymn writer, Margaret Clarkson, who saw almost all her life's output discarded as 'not so good' by this single criterion. I knew only too well how she felt. My first collection of texts had been published that year, and it was with similar incredulity and indeed horror that I heard my American publisher explain to me, as gently as possible, that if my texts were to be published, let alone sung by US congregations, I must undertake an extensive revision in the interests of inclusive language. I was fortunate; the warning came just in time. I began to catch a glimpse of the very strong feelings behind this issue, and the reasons for them. I have become more persuaded as the years pass that it is at least a courtesy owed to those who feel demeaned, excluded, by the generic 'man', to avoid its use however technically unimpeachable; and I find in practice that it is not impossible to do so.

The rub comes, of course, not in the loss of expressions like 'Rise up, O men of God' or 'Brother clasps the hand of brother' but in the difficulty of elegantly and succinctly contrasting the human and the divine. On these terms 'God with man is now residing', a marvellously compressed affirmation of the incarnation, becomes not so good. For myself, then, I recognize in the generic 'man' an entirely proper use of English, as the King James Bible and Shakespeare alike bear witness; but I have largely renounced it in hymn writing because some find it hurtful, and it limits the usefulness of the text. Elizabeth Cosnett addressed the 1990 Conference of the Hymn Society on this subject in some detail, and my own experience echoes her conclusion: 'I constantly try to balance my integrity as a writer with what I judge to be acceptable to a general congregation': and she describes this as being 'all too often a frustrating negative experience of linguistic renunciation'.[38]

But to apply any such principle retrospectively and without discrimination is almost always mistaken and leads to all manner of infelicities, even if not quite to the extent that Baring-Gould's line 'Brother clasps the hand of brother' should now read 'Sibling clasps the hand of sibling...'. Experience shows that there are traps for the unwary in the desire to be 'inclusive' at all costs. Because of it, we have had 'gingerbread persons' on sale in supermarkets; while the Mayor of New York, so it was reported, had to ask his council to reverse their decision to rename 'manholes' as 'personholes' on the ground that this had made the city ridiculous throughout the world.[39] Hymnal committees can suffer from the same inability to see the unintended consequences of alterations made with the highest intentions. A current hymnal includes the familiar 'Angel voices ever singing' published in the 1860s 'for the Dedication of an Organ or a Meeting of Choirs' and it remains today a hymn of choice for musical occasions. Here is the second verse just as Francis Pott wrote it, and as it has been sung ever since:

> Thou who art beyond the farthest
> Mortal eye can scan,
> Can it be that thou regardest
> Songs of sinful man?
> Can we know that thou art near us,
> And wilt hear us?
> Yea, we can.

The 2011 revision of this verse begins:

> Thou who art beyond the farthest
> Mortal eye can scan,
> Can it be that thou regardest
> Sinful woman, man?

The trouble lies not only with the *double entendre*, which will amuse the choirboys, but in the loss of all reference to songs or singing, which is the whole theme of the hymn.

Equally if not more contentious with inclusive language of persons is inclusive language of deity: should we use only masculine pronouns to refer to God? One newspaper back in 1995 neatly mocked both the feminist concerns on this issue, and the establishment desire to be seen to be taking them seriously: 'God,' said the Dean of Gloucester, 'does not have any gender. He is neither male nor female.'[40] Much ink has been spilt over this question; whole books have been written.[41] Erik Routley described it as 'the only example I know of in history where an attempt has been made to reconstruct a living language in the interests of a pressure group'.[42] For myself, I think the Dean of Gloucester's statement doubly correct, though I am not sure this was just what he intended. We are right to think that God has no gender; but equally right to refer to him by masculine pronouns, since this is what the Lord Jesus did himself and, in the prayer he taught his disciples, provided for us to do. In short, the surest way to address God, or speak about him, is in the language of revelation: God is Father. The Bible does, of course, include female *imagery*, just as Jesus compared himself to a mother hen when mourning over Jerusalem; but it is entirely consistent in its use of such words as 'Lord' or 'King' and pronouns such as 'he', 'him', and 'his'. I take this as clear guidance that we cannot be wrong to do the same. Some thirty years ago, when this fever was at its height, a major American hymnal included my text based on the Magnificat, 'Tell out, my soul, the greatness of the Lord.' Unknown to me they revised it so as to replace the masculine pronoun 'his' on all eight occasions with the noncommittal 'God's'. Verse two read:

> Tell out, my soul, the greatness of God's name!
>   Make known God's might, who wondrous deeds has done;
> God's mercy sure, from age to age the same,
>   God's holy name, the Lord, the mighty One.

By an isolated administrative oversight they were within their legal rights to make these changes: but apart from a doctrinaire approach to inclusive language of deity, who would really feel them to be an improvement? It qualifies, I fear, for the rare word 'hymnicide', which the Oxford dictionary defines as 'the "murdering" of a hymn, i.e. by alteration'. Only one example of the use of the word is quoted, from 1862: 'We have here a new illustration of the unhappy practice of hymnicide, which is as unjust to the authors of hymns, as it is generally detrimental to poetry.' I am glad to say that in a later publication the editor included an apology for this 'botched paraphrase'.

This is a contentious subject. Feelings in some quarters do run very high, and some would hold that any male, simply by his masculine nature, is unable to do justice to the feminist argument. Nevertheless, let the last word be with Fred Pratt Green, who wrote these pertinent verses for the International Hymnody Conference in Oxford, 1981:

>   How can we sing the praise of Him
>   Who is no longer He?
>   With bated breath we wait to know
>   The sex of Deity.

> Our Father is our Mother now,
>   And Cousin too, no doubt.
> Must worship wait for hymnodists
>   To get things sorted out?
>
> O rise not up, you men of God!
>   The Church must learn to wait
> Till Brotherhood is sisterised,
>   And Mankind out of date.
>
> O may the You-know-who forgive
>   Our stunned ambivalence,
> And in our sexist anguishings
>   Preserve our common-sense.[43]

© 1981 Stainer & Bell Ltd for the world excluding US and Canada, and Hope Publishing for US and Canada. All rights reserved. Reproduced by permission of Stainer & Bell Ltd, London, England, www.stainer.co.uk

* * *

Inevitably certain hymns, however popular, have strictly to be classified as not so good because of technical errors and infelicities. Sometimes such errors will mar hymns which are otherwise strong in warmth, colour, and devotion. But these, on the whole, are not the faults commonly cited as making the hymn 'usually a second-rate type of poetry'. This wounding assessment from Lord David Cecil, in his Introduction to his *Oxford Book of Christian Verse*,[44] seems to me to betray a basic misunderstanding, not of course of poetry, but of hymnody. Had he said, 'a different type of poetry' I would have little quarrel with him, but in the opening paragraph of his Introduction he goes further: 'The average hymn is a by-word for forced feeble sentiment, flat conventional expression.' That I firmly deny. C. S. Lewis, no lover of hymns, took up the point in reviewing the book.[45] Of course, one can find examples, particularly of 'flat conventional expression'; but who is to say whether the sentiment is 'forced'? And a few poor examples do not represent 'the average hymn'. In a letter of 1956, Lewis set the matter where it truly belongs, in the field of spirituality; or, to use a better phrase, of Christian devotion and discipleship:

Concerning hymn singing and organ playing: if they have been helpful and edified anyone, then the fact that they set my teeth on edge is infinitely unimportant...the test of music or religion or even visions if one has them is always the same—do they make one more obedient, more God-centred, and neighbour-centred, and *less self-centred*?[46]

This is in harmony with one of those thought-provoking insights that can stop us in our tracks when we are tempted to moan about being asked to sing a hymn which is not among our favourites. It comes, once again, from Bernard Manning: 'Reverence is due to hymns as to any sacred object. The hymn that revolts me, if it has been a means of grace to Christian men, I must respect as I should respect a communion cup, however scratched its surface, however vulgar its decoration.'[47]

For many centuries, the words of hymns have found a place in private devotion. There was a period when I used to end my morning prayers with Charles Wesley's hymn entitled 'Before work'. It is found in many hymn books as 'Forth in thy name, O Lord, I go'. Lionel Adey has explained how this hymn was written before the industrial revolution had turned daily work, for so many, into the misery of dehumanizing drudgery;[48] and it seemed to me particularly suitable for 'work' undertaken in what is laughingly called retirement:

> The Task thy Wisdom hath assign'd
>   O let me chearfully fulfil,
> In all my Works thy Presence find,
>   And prove thine acceptable Will.
>
> For Thee delightfully employ
>   Whate'er thy bounteous Grace hath given,
> And run my Course with even Joy,
>   And closely walk with Thee to Heaven.

But such a practice does not contradict the basic truth about hymns, that they are designed to be sung *together*. The Methodist scholar W. F. Lofthouse summed it up in an article for the *Congregational Quarterly* in 1953, and I will leave to him the final word in this discussion of good and not-so-good hymns, always remembering his admonition that 'since the words, like the tune, of a hymn are what we are bold enough to ask God to listen to, the emotions they express must wear, so to speak, their Sunday clothes.'

Singing hymns means singing them together...we are not like the ignorant Corinthian Christians, bringing their own lunch to the Lord's Table, and eating it in their own corner. We share the bread and wine of our devotion together. We leave our favourite little song-books behind. It is—indeed, it must be—common prayer and common praise, that are offered to the common Lord.... What helps my brother in making his way to the Lord's side, helps me. Out in the street I might not admire the cut of his coat. I might congratulate myself that I go to a different tailor. But when, within the sacred walls, I see the wedding garment which the Master of the feast has given him, who am I that I should shrug my contemptuous shoulders? If he rejoices to sing 'Count your blessings' while I long for Addison's 'When all thy mercies, O my God', the sentiment is the same. Is Addison's the only language understood in the heavenly courts?.... there is nothing that opens more widely the door of worship than to exchange the attitude of 'I prefer this' to 'God evidently accepts that.'[49]

AFFIRM ANEW THE THREEFOLD NAME

AFFIRM ANEW the threefold Name
    of Father, Spirit, Son,
our God whose saving acts proclaim
    a world's salvation won.
In him alone we live and move
    and breath and being find,
the wayward children of his love
    who cares for humankind.

Declare in all the earth his grace,
    to every heart his call,
the living Lord of time and place
    whose love embraces all.
So shall his endless praise be sung,
    his teaching truly heard,
and every culture, every tongue,
    receive his timeless word.

Confirm our faith in this our day
    amid earth's shifting sand,
with Christ as Life and Truth and Way,
    a Rock on which to stand;
the one eternal Son and Lord
    by God the Father given,
the true and life-imparting Word,
    the Way that leads to heaven.

Renew once more the ancient fire,
    let love our hearts inflame;
renew, restore, unite, inspire
    the church that bears your Name;
one Name exalted over all,
    one Father, Spirit, Son,
O grant us grace to heed your call
    and in that Name be one.

© Timothy Dudley-Smith in Europe and Africa. © Hope Publishing Company in the United States of America and the rest of the world. Reproduced by permission of Oxford University Press. All rights reserved.

CHAPTER 5

Words and Music

> A song is a magical marriage between a *lyric* (some words) and a *melody* (some notes). It is not a *poem*. It is not *music*. It is in this gray area of synthesis between language, rhythm and sound that some of the most acute of all sensors of human emotion lie.*
>
> Jimmy Webb, 1998

A STORY IS TOLD of how the Hammersteins and the Kerns were fellow-guests at a dinner party; it may well be apocryphal, since I gather it is told of other song-writing partnerships. Mrs Hammerstein overheard a neighbour congratulate Mrs Kern on her husband's song, 'Ol' Man River'. She interrupted their conversation with, 'Jerry Kern didn't write "Ol' Man River", *my* husband did. What Kern wrote was dum-dum-*dee*-dum.'[1] It illustrates the difference in viewpoint between those who would give priority to the music, or to the words. Again, when Sir Arthur Sullivan died in November, 1900, *The Times* in a long obituary raised the question as to which of the celebrated partnership had contributed more to the extraordinary success of the Savoy Operas. The writer concluded, perhaps predictably, that it was 'impossible to say... still, there can be no doubt that if associated with dull or unattractive music, even Mr Gilbert's funniest ideas would have failed of their object'.[2] As it happens, one proof of this is on my bookshelves. Alongside the texts of the Savoy Operas there stands *The Bab Ballads*, a collected edition of Gilbert's comic verse. The lyrics from some of the operas leap from the page as familiar friends, but the rest has vanished into oblivion: who reads *The Bab Ballads* today? My father used to read *The Yarn of the 'Nancy Bell'* ('Twas on the shores that round our coasts/From Deal to Ramsgate span...') to his class at school, but that is almost the only one I have ever read or heard. Yet if Sullivan had set them to music, they might be known alongside 'Take a pair of sparkling eyes' or 'A policeman's lot is not a happy one'. In all songs and hymns, words and music each have a part to play; and this, it seems, is rooted in antiquity. C. S. Lewis has described how in Homer's day, 'All poetry is oral, delivered by the voice, not read, and so far as we are told, not written either. And all poetry is musical. The poet delivers it to the accompaniment of some instrument...' Lewis goes on to compare this solemn, public, ceremonial, and so almost theatrical experience with 'the solitary, private, and armchair associations which the word "poetry" has for a modern'.[3] If we ask ourselves where, today, we find verse set to music and sung in a solemn public setting, one obvious reply is 'when hymns are sung in church'.

Back in the 1970s and 1980s when I was beginning to give the occasional talk about hymns, I was glad to hit on the idea of 'happy marriages' to provide a framework.

There is the marriage of words and music, as in this chapter; and of content and form, or creativity and criticism, which come later in the book. There are other partnerships, too, some of which will find mention: sound and sense, poetry and piety, aspiration and reality, objective and subjective, and so on. It was only much later that I found this metaphor of marriage was by no means original. Professor Henry Chadwick used it (and may well not have been the first to do so) in a celebrated lecture to mark the seventy-fifth anniversary of the Church Music Society:

> Music can be married to words without taking away from their force; indeed, it has the capacity to increase their force, their power to stay in the mind and to haunt the memory... Marriage is not too strong a word to describe the relationship.[4]

In essence it is this relationship which distinguishes verse from prose. Sir Arthur Quiller-Couch told his students in a Cambridge lecture:

> Always you must come back to this, that the first poets sang their words to the harp or to some such instrument: and just there lies the secret why poetry differs from prose. The moment you introduce music you let in emotion with all its sway upon speech. From that moment you change everything...[5]

To work well, of course, words and music must live together in harmony; it must be a *happy* marriage. When a text, however good in itself, is set to a poor or unsuitable tune, they sink together. Worse, as Erik Routley pointed out, 'If the music is so eloquent as to drown the sound of the words, the words, no matter what nonsense they may talk, will go clear past the critical faculty and into the affections.'[6] Even where the words lack nothing in content and craftsmanship, it is still easy for a congregation to lose all sense of what they are singing, carried along by the music and the pleasure of participation. This can be painfully obvious, sometimes, when the theme of a hymn changes from one verse to the next; say, from the joy of Christ's birth to the pain of his death. Unless the worshippers are given a conscious hint beforehand, or perhaps a change in volume or key from the organ or piano, they can sing blithely on, just as thoughtless when singing of the one as of the other. Martyn Lloyd-Jones, Minister of Westminster Chapel, London from the 1940s, used to see it filled to its galleries, Sunday by Sunday, with huge congregations. He was known on occasion to stop the singing in the middle of a hymn, warning the congregation against 'singing the tune instead of the words'. His biographer recounts how 'he would not tolerate, for example, an exuberant or hearty singing of such words as "False and full of sin I am" in Charles Wesley's "Jesu, Lover of my soul".'[7]

Not every poet is happy with the idea of marrying their words to music. Philip Larkin is quoted in an interview as saying, 'Musicians like things that don't mean too much',[8] which is a shaky foundation for matrimony. Perhaps he had in mind the power of the music to dominate, even obliterate, the best efforts of the writer of the text. There is a story of how George Moore came across W. B. Yeats one afternoon in London near the Albert Hall. Yeats was looking distraught: 'Moore,' he explained, 'I have just heard my poem, "The Lake Isle of Innisfree" sung by a choir of ten thousand boy scouts!'[9] In fairness to the scouts, one ought to note that Yeats is on record as having hated all his early poems, and 'Innisfree' most of all.[10]

A. E. Housman, to take a notorious example, complained bitterly about the settings of some of the poems in *A Shropshire Lad*, which proved highly attractive to a variety of composers. In 1920, he wrote to his publishers to complain that Vaughan Williams had cut two verses out of 'Is my team ploughing?'; adding, 'I wonder how he would like me to cut two bars out of his music?' Two years later we find 'Vaughan Williams has mutilated another poem just as badly, to suit his precious music.'[11] Perhaps it was this that contributed to either 'total indifference' or else 'pain or anger', which seem to have been his usual response to musical settings. His friend Percy Withers tried an experiment:

> Since he had so often and so unaccountably allowed his verses to be set to music, and never as I knew experienced the results, it occurred to me that he might like to hear the gramophone records of Vaughan Williams' settings sung by Gervase Elwes. I was oblivious of the effect until two of them had been played, and then turning in my chair I beheld a face wrought and flushed with torment, a figure tense and bolt upright as though in an extremity of controlling pain or anger or both.[12]

One set of his verses Housman did intend to be sung, No. XLVII in *More Poems*:

> O Thou that from thy mansion,
>   Through time and space to roam,
> Dost send abroad thy children,
>   And then dost call them home...

He gave the text to the Dean of Trinity College, Cambridge, in a sealed envelope marked 'for my funeral'. In his MS book he noted sardonically below the text his gloomy expectation that the choir, 'unless forcibly restrained' would want to add a Gloria.[13]

Housman illustrates an aspect of the choice of words in poetry which also applies to hymnody, the musical value of proper names. I once did a quick count in *A Shropshire Lad*, and found in its sixty-three poems about seventy references to the proper names of people, places, rivers, and so on. Shakespeare did this in the *Sonnets* so that 'the inclusion of particularity within the universal contributes to their unique force'.[14] Walter Scott (think of the titles of his books) was another, as was Tennyson ('Maud', 'Camelot', 'Edward Gray', and the Idylls). Erik Routley, writing of hymns rather than poetry, believed that 'the careful use of proper names, as Milton knew and Watts after him (for example, in "There is a land of pure delight"), lends always power and picturesqueness'.[15] I think of that as 'vividness', a colourful and almost definite glimpse of the particular in the mind's eye. Of course many names have magic simply in the sound. Generations of children must have felt the resonance of W. J. Turner's poem 'Romance', found in many a school anthology, with the opening line 'When I was but thirteen or so' and the names, almost as an incantation, of Chimborazo, Cotopaxi, and Popocatapetl. In hymns this seems to be especially true of names drawn from the Gospels. Professor Watson, in his inaugural lecture, cited D. H. Lawrence, perhaps an unlikely witness: 'To me,' wrote Lawrence, 'the word Galilee has a wonderful sound. The Lake of Galilee!'[16] Think, too, from our hymn books of those 'Southern seas', of Sinai, Jordan, Bethlehem, and Calvary, and of Whittier's

> ...faith has still its Olivet,
> And Love its Galilee.[17]

I could wish I had realized this earlier, though I find that my hymn texts do have occasional references to Bethlehem and Nazareth, to Galilee and the Jordan, and so on.

Names of people feature rather more: Michael the Archangel, Moses, Levi, Solomon, David, Elijah, Jonah; Mary and Joseph, John the Baptist, the four evangelists, Andrew and Peter, Simeon and Anna, Paul and Barnabas, Thomas and Mary Magdalene; together, tragically, with Pontius Pilate in a hymn based on the creed. One could add to these Apollyon and Giant Despair, with a few others borrowed from *The Pilgrim's Progress*. Titles, chiefly of Christ himself, seem to be more frequent: Holy Child, High Prince and Potentate, Shepherd King, Eternal Word, Man of Sorrows—and many more. A couplet of mine, depending on a place name, is:

> and make of life's brief journey
> a new Emmaus road.[18]

which uses the name from Luke 24.13 to evoke the companionship of the risen Christ. For many years now, sadly, we have been unable to rely on every singer understanding such allusions, let alone being moved by them as Lawrence was. Back in the 1930s, Bernard Manning was making just that point from the hymns of Charles Wesley:

He knew that the use of a proper name with associations may start or clinch a train of thought more effectively than a flood of colourless words will start or clinch it. To you and me, with our beggarly knowledge of Holy Scripture, this magic is less potent than it was to Wesley. What was once moving may seem to us only quaint.[19]

In this, as in so much else in hymnody, Charles Wesley was a master. The Methodist scholar J. E. Rattenbury compares his use of proper names with a poem of Kipling's:

He was sensitive to the beauty of words and the dramatic value of names. He wrote 'Jeshurun's God' instead of 'Israel's', not only because the word is to be found in the passage he was paraphrasing, but because it was melodious, just as Kipling found the names 'Stormcock, Claribel, and Unity' to be.[20]

I was amused to read how Winston Churchill aboard a destroyer at Scapa Flow in the early days of the war quoted a few lines of this poem—very appropriate at that moment—to his Flag Commander, who was able to carry on correctly with the names of the five minesweepers, *Unity, Claribel, Assyrian, Stormcock*, and *Golden Gain*.[21]

It is a hymn writer's privilege to choose the opening line of a text, by which thereafter the hymn is known. Sometimes, indeed, hymn texts have been given titles as well, which is a fruitful source of confusion for editors and indexers. In the same way, the composer gives a name or title to the tune. I take it as a great compliment that I have sometimes been asked to suggest a name for a new tune to one of my texts; and that composers have chosen to name tunes TIMOTHY, ARLETTE (after my late wife), and RECTORY MEADOW and ASHLANDS from places where I have made my home. Wesley Milgate, the Australian hymnologist, found tunes named from a variety of sources: from the composer's birthplace (DOWN AMPNEY) or where he honeymooned (LITTLE CORNARD) or—posthumously, perhaps?—where he died (MOSCOW). There are tunes named after a street, a cottage, a friend, a publisher, innumerable saints and churches, schools and universities, a fishing stream, a character in a novel, a plant, a bird, a hostess; and, famously, a tune called SINE NOMINE, 'without a name'.[22]

The relationship of words and music in a hymn has been compared to the bicycle. As the name implies, two wheels are essential; they complement each other. If the bicycle is a penny-farthing, the picture is a little different. Both are still essential but one is very noticeably larger; and to me that would represent the words, the lyric, what hymnologists call the text. The idea of the bicycle was used rather differently by R. Thurston Dart, who founded the music faculty at King's College, London. I owe this to Paul Burbridge, Dean of Norwich during my time in the diocese, who described in the *Cathedral Newsletter* his personal recollection:

> '*The bicycle upon which the liturgy rides...*' That was the telling description of church music I once heard used by that most distinguished musician, the late Thurston Dart—and what an apt epithet that is! In that brief phrase he succinctly made two important points: (1) That in church music the music must always be strictly governed by the text; (2) That the music should transport the worshipper beyond the text.[23]

It is the same conclusion we find in the Report of the Archbishops' Commission on Church Music a few years later: 'Words will continue to have priority in our worship. Music will be used primarily for their enhancement. There can be no more powerful partnership than these two forms of expression.'[24] I cannot myself think of a partnership where the music is unduly dominated by the text; though allied to a poor text any music is bound to be diminished. But are there not occasions when the music 'takes over' and any real partnership is lost? Henry Chadwick ended the lecture quoted above with the following warning, much as Augustine himself might have done. It was a brave statement to an audience presumably composed largely of musicians:

> We need music in Church; it does something for us which is integral and indispensable; we fear when it takes over, not merely because it may obliterate the distinctively Christian, but because it may end by the mere glorification of man himself. And man being held in honour is uncommonly akin to the beasts that perish.[25]

Words have suffered in our generation. They are devalued by two comparisons: with the *act* and with the *image*. Yet in Scripture, words carry power. This is pre-eminently true of God himself, where his creative *fiat* is word and act in one, and of the Lord Jesus Christ ('Rise; take up your bed and walk') and his apostles ('In the name of Jesus Christ of Nazareth, rise up and walk').[26] But all through Christian history it is the word of the gospel, often the word preached, which the Holy Spirit deigns to use. When Hosea is beseeching a wayward Israel towards repentance, his plea is 'Take with you *words* and return to the Lord'; and when the Twelve asked Jesus to teach them to pray he gave them *words* to say—'Our Father...'.[27]

Again, the psalms are full of words which are not just exclamations of praise, but explanations also. John Stott made this point, perhaps to their surprise, in a talk to students. He asked if they knew that song 'when you sing Hallelujah about twenty times'; and went on to say 'without fear of contradiction', that it was totally unbiblical. 'Now don't misunderstand me. The word Hallelujah is biblical but you have to sing it in its context... you have got to declare what you are singing it about, then you can sing Hallelujah.'[28] Our praise as well as our prayer needs to find expression in words which bring before our minds what we are praying or praising for, and who it is that we are addressing. Perhaps there are those much further down the road of sanctity who do not need such words, but the whole weight of Scripture suggests that most of us do. Again, for most of us, it is by words that we arrive at some self-understanding. Years ago

I came across this passage in a novel of Eric Linklater's, and it has stayed with me, adding to its meaning as the years pass. The speaker is a Danish educationalist, Bishop Grundtvig:

> Teach him his own language in such a way that he will learn the spirit of it: not only because words are the principal condition of social life, but for this reason: whenever a man makes one of those lonely journeys into his own mind and the secret places of his will, he takes with him, like a lamp to explore them, his native language.[29]

For many people, though, the *word* takes very much second place compared with the *image*. Since the arrival of photography, films, TV, and a multiplicity of visual media, the *word* has come to mean less and less to more and more people, as evidenced by the sort of 'library' where there are more screens than books or even no books at all. The power of the image lies in its ability to *show*—'before our very eyes'—what we take to be reality; since there remains for most of us a residual feeling which we might be quick to deny that the camera cannot lie. 'I saw it for myself' is a kind of gold standard of veracity. But the chief drawback of the image, particularly when we enter an abstract, mental, or spiritual world, lies in its denial of the individual *imagination*: it gives to a universal idea a single concrete form. We find it more difficult to form our own conceptions of something we have seen depicted, and the truth of Scripture—by God's providence, as I believe—comes to us in words, leaving us all to make the pictures for ourselves. It was pointed out, for example, that when Zeffirelli's film *Jesus of Nazareth* was released, the visual images became determinative. 'Jesus, for many people,' wrote Derek Weber at the time, 'bears a striking resemblance to Robert Powell...direct [that is, visual] communication is more than merely inadequate, it is a distortion of the truth.'[30] This is how 'Vernon Lee' (the pen name of Violet Paget) expressed it in her work on literary psychology:

> Think of such a word as *Sea*. It awakens in our mind an incredible number of possible visual, audible, sensible, and emotional impressions: wide, deep, wet, green, blue, briny, stormy, serene, a thing to swim or drown in, connecting or severing countries...[31]

The *word* has a flexibility which no single *image* can achieve because it liberates and inspires the individual imagination. C. S. Lewis, whose own powers of imaginative creation were legendary, used to describe the imagination as 'the gatekeeper of the human soul'.[32] In the realm of the spirit, I believe we need to be nourished with words and the concepts they convey, including, of course, the words of Scripture, liturgy, and hymns; and also to protect it from some of the visual assaults that threaten to overwhelm it. I think this may have been what the broadcaster Terry Wogan had in mind, when he said that television contracts the imagination, while radio expands it.[33]

Again, it was C. S. Lewis, you remember, who wanted shorter hymns; but compared to most forms of writing, hymns are inevitably short. Charles Wesley, to be sure, wrote some very long hymns: 'Soldiers of Christ, arise' as we sing it today is a fraction of the whole 128 lines. But when words are few, it becomes more than ever important that each word be right, chosen with precision. Nevil Shute, whose gift of narrative ensured that his books were best sellers, compared a piece of writing to a camera: 'the smaller it is, the more carefully it has to be made'. He adds: 'In a short poem [Christopher Idle, to whom I owe this, added the words "or hymn"] every word must play its part and be exactly right, and the temptation to use the wrong word for the sake of rhyme or rhythm is very great.'[34] This is where, for the hymn writer, an apprenticeship in light or comic verse can be of real value. Perhaps this is not universally true; there are Victorian hymn writers whom it is hard to imagine as contributors to *Punch*. But Ronald Knox was a master of light verse before he wrote for the *Westminster Hymnal*; and often what is known of William Cowper's writing is not so much his *Olney Hymns* as his comic story of John Gilpin, verses that used to be in every school anthology. In light verse, you learn a lot about metre and stress, rhyme, structure and precision, inversion and word order, what works and what does not. Kingsley Amis in his Foreword to *The New Oxford Book of Light Verse* called such verse 'the most severely technical work known to authorship',[35] and of the lyrics of a song A. A. Milne wrote: 'If you can find words which keep time to the music and which are just the words you want to say, then the verses you write are verses which will sing themselves into people's heads and stay there...'[36]—an almost exact description of the work of the hymn writer. Erik Routley, writing in the serious-minded *Congregational Quarterly* of the 1950s, quoted the Canadian economist and humourist, Stephen Leacock, and applied his words to Wesley, Watts, Doddridge, and Montgomery. Leacock wrote: 'If you examine comic verse with a view to writing it you will see that the essence of its literary appeal lies in the extraordinary correctness, aptness and simplicity of its words and phrases.'[37] For the hymn writer, too, this is a prize to strive for.

A. E. Housman, whose name reoccurs in these pages, was for me an early model in his depth of feeling, his brevity and precision, his powers of description and allusion. Some of this will have sprung from his unparalleled grounding in the classics as Professor of Latin both in London and Cambridge but some, I like to think, from the skills he had honed in comic verse. When his brother Laurence published a book of devotional poetry, Housman mischievously wrote to his stepmother to say that he was himself thinking of doing something of the same kind himself, perhaps for the Salvation Army, which was then becoming prominent, and enclosed two sample verses:[38]

> 'Hallelujah' was the only observation
> That escaped Lieutenant-Colonel Mary-Jane,
> When she tumbled off the platform in the station
> And was cut in little pieces by the train;
> Mary-Jane, the train is through ye,
> Hallelujah! Hallelujah!
> We will gather up the fragments that remain.

And this:

> There is Hallelujah Hannah
> Walking backwards down the lane,
> And I hear the loud Hosanna
> Of regenerated Jane;
> And Lieutenant Isabella
> In the centre of them comes,
> Dealing blows with her umbrella
> On the trumpets and the drums.[39]

Even in this latter trifle his skill is noteworthy and presumably effortless. Mark the natural word order, the single emphatic inversion, the precision of stress and metre, which in hymnody we would identify as 87 87 D. Note also the accuracy of the rhyme, helped by the use of proper names, and the alternate feminine rhymes. There is, too, multiple alliteration, with the aspirate H four times in the first three lines, the G and J of the fourth, and the labial L dominating lines five and seven. Finally, the 'um' rhyme of lines six and eight is echoed internally in both 'umbrella' and 'trumpets'. Little of this, surely, would have been carefully devised and constructed; it would have been recognized and accepted as the verse took shape in his head. But if Housman did this for fun, what might such a talent have done for hymnody?

Before this chapter moves on to consider briefly what music adds to words in hymnody, there are two more samples of verse to complete this section. The first carries a reminder that words require listeners. I suppose we have all known the experience of finding ourselves at the last verse of a hymn with no recollection of what we have been singing. This is not simply a failing of increasing years; though I do now empathize with whoever said, 'Sometimes when my mind wanders, I wonder whether it will ever find its way home.' Here is Thomas Hardy, conjuring up 'Afternoon Service at Mellstock' about 1850, with singers oblivious to the words of the psalm:

> On afternoons of drowsy calm
>   We stood in the panelled pew,
> Singing one-voiced a Tate-and-Brady psalm
>   To the tune of 'Cambridge New'.

The crunch comes in the final verse, which begins: 'So mindless were those outpourings!' The tune engages their attention, while the words pass them by. A century later it was well summed up in four lines quoted by Fred Kaan in a discussion on hymnody. He attributed them to Nathaniel Micklem adapting a vesper hymn, and used them as a description of how 'the melodies of our hymns sometimes get in the way of what the hymns are trying to say':

> Lord, keep us safe this night
> Beneath the stars and moon,
> Pay thou no heed to what we say,
> We only like the tune.[40]

* * *

Brian Castle, Bishop of Tonbridge when I first knew him, spent some years as a parish priest in Africa. He describes how he was discussing whether to include a mid-week 'said' Service of Holy Communion in one of his churches in the Copperbelt town of Northern Zambia: 'I was told quite firmly by a young Zambian, "It is not possible to worship Almighty God without singing".'[41] One can understand this in an African culture but it is altogether too sweeping. It brings to mind an occasion in the 1980s when I was working towards my first collection of hymn texts. Cyril Taylor was then a name to conjure with. He had worked for the BBC and the Royal School of Church Music and had been Precentor at both Bristol and Salisbury Cathedrals. Salisbury has a fine carved stone memorial to him in the cloisters, complete with a BBC microphone and the opening notes of his ABBOT'S LEIGH, one of the great hymn tunes of the twentieth century. By the 1980s he had retired to Sussex, and though I had never met him I wrote to say that I was staying nearby and asked if might visit him. I spent a delightful morning sitting at his feet and talking hymns. As a suffragan bishop in a rural diocese I was often sharing Sunday worship in remote villages with historic churches and tiny congregations. Indeed our own parish church, just at our garden gate since we lived in a former Rectory, seldom seemed to have more than a faithful dozen or so.

One of the questions I particularly wanted to ask Cyril Taylor was his advice on what to do about hymns in such country churches, often in very small communities with few to sing and limited musical accompaniment. His immediate response was, 'Say them!'—a considerable surprise from so distinguished a church musician. He went on to suggest that there should be perhaps only two hymns sung, both shortish and familiar, and that another one or two should be said just as one might say the psalms, seated, slowly and thoughtfully, perhaps with a word of introduction or comment. Because no singing was involved, it was easy in this way to introduce even the most conservative congregation to parts of their hymn book which they had yet to discover.

This advice was very welcome to me, as I expect it might have been to earlier hymn writers who had no ear or skill for music. There are more of these than one might think, though I have sometimes sensed a kind of unspoken agreement with the mathematician, G. H. Hardy, that 'Musical incapacity is recognized (no doubt rightly) as mildly discreditable'.[42] Philip Doddridge, for example, who gave us 'Hark the glad sound! the Saviour comes', was described by his first biographer as 'a Man who had no ear for Musick'.[43] Of the scholarly John Keble, Georgina Battiscombe writes:

> His ear for music was notoriously poor and so too was his ear for poetic rhythm and the value of words. His poetry is like nothing so much as a piece of music written by someone who is a master of the technical side of harmony, but yet tone deaf.[44]

Her criticism of his poetry is surprising, not least because two pages earlier she quotes A. E. Housman as saying, 'Keble is a poet; there are things in *The Christian Year* that can be admired by atheists.' Again, it was said of Christina Rossetti, whose 'In the bleak midwinter' is always a Christmas favourite, that 'neither she nor Maria [her sister] manifested any music ability whatsoever'.[45] The American Quaker, John Greenleaf Whittier, who gave us 'Dear Lord and Father of mankind', admitted this of himself: 'I am really not a hymn-writer' he said, 'for the good reason that I know nothing of music.'[46] The same was true of Mrs Alexander, whose texts include 'Once in royal David's city', 'There is a green hill far away', and 'All things bright and beautiful'. Her daughter wrote that 'Music to her was measure, not melody.'[47] I have long felt this to be a remarkably exact description of my own experience. More recently, I learn that something of the same—at least as regards singing—can be said of the evangelist Billy Graham. He described how, as soon as he became a Christian, 'I knew something was different... I got hold of a little hymn book and began to memorize those hymns. I would say them because I couldn't sing.'[48] 'Anyone who knows me,' he wrote later, 'is well aware that I cannot even carry a tune. I once said that when I get to Heaven, I will be able to sing like George Beverly Shea. But the response from the team was, "It will *take* heaven to do that!"'[49]

As we have seen, it is not uncommon for poets to have problems with music. Robert Frost was one such. In almost his last public appearance he said that poetry was 'at war with music' since the poem was a song in itself. His biographer wryly adds that he may have had in mind the recent experience of hearing some of his poems in settings by a contemporary composer.[50] Fred Pratt Green, a practising poet before becoming a hymn writer, set out his own experience of the problem in an early article for an American journal: 'To write strictly to a metre is extremely irksome to a poet', he explained, because the need for the stresses to fall equally in each verse deprives the writer 'of those subtle variations in rhythm that save poetry from monotony.' And he adds, from experience gained, that 'the wise hymn writer writes to a tune'.[51] That tallies exactly with what it took me some time to discover for myself. In my early days, I often wrote verses with no intention or expectation that they might one day be hymns; and when I began to write hymn texts for Michael Baughen's collections I was very fortunate that he allowed me to write the words first. He would then, as often as not, write the tune himself. It is to this partnership that I owe tunes of his such as DAVOS to 'I lift my eyes to the quiet hills', and the tune LORD OF THE YEARS. For some of this time he was in Manchester, as Rector of Platt, and I was still in London. One evening, I remember, I had heard on TV a pop song with a distinctive beat. On my late-night walk 'round the block', this stayed in my head until I wrote some words roughly to the same rhythm, and sent them off to Manchester. Michael was soon on the telephone: 'Timothy, this seems a very unusual text you've sent me. You must have had some sort of tune in mind when you wrote it?' I thought this was rather discerning of him, and explained about the pop song. 'Sing it to me' said Michael. 'Michael, you know I don't sing.' 'Well, hum it to me then'; and when I still hesitated, 'It's only over the 'phone. No one's going to be listening.'

So I took a deep breath, made sure I was alone, shut my eyes and hummed what I could remember. There was then a considerable pause before, doubtfully, Michael asked, 'Is it meant to be all on one note?'

Few Poets Laureate have added significantly to our stock of hymns since Nahum Tate, who died in 1715. Tennyson, to be sure, has a slightly tenuous hold in contemporary hymnals, and John Masefield had a text in *Songs of Praise*, 1931. Robert Bridges is the great exception, but he died in 1930. Bridges is an interesting example of how dissatisfied many church musicians seem to have been with the music they found in church. Bridges, though a great poet, always gave first place to the music and in an article of 1899 he described what he was looking for:

...a music whose peace should still passion, whose dignity should strengthen our faith, whose unquestion'd beauty should find a home in our hearts, to cheer us in life and death; a music worthy of the fair temples in which we meet and of the holy words of our liturgy...what power for good such a music would have! Now such a music our Church has got, and does not use; we are content to have our hymn-manuals stuff'd with the sort of music which, merging the distinction between sacred and profane, seems design'd to make the worldly man feel at home, rather than to reveal to him something of the life beyond his knowledge.[52]

Not only poets but musicians have expressed their misgivings over what is sung in church. Augustine himself, for whom listening to singing proved a decisive moment, was cautious about the place of music in Christian worship, not because of any lack of quality but rather the reverse. He felt music to be so powerful in its appeal to the emotions that it was accompanied by spiritual perils. He wrote:

...my physical delight, which has to be checked from enervating the mind, often deceives me when the perception of the senses is unaccompanied by reason, and is not patiently content to be in a subordinate place. It tries to be first and to be in the leading role, though it deserves to be allowed only as secondary to reason. So in these matters I sin unawares, and only afterwards become aware of it.[53]

That is from Henry Chadwick's translation, and he adds a footnote that 'there was deep disagreement in the churches of North Africa at this time whether any music should be admitted to worship'. In our own day Jeremy Begbie has reminded a new generation that even sacred music making is not immune from the perils that attend all human endeavour in a fallen world. He explores the hostility that Christian people have sometimes shown towards such music and its instrumental accompaniment, and cites the prophets of the Old Testament. The reason for God's 'I will not listen' (Amos 5.23) is easily explained:

Music had become an abomination because it was part of an indulgent lifestyle that deafened God's people to the corruption and injustice that surrounded them—a kind of drug that dulled their spiritual sense so that they could no longer discern the deeds of the Lord. The attack is on the abuse of a gift, not the gift itself.[54]

As for the gift, Robert Browning summed it up in verse. It comes from his poem 'Abt Vogler', an imaginary soliloquy by the court chaplain at Mannheim as he sits at the organ he has devised:

> But here is the finger of God, a flash of the will that can,
>   Existent behind all laws, that made them and, lo, they are!
> And I know not if, save in this, such gift be allowed to man,
>   That out of three sounds he frame, not a fourth sound, but a star.

Ralph Vaughan Williams, who along with much other music, gave us hymn tunes such as DOWN AMPNEY to 'Come down, O Love divine', SINE NOMINE to 'For all the saints', or MAGDA to 'Go forth for God', was Musical Editor for *The English Hymnal*, to which he also contributed numerous harmonies and arrangements. In his section of the Preface he famously threw down the gauntlet by declaring that the quality of a hymn tune was 'a moral rather than a musical issue':

No doubt it requires a certain effort to tune oneself to the moral atmosphere implied by a fine melody; and it is far easier to dwell in the miasma of the languishing and sentimental hymn tunes which so often disfigure our services...it ought no longer to be true anywhere that the most exalted moments of a church-goer's week are associated with music that would not be tolerated in any place of secular entertainment.[55]

He goes on to write of the difficulties of removing 'old favourites'; and it was an open secret that a section entitled 'For Mission Services: Not for ordinary use', with tunes like HOLD THE FORT and TELL ME THE OLD, OLD STORY, was known to him as the 'chamber of horrors'. Fifty years later, Erik Routley was underlining this view: 'There is in fact, as the early Fathers of the Church were never tired of pointing out, an uncomfortably close connection between cheap music and cheap faith.'[56] Sir Sydney Nicholson, founder of what is now the Royal School of Church Music, would have agreed. 'It is sometimes argued,' he is reported as saying, ' "Why should the devil have all the best tunes?" My reply is that it would be no bad thing if the major part of our so-called Church Music were entrusted to his care.'[57] Charles Wesley for one was certainly not prepared to let the devil have it all his own way. There is a story of how at a certain seaport his open-air preaching was disturbed by a crowd of half-drunken sailors. As soon as a hymn began they drowned the words with 'one of their lewd songs called *Nancy Dawson*'. Charles memorized the metre and melody and at the following Service his people sang new words to the sailors' tune, published later by Charles as 'The True use of Musick'. In this opening verse, note the word 'prest', as something with which sailors of the 1740s would be all-too-familiar:

> Listed into the Cause of Sin,
>   Why should a Good be Evil?
> Musick, alas! too long has been
>   Prest to obey the Devil:
> Drunken or lewd or light the Lay
>   Flow'd to the Soul's Undoing,
> Widen'd and strew'd with Flowers the Way
>   Down to Eternal Ruin.[58]

In May 1988 I was invited to lead one of the very popular 'Come and Sing' lunch-hour sessions in Westminster Abbey, to mark both the bicentenary of Charles Wesley's death, and the 250th anniversary of the conversion of the two brothers. 'The True use of Musick' was among the hymns I chose, partly as a reminder of his courageous 'field preaching', and partly to illustrate his versatility. John Wilson was in charge of the music and after some research reconstructed the tune *Nancy Dawson* along the lines of 'Here we go round the mulberry bush'. I guess it would have been a hymn new to the Abbey's repertoire!

* * *

It is very clear to me that when it comes to music I am quite unqualified to express an opinion, or even to claim more than a very shallow grasp of the issues. Of course I believe, and as a hymn writer seek to make it my practice, that all our creative offerings to God, especially in the field of congregational worship, should be the best that in us lies. Given this, though, it seems that God is prepared to bless and use what many editors, for the highest motives, would reject. I remember how in the 1950s the young Patricia St John was a pioneer missionary, alone in a small mountain town. Little by little she gathered a group of village children who met regularly in her home, and to whom she taught the stories of Jesus. This is what she wrote of those children, forty years on:

Sometimes even now, when I return for a few weeks each year to Morocco, I find one of them again. They nearly always remember just one thing from those old days—the little hymn that we sang almost daily in Arabic:

> There is a beautiful country.
> The gates are closed. No sin can go in.
> O Lord my God, give me a clean heart.
> Take away my sin in the blood of my Saviour.
> Lead me on the road to your house, O God.
> Then receive me with joy.

They repeat the words with laughter and enjoyment, for those old days were happy ones. How much they understand I do not know. But I remember that the thief on the cross knew much less theology than what is contained in that little hymn.[59]

Hymns are indeed, very often, 'the poor man's poetry... the ordinary man's theology'.[60] It is part of the reason why we of today's generation must prize and defend them—and seek to develop and continue their tradition of words and music in a happy marriage. Donald Hustad, who in his day was doyen of serious church musicians among American Baptists, reminds us in one of his books that 'singing in worship is not reserved for priests or for "singers"; singing is for believers. The crucial question is not "Do you have a voice?" but "Do you have a song?"'[61]

WE BRING YOU, LORD, OUR PRAYER AND PRAISE

WE BRING YOU, LORD, our prayer and praise
    that every child of earth
should live and grow in freedom's ways,
    in dignity and worth.

We praise for such a task begun
    to serve each other's need,
for every cause of justice won,
    for every fetter freed.

Our prayers are for a world in pain
    where force and fear prevail,
the plough becomes the sword again,
    and hope and harvest fail.

Alike our prayer and praise express
    the wants of humankind,
that those in bondage and distress
    their larger freedoms find.

So may we still maintain the fight
    till earth's oppressions cease
before the universal right
    to liberty and peace.

In Christ we learn to love and care
    and spread his truth abroad;
and in his Name we lift our prayer:
    'Your kingdom come, O Lord.'

© Timothy Dudley-Smith in Europe and Africa. © Hope Publishing Company in the United States of America and the rest of the world. Reproduced by permission of Oxford University Press. All rights reserved.

CHAPTER 6

Content and Form

> Much discussion of hymns has been concerned with their content, but a more appropriate criticism would acknowledge that form and content are inseparable: that the images and language used actually determine our sense of what those ideas are.*
>
> J. R. Watson, 2004

AMONG THE HAPPY MARRIAGES scattered through this book, the union of content and form must rank very high. It applies, of course, not only to hymnody, nor even to literature alone, but to all art. Since I discovered it—as I supposed, for myself—I have found it cropping up in my reading with surprising regularity. To say 'I discovered it' is an exact description. I vividly remember how it came about. It seems strange, looking back, that the penny took so long to drop but I can date it exactly as 14 February 1984. That evening I was watching on TV the winter Olympics from Sarajevo, when Jayne Torvill and Christopher Dean won the gold medal for ice dancing. As the last strains of Ravel's *Bolero* died away, the entire stadium rose to their feet, flowers were thrown onto the ice, and the couple retired to await the verdict of the judges. There were nine judges, and they each held up large cards to display the points they awarded. They did this twice, with one set of points for artistic impression, and one for technical merit; as I recall, in the first of these categories they all awarded the highest possible mark. But when the euphoria died down a little I found myself pondering 'artistic impression' and 'technical merit' and renaming them content and form. It was then that I realized that they are applicable to everything which combines some personal vision with the desire to communicate it.

I know now that this is a commonplace, but it was new to me. Since then I have found it expressed, in only slightly differing ways, by or about writers, musicians, performers, and artists of all kinds. John Betjeman, for example, described the frustration when the two are not in balance. In his verse autobiography, written in his fifties, he looked back to the young schoolboy Betjeman, perhaps only seven or eight but even then set on being a poet, and how he was captivated by tripping lines, internal rhymes, and what he regarded as poetic words: o'er, and ere, and e'en:

> My urge was to encase in rhythm and rhyme
> The things I saw and felt...

He sums it up a few lines later in an experience which most creators at some time in their early days will have found only too familiar:

> The gap between my feelings and my skill
> Was so immense, I wonder I went on.[1]

Peter Ackroyd, in his biography of T. S. Eliot, tells how a very different poet had a very similar experience. He describes how in Eliot's early unpublished verse 'the desire to make a statement is stronger than the ability to formulate that statement in a melodic and convincing way'.[2] Here, the desire is about content, and the ability about form. They share a number of different names: conception and expression, vision and execution, inspiration and craftsmanship. Perhaps the most succinct and cogent summary of these that I have come across was in a review of C. Day-Lewis's *Overtures to Death* (poetry, rather than one of the murder mysteries he wrote as 'Nicholas Blake') when the old *Manchester Guardian* wrote of 'an authentic emotion controlled by an assured art'.[3] What poet, what hymn writer—what creator of any kind—could ask more than that?

Philip Larkin is another who has written on this relationship. In an interview with the *Paris Review* he was forthright: 'On any level that matters, form and content are indivisible. What I mean by content is the experience the poem preserves, what it passes on.'[4] For the hymn writer such 'experience' may, as we have seen, take many different forms, often less subjective than the content which inspires the poet. But elsewhere Larkin set out three stages in the life of a poem, which apply also with a minimum of adjustment to the text of a hymn. The first he calls 'obsession' with an emotional concept, which to the hymn writer is the grasping of some new aspect of praise, some insight into narrative, or perhaps some particular but universal application of spiritual experience or biblical truth. Then, says Larkin, the poet has to construct 'a verbal device that will reproduce this emotional concept in anyone who cares to read it'; and the third stage is when others re-create in themselves the emotion—we could add the idea, the concept, the insight—which inspired the work. He adds that 'the stages are interdependent and all are necessary. If there has been no preliminary feeling, the device has nothing to reproduce and the reader [we could say 'singer'] will experience nothing.' Similarly, the device 'may not deliver the goods'; and if there is no third stage 'the poem can hardly be said to exist in a practical sense at all'.[5] We, too, are aware that in its fullest sense a hymn only exists as a hymn when it is sung by believing worshippers.

What then describes the content we may expect to find in a good hymn? John Ellerton, one of the most respected hymn writers of his day, was among those who wished to see 'a National Hymnal worthy of the Church of England'. In his paper 'On the Principles on which a Hymn-b00k should be Constructed' he set out 'a few particulars in which the excellence of a hymn may be said to consist' and lists sincerity, vigour, simplicity, brevity and suitability to be sung.[6] Not content with that, he went on to list 'the worst vices of modern hymns'—this was in the 1860s—as softness, sentimentalism, unreality, and sensuousness;[7] and believed that editors should be looking for a congregational hymnody which is 'simple, calm, comprehensive, and objective':[8] the more fervent, personal, and devotional hymns he would assign to collections for private use. Anyone today seeking to list the attributes of a good congregational hymn might well take Ellerton as a starting point. For myself, as regards content, I am in considerable agreement, though the five points he names as 'a few particulars' are not exactly those I would choose. He begins with sincerity; I prefer to say 'heartfelt', as including not only sincerity, but spiritual reality or genuineness, and aspiration. This is surely an essential prerequisite.

It is strange to think that there might be hymns which are not both heartfelt and genuine, at least as regards the writer. Whether the singer can always enter into the same sincerity cannot be guaranteed, but the thought should never be far from the hymn writer's mind, and there have been instances when even the writer's sincerity is subject to question. Like Queen Elizabeth I, 'We would not open windows into men's souls' but sometimes it is no secret that the writer of a text to be found in our hymnals does not profess faith in Christ. This is notoriously so of a few of the poets in Percy Dearmer's *Songs of Praise*—Shelley, for example, or Thomas Hardy—but their poems, I believe, are almost never sung in church today, and probably very seldom have been. More difficult, and nearer to our own time, is the instance of Joyce Torrens, born Joyce Anstruther, who after her second marriage became Joyce Placzek. She wrote under the name of Jan Struther, a combination of her initial and her maiden name, and to the generation of World War II was most famous as the author of *Mrs Miniver*, a patriotic novel made into a celebrated film. Her hymns, mostly commissioned by Percy Dearmer for *Songs of Praise*, are still represented in hymnals published today, notably the popular 'Lord of all hopefulness, Lord of all joy'. Her texts tend to celebrate nature rather than grace; and though they do not usually depend much on Scripture, they speak of Christ as King and Lord, as the herald, the 'star of day', and indeed as risen. But her granddaughter, her most recent biographer, describes her as 'standing back from Christianity', and adds that lovers of her hymns 'who discover that their author was not herself a churchgoer feel a sense of betrayal. The favourite hymn sung at their wedding or at their grandfather's funeral turns out to be, so to speak, a fake.'[9] And this is only to parallel among text writers a situation yet more prevalent among composers, with Vaughan Williams' well-documented agnosticism a case in point. He made no secret of it, and it finds mention in the *Dictionary of National Biography*. But whatever statement music may make, it does seem that if a hymn text is to be sung with integrity it should be the work of a writer who can sing it in the same way. People's views change; only God sees the secrets our hearts; perhaps what Jan Struther wrote for Percy Dearmer she at least thought she then believed. I remember, too, that Dorothy Sayers wrote pungently about how to the critic it is the work, rather than the creator of it, that really matters. In her Introduction to the published scripts of her celebrated radio plays, *The Man Born to be King,* she writes: 'When a story is great enough, any honest craftsman may succeed in producing something not altogether unworthy, because the greatness is in the story, and does not need to borrow anything from the craftsman; it is enough that he should faithfully serve the work.' And a few pages later:

I have assisted now at the production of a good many religious plays, and it is my considered opinion that in the matter of awareness of what he is about and a sense of dedication in doing it, the professional actor can give the average professional Christian cards and spades.[10]

Nevertheless, when it comes to putting words into the mouths of what may be many congregations over many decades, I stick with my conviction that the words should be 'heartfelt' by the writer; even though, thankfully, it is not ours to say what God may be gracious enough to use.

'Heartfelt', in my thinking, includes genuineness, which differs slightly from sincerity, in that a text may be sincere in intention, but in fact unreal. When F. W. Faber concluded a text with the words,

> If our love were but more simple,
> We should take him at his word;
> And our lives would be all sunshine
> In the sweetness of our Lord.[11]

he asked us to affirm what few could say from the heart—and indeed we would have our misgivings about any who did. The *Companion* to the Methodist book *Hymns and Psalms*, a book which emends this to:

> And our lives would be illumined
> By the presence of our Lord,

adds the comment that this is 'a considerable improvement on Faber's sentimental imagery; it is also true, whereas Faber's conclusion is not'.[12] Thirty years on, these lines seem to me to leave room for further improvement, even allowing for the fact that the archaic word 'illumined' is being woven into a nineteenth-century hymn. Nevertheless, the editors have rescued a generation of Methodist worshippers from being asked to sing what few could place their hands on their hearts and declare they really believed. Truer to most Christian experience are the lines from Francis Rawley's American gospel hymn of 1886, 'I will sing the wondrous story', which is still in common use. His original text includes the couplet:

> Days of darkness still may meet us,
> Sorrow's path I oft may tread,

leading on to:

> But his presence still is with me,
> By his guiding hand I'm led.[13]

In describing faith rather than feelings, that couplet is helping us apply to our present discipleship what the people of God have always believed, often in circumstances more difficult than our own.

'Heartfelt' should apply very particularly to those hymns which are really acts of commitment or prayers in song. We are warned by 'the Preacher' in Ecclesiastes (5.5) that 'it is better that you should not vow than that you should vow and not pay. Let not your mouth lead you into sin...' I know it is easy to caricature the comfortably-off citizen feeling for some loose change, while singing blithely

> Take my silver and my gold;
> Not a mite would I withhold...[14]

but this, and the explanations sometimes given from the pulpit that it does not mean what it appears to say, does not quite dispose of the matter. More helpful, I find, is Susan Drain's comment, when researching the story of *Hymns Ancient & Modern*:

Any public form of words carries a real danger of insincerity or sheer inappropriateness. The choice of a hymn must take into account all the circumstances of its use: the identity and experience of the singers and the occasion of the service... The hymn need not always reflect what its singers are; it may reflect what they aspire to be, and thus be an affirmation both of individual and of common purpose, and a statement of faith in what is greater than themselves.[15]

The same passage goes on to cite Dame Helen Gardner as seeing in a hymn 'a common ideal of Christian feeling and sentiment which the congregation acknowledges as ideal... Sincerity is measured by how wholeheartedly the singer accepts the ideal.' I learned something of this from my mentor, Derek Kidner, when in 1982 I sent him a draft of a metrical version based on Psalm 63. The first verse runs:

> God is my great desire,
>   his face I seek the first;
> to him my heart and soul aspire,
>   for him I thirst.
> As one in desert lands,
>   whose very flesh is flame,
> in burning love I lift my hands
>   and bless his Name.

My note attached to the draft mentioned my hesitation in thinking this could be a congregational hymn, 'using words which I suppose all of us reach only at moments, if then'. I wondered whether it would be better to cast the hymn into the plural ('God is *our* great desire'), which might do something to alleviate this concern. Derek's reply, as always, was helpful, cogent, and succinct. 'Don't worry,' he wrote, 'the psalms are for singing, and they beckon us to heights we haven't often reached, if at all. I would keep the singular...'

Together with 'heartfelt', my word of choice would be 'biblical' and my exemplar would be Charles Wesley. John Wesley claimed for his brother's hymns that they were 'scriptural';[16] and modern critics have shown how almost every metaphor or striking turn of phrase can be traced to a biblical origin. Two or three examples will illustrate the point. The first is from the well-known and much-loved hymn, 'O Thou who camest from above': but how many who have often sung the hymn know of its source? It is in fact closely based on the exposition by the seventeenth-century commentator Matthew Henry of 'the law of the burnt-offering' in Leviticus 6.13. Whole phrases and metaphors in the text can be traced to Matthew Henry: the fire of holy love always burning, the stirring up of the gift, the acts of piety and devotion, the readiness for every good word and work. It is typical of Wesley's genius that he should have given us, in a line of eight syllables, the six-syllable 'inextinguishable'; and that in the phrase 'stir up thy gift in me' he should look beyond the Old Testament to Paul's second letter to Timothy, and find there in the Greek the word meaning 'to blow coals to a flame'. It is one example of how the whole hymn uses fire as a metaphor for love. Nor is this an isolated instance: in his familiar two-verse hymn 'A charge to keep I have', Charles turns again to Leviticus, and again to Matthew Henry. He borrows not only the main theme and structure, but key words and phrases, often slightly altered but very recognizable: 'a charge to keep... God to glorify... immortal soul... daily care... Master... account... betray the truth we are charged with'. For a third example, perhaps even more telling, think of those lines in 'Soldiers of Christ, arise':

> And take, to arm you for the fight,
> The panoply of God.

'Panoply' is an unusual word. We can imagine Charles, perhaps on his 'poney', his mind preoccupied with the sixteen verses of this hymn on 'The Whole Armour of God' from Ephesians 6. Paul's imagery is all there, rehearsed in succeeding verses: 'Let Truth the Girdle be...The Gospel Greaves...Faith's victorious Shield...', and so on. But in the Authorized Version, the translation of Charles's day, there is no mention of 'panoply': where did the word come from? The answer is not hard to find. It is there in Paul's Greek text as *panoplia*, the exact word for 'full armour'. The word would be familiar to Charles from his classical reading, perhaps in Plato or Herodotus. He may have had his Greek New Testament to hand, even on horseback, just as he had his pencil, and 'a card kept for the purpose'; but it is much more likely that he was so familiar with the Greek New Testament that he could work entirely from memory, weaving a word found there, suitably anglicized, into his verse. The Methodist scholar W. F. Lofthouse sums up just how deserving Charles Wesley's hymns are of his brother's epithet 'scriptural'. He describes how Charles Wesley 'rarely wrote a verse without some allusion to an incident or passage out of the Bible. In some hymns they appear in almost every line...Sometimes two or three passages are laid under tribute for one sentence.'[17] In other hands, this might seem contrived, obscure, and even dull. We have to admit that examples are not hard to find. Erik Routley wrote disparagingly of some of Cowper's hymns (surprisingly enough) as reading 'like a versified concordance',[18] while another critic, like Routley an admirer of Cowper, had to admit that 'he wrote many hymns that are mere rhymed Calvinism'.[19] Nevertheless, William Cowper's place is secure as one of our most poetic hymn writers.

By contrast with any suggestion of 'rhymed concordance', Charles Wesley's use of Scripture helps us to lay hold on it as the word of life. Archbishop Rowan Williams, preaching in Westminster Abbey to mark the tercentenary of Charles's birth, described his hymns as 'an irreplaceable and inexhaustible treasure of classical Christian wisdom'.

What is here illustrated from Charles Wesley should surely characterize the great majority of Christian hymns. There will always be exceptions; but to me these owe their inclusion to the company they keep. We can afford to admit them because so much of our hymn books is securely based on revealed truth, which makes our best hymns what Bernard Manning called 'the safest protection and the surest vehicle of orthodoxy'.[20] Not so long ago such a view was thought to be old-fashioned. When *Congregational Praise* was published in 1951 a *Companion* followed it shortly afterwards. The General Introduction included a section on 'Yesterday, To-day and Tomorrow' which spoke of 'the divorce of the union which wedded the hymn-book to the Bible', and confidently affirmed that 'the nineteenth century saw the end of this biblical tradition'.[21] In fact this was written on the very brink of the 'hymn explosion' which has seen many writers return to the 'marriage' of hymnal and Bible, in a renewed determination to offer congregations a form of praise which springs from Scripture. Henry Bett, that perspicacious student of the Wesley hymns, describes some as 'a mere mosaic of biblical allusions'.[22] 'Mosaic' I accept; 'mere' I refute. Lord Byron—surely not known as a lover of hymns—put his finger on a tender spot in his poem 'The Sabbath Bard', a sardonic portrait of a well-meaning versifier who

> Breaks into blank the Gospel of St. Luke,
> And boldly pilfers from the Pentateuch;
> And, undisturbed by conscientious qualms,
> Perverts the Prophets and purloins the Psalms.

This was written, however, not about the Wesleys, but as response to James Grahame's poem, 'The Sabbath'. It was a tradition in the family that James's literary gifts passed to his great-grand-nephew Kenneth, finding their eventual flowering in *The Wind in the Willows*.[23]

The description 'biblical' implies that such hymns are also 'evangelical', not in a partisan sense of the word, but as conveying 'good news', the gospel. Perhaps at times this may make them seem simplistic, but if they are to present the Christ of revelation, rather than the Jesus of contemporary imagination, they will never stray far from the central truths of the Gospels. Max Warren, the pre-eminent missionary statesman of the twentieth century, paid tribute to this:

> I can never thank God enough for the fact that these simple evangelical hymns were the ones with which I first entered into a conscious and deliberate discipleship... they do not represent the whole gospel: they do not look beyond a deep personal experience: they lack the horizontal dimension. But continuing discipleship brings in the horizontal. I believe with all my heart that we must start with the vertical... God comes first in the Bible and it is of far-reaching importance that God—the Other—comes first in experience.[24]

This is to echo some words in a rather touching private letter, written in 1909 by Randall Davidson, Archbishop of Canterbury, to Cosmo Gordon Lang, the just-appointed Archbishop of York:

> I grow increasingly sure as time runs on that the simplest of the old gospel truths and lessons of our childhood are the most effective too for our daily need.[25]

It is the more striking since neither man strikes the church historian as particularly childlike. Hensley Henson, always something of an *enfant terrible*, was once looking with Lang at Sir William Orpen's rather imposing full-length portrait of him. Lang said that he disliked it, because it made him appear 'proud, prelatical and pompous'. 'May I ask,' said Henson, 'to which of those epithets does your Grace take exception?'[26]

It was with the university Christian Union in Holy Trinity Church, Cambridge, where ten years earlier Max Warren had been vicar, that I recall singing just such a hymn of 'simple gospel truth', not conscious that I had ever met it before, but finding as the student congregation sang around me that it expressed what was in my heart. The hymn was Elizabeth Clephane's 'Beneath the cross of Jesus'. The closing verse begins 'I take, O cross, thy shadow/For my abiding place' and ends:

> ...Content to let the world go by,
>   To know no gain nor loss—
> My sinful sense my only shame,
>   My glory all the cross.

That is for me, I remember thinking, and in my better moments I think so still.

What more can be asked, in terms of content, of a hymn which is both heartfelt and biblical? My other suggestions can be disposed of more briefly. Ellerton looks for simplicity, and in one sense, probably the sense he had in mind, I agree with him here too. The congregation should grasp the sense of what they are singing even when meeting the text for the first time. This is very different from saying that they will discover its whole meaning, if indeed such a thing is possible. Ideally, aided by the Good Spirit, they will find that the same words, direct and simple though they may be, speak to them in different ways at different times, according to their growth in grace and their particular needs. This is surely a canon of all true poetry, and even more so of those hymn texts which aspire to a heightened vision in what they say. Let there be simplicity, directness, by all means; but there should also be sufficient depth, or at least some hint of depth, to encourage readings which may not have been part of the author's intention when the text was written. I cannot find a better word for this than 'depth', though moderns might use the more technical term 'layers'; and I would want to add the word 'colour', as a rather inadequate way of describing that quality, perhaps conveyed through a single word, which lifts the text above the commonplace and gives something for the imagination to work on. Andrew Motion has summed up an experience widely shared when he described how, as a boy at school reading Philip Larkin's poems for the first time, 'I enjoyed the poems as much as Hardy's; they gave me the same mysterious feeling of discovering things I didn't realize I already knew.'[27] The judgement of how this is to be achieved is a matter of very nice discrimination, since too much poetic diction in a hymn can be as detrimental as dull mediocrity. Erik Routley had this in mind, surely, when he described a hymn text as 'lyric under a vow of renunciation'.[28] In this he is following Isaac Watts' admission:

I confess myself to have been too often tempted away from the more spiritual designs I proposed, by some gay and flowery expressions that gratified the fancy; the bright images too often prevailed above the fire of divine affection; and the light exceeded the heat; yet, I hope, in many of them the reader will find, that devotion dictated the song, and the head and hand were nothing but interpreters and secretaries to the heart...[29]

Interestingly, it seems that this can be a problem as much for novelists as for hymn writers. C. P. Snow has described how an examination of Anthony Trollope's manuscripts reveals how 'time and time again' Trollope strikes out a picturesque word to repeat one already used: 'It was one of the most thorough, and in appearance sacrificial, revisions in literary history.'[30]

In looking for the qualities that mark a good hymn, I think we must add 'uncontroversial'. The examples given earlier of hymns designed to win an argument surely prove this. There are exceptions, of course, where hymns which formed part of a current controversy have survived when the controversy itself no longer rages. Henry Bett has pointed out that many Wesley hymns are used today by 'those religious communities which have a Calvinist tradition, without any realization of their polemical intention'.[31] 'Rock of Ages, cleft for me', Toplady's great hymn, would be a similar case. But a good hymn should unite believers, not divide them. It should serve that unity for which we pray in the Book of Common Prayer, 'that all they that do confess thy holy Name may agree in the truth of thy holy Word, and live in unity, and godly love'.[32] I confess that it was a sadness to me, as an admirer of Keble's hymns, to discover that on his deathbed he was persuaded (under what pressure, one wonders, from his more extreme Tractarian friends?) to make an alteration in his immensely popular *The*

Christian Year, a book which went through ninety-six editions in his lifetime.[33] In Keble's day, at the height of the Oxford Movement, the Prayer Book still included a form of Service giving thanks for the failure of the Gunpowder Plot of 1605, and Keble's poem bore the title 'Gunpowder Treason'. The verse in question runs:

> O come to our Communion Feast:
>   There present in the heart,
> Not in the hands, th' Eternal Priest
>   Will His true self impart.

Keble was persuaded to change the third line to read 'As in the hands...' in the interest of a sacramental theology more Roman than Anglican. His biographer recounts how

a well-known Evangelical divine, Canon Tristram, was in the habit of presenting a copy of *The Christian Year* to each of his many children on the occasion of their confirmation. After this alteration was made he was obliged to spend much time and trouble hunting for second-hand copies of earlier editions so that the minds of his offspring should not be contaminated by such Popish sentiments.[34]

Controversy, even when necessary, is a sad business and seldom at home in hymnody. Do we not find, too, that there are subjects better suited to our intercessions than to our hymn singing? The two can overlap, as in Fred Pratt Green's moving text:

> Pray for the church, afflicted and oppressed,
> For all who suffer for the gospel's sake...[35]

But sometimes, in their zeal to keep the global troubles of our society firmly before the worshipping community, some hymns become more like protest songs, even with hints of a party-political manifesto. However good the cause or worthy the motive, I would want to look very closely at such texts in the light of the pastor's knowledge of those who will be asked to sing them. It is a fine line between the desired end—peace on earth, for example—which commands universal agreement, and a particular means—unilateral disarmament, say—on which members of a congregation may have strongly divergent views. I have myself responded to a request for a text to celebrate the fiftieth Anniversary of the Declaration of Human Rights; but such a text, like the Declaration itself, is concerned with ends rather than means.[36]

Archbishop Donald Coggan was quoted as saying that a good sermon should have a good beginning and a good ending—and not too much in between. Something of the same is true of a hymn. Excessive length, save in hymns designed to be sung in procession, is generally a weakness, as John Wesley knew well when he came to edit his brother's hymns for inclusion in his famous 1780 *Collection*. As for the opening of a hymn, that is the line which is also its title; by that it will be known, announced, and indexed. It is a source of confusion, as I soon discovered by experience, to allow a hymn any title other than this opening line: Blake's 'Jerusalem' and Kipling's 'Recessional' defy this, but neither was written as a hymn. A further trap for the unwary lies in the fact that the same hymn may be composed of a different selection of stanzas in different books, and so have different opening lines. John Keble's 'New every morning is the love' is the first line of the familiar hymn, for example, but is taken from the sixth stanza of his poem 'Hues of the rich unfolding morn'. Charles Wesley's 'Jesus, the name high over all' is the ninth stanza of 'Jesu, accept the grateful song'; while 'Come, let us join our friends above' appears in Methodist hymn books as Wesley wrote it, but the same hymn elsewhere is often printed as 'Let saints on earth in concert sing' (Wesley wrote 'Let all the saints terrestrial sing') adapted from line 5 of the first eight-line stanza.

Another distinguishing general principle, though again there are plenty of exceptions, is that a good hymn will usually begin with God, rather than with me. As with the Prayer Book Collects, we can then fix our minds on who it is whose praise we are singing, whose grace we seek, before going on to relate the hymn to our own circumstances and concerns: in a word, the hymn should be objective before subjective. It is after we have reflected on the God 'who camest from above, the fire celestial to impart' that we go on to ask that he will look on us, and warm our hearts with his 'sacred love'. There is a story of how an old-fashioned printer could not continue typesetting a work of autobiography because he had run out of the letter 'I': sometimes it seems that it is only modern technology that has saved the printers of some contemporary worship song collections from the same predicament.

Endings are just as important as openings; perhaps even more so, since they remain with us when the hymn is over. In one of his letters, Philip Larkin wrote of how he would like to add Handel's *Messiah* to his substantial collection of LPs, and how 'it gets better toward the end—this is almost a *sine qua non* of good art'.[37] Not only should it get better, but it should bring the whole to a climax. Good preachers know this from their sermons. Without adequate preparation they can find themselves like aircraft endlessly circling trying to make a landing. It gives rise to the definition of an optimist as a lady who, when the preacher says 'In conclusion...' starts looking for her shoes. So it is with hymns: the final verse or couplet or line is crucial. The example that always comes to mind is Mrs Alexander's Christmas text, masterly in its simplicity, 'Once in royal David's city'. Had she known it would find a place in almost every hymn book for a century and more, surely she would have tried harder to find a fitting climax, something more conclusive than:

> When like stars, his children crowned,
> All in white shall wait around.

Or is it that language has changed since she published her *Hymns for Little Children* 130 years ago? Might the word 'wait' have then more the connotation of service, as in 'waiter', rather than the idle street-corner image that 'wait around' suggests today? The elusive ideal must be to emulate Charles Wesley's gift for 'closing a hymn with solid finality, with no lingering impression that he might have gone on for a few more verses'.[38]

It used to be thought that this finality could be achieved by adding an Amen, 'so let it be', to the end of a hymn; and indeed Isaac Watts wrote of how 'we are taught in several places of Scripture to conclude our prayers [note, *prayers*] with Amen, as implying faith, desire, a solemn profession on our part, and a sure expectation'.[39] The first editors of *Hymns Ancient & Modern* printed an ' Amen' almost invariably but this has long been discontinued, even at the end of petitionary hymns or of a doxology. Such a change is in keeping with Erik Routley's view of the practice as 'an episcopal mistake... unhistorical, unmusical, and unliturgical', introduced to our hymnody only in the 1850s by those who believed 'that medieval practice was the right guide for everything in the modern church'.⁴⁰ Without this device, the ending of the hymn itself becomes even more important, and it is no accident that this often implies the kind of completion found in journey's end, and indeed in the homecoming that concludes the Christian's final journey. Professor Watson, lecturing on this theme, adds to this the thought found in so much literature of love and marriage, the traditional 'happy ending' raised to the sublime:

> We approach here the greatest mystery of all, the marriage-supper of the Lamb from Revelation 19. And if I have taken the suggestion of marriage and love from Shakespearean comedy, I must end with a greater example of triumphant love, *The Divine Comedy* . The wonderful Canto XXIII of the *Paradiso* is Dante's vision of the radiance of heaven... So it is with hymns. Some of the most effective endings are those in which the soul is transported and enraptured, dazzled with the love that Dante writes of, 'the love that moves the sun and stars'. It is in this splendour that Charles Wesley will end 'Love divine, all loves excelling': Lost in wonder, love and praise.⁴¹

* * *

I have given much of this chapter to content, but as we have seen already, content must be matched with form. That implies craftsmanship, the learning and practising of a skill, as in the admission of John Betjeman a few pages back, 'The gap between my feelings and my skill was so immense, I wonder I went on.' Walter de la Mare had a word for the painstaking and concentrated work so often required to shape a poem into its proper form; he called it 'gruelling', and a recent biographer wrote of him as 'a craftsman in verse who weighed every nuance of every syllable in conscious choice'. It was to Naomi Royde-Smith, with whom he shared a unique and passionate friendship, that he wrote in comment on a poem she had sent him (she was herself Literary Editor of the *Saturday Westminster*): 'I don't believe that *you* really know what downright *gruelling* at a poem means.'⁴² The word signifies what is exhausting, even punishing. Lord David Cecil described de la Mare as one of those authors 'who speak to us, as it were, on a private line', to whom 'we owe a particular debt'. It is the more surprising that in the same lecture he should have gone on to describe Walter de le Mare's technical equipment as inadequate to his inspiration: 'a disproportion between his mind and imagination, on the one hand, and his gift of expression on the other'.⁴³ This is exactly the partnership of content and form, and it is clear that de la Mare did in fact take immense pains to clothe his unique imaginings in a fitting dress. One example would be his famous lyric, often anthologized, 'Very old are the woods' which includes the lines:

> Oh, no man knows
> Through what wild centuries
> Roves back the rose.

Robert Graves asked him about the last line, whether he had tried 'all sorts of things to get *roves* right, [*roams* would be one example] and failed and been content with the nearest'. De la Mare told him that it had been a 'nightmare to him and remained unresolved'.⁴⁴ Perhaps this is what David Cecil meant by suggesting that his mastery of form did not match his inspiration; yet just as he acknowledged 'a particular debt', so W. H. Auden once named de la Mare's poems, which he read as a schoolboy, as having taught him, more than any book he had read before or since, what poetry was.⁴⁵ It seems very fitting that when Walter de la Mare was once asked, supposing he could choose his forebears, who would be his choice, he named John Wesley and 'the author of "When I survey the wondrous cross"'—namely Isaac Watts.[46]

I do not myself see an unequal partnership between content and form in de la Mare's poetry; but when, as sometimes happens, I am sent hymn texts in draft and asked to comment, I often have to say something like, 'You stopped work too soon.' Robert Frost thought that Emily Dickinson might be a case in point. He appreciated her 'wilfulness, the unmanageability of the thought by the form', but felt it was sometimes indistinguishable from carelessness: 'she gave up the technical struggle too easily'.[47] To some of my correspondents, form is an adversary; so that wrestling with form becomes an unsatisfactory and ultimately frustrating experience. Of course, this must surely be so at times with most writers, of hymns or poems or anything else. But, whatever the difficulties, form should not be seen as the enemy. C. Day-Lewis described it as a discipline which helps selection, but adds that

form is not always merely selective and disciplinary: many poets have observed...that the need for a rhyme in a certain place, or the exigency of a metre, has thrown up a revealing phrase, a creative idea, which might well not have come into existence without the prompting of the formal agency. Form, in a word, not only restrains but stimulates.[48]

Among the 'many poets' would be Auden. One of his biographers includes a chapter of what he calls Auden's *obiter dicta*. A number relate to content and form, for example:

I always have two things in my head—I always have a theme and the form. The form looks for the theme, the theme looks for the form, and when they come together you're able to write. I can't understand—strictly from a hedonistic point of view—how one can enjoy writing with no form at all. If one plays a game, one needs rules, otherwise there is no fun.[49]

William Wordsworth, writing in 1827 to a friend who had sent him some verses, advised him that what he called 'the logical faculty' had a crucial place in composition, a faculty which included the handling of form. 'Indeed,' he wrote,

as the materials upon which that faculty is exercised in Poetry are so subtle, so plastic, so complex, the application of it requires an adroitness which can proceed from nothing but practice, a discernment which emotion is so far from bestowing that at first it is ever in the way of it...[50]

This applies equally to the hymn writer. No matter how perfect the form, a hymn is valueless to a congregation unless it helps them to express something they wish to say. But, as we have seen, content without form may be equally fruitless when it fails to communicate the vision of truth. The two are not separable; conception and execution are part of a single whole. William Dunbar, the Scottish poet and priest who is believed to have fallen at the battle of Flodden in 1513, has been described as 'professional through and through...the last line of each poem was in view before he wrote the first'.[51] This is a hard test, surely, for the hymn writer who, at least in my experience, cannot always see the end from the beginning; and I understand that it conflicts with the experience of some contemporary poets and artists. It is sometimes said of Paul Klee that he began with a point, extended it to a line, and would then 'take it for a walk' wherever it chose to go. But, at least for me, the constraint of form helps in the search for the fitting conclusion; though I learned, again from C. S. Lewis, that there is a higher law than form:

A supreme workman will never break...the living and inward law of the work he is producing. But he will break without scruple any number of those superficial regularities and orthodoxies which little, unimaginative critics mistake for its laws. The extent to which one can distinguish a just 'licence' from a mere botch or failure of unity depends on the extent to which one has grasped the real and inward significance of the work as a whole.[52]

Here, I believe is one explanation of how Charles Wesley can sit so lightly to what we see as purity of rhyme, in a way which in lesser hands would qualify for Lewis's condemnation as 'botch'.

Another important aspect of form is the appearance of the printed page. I suppose it is because I am a text-writer that I believe so strongly that the text should be printed, as a poem is printed, complete upon the page. By all means let the words appear also between the staves if that helps the singers; but when that is the style adopted for just the opening verse, that verse should still be printed with the text. I find it sad if in order to read a new hymn unknown to me, I have to pick out the words from between the staves; or do that for the opening verse, while the rest of the truncated text appears alongside. Churches in North America, I discovered to my surprise on a first visit to their Hymn Society, rarely print 'words only' hymnals, since the whole congregation likes to have music in front of them, and indeed often cannot sing without it. A churchful of their Hymn Society members, I cringe to recall, made a very poor shot at singing a new text of mine to ST GERTRUDE (familiarly set to 'Onward, Christian soldiers') because they had only the words in front of them, and I had imagined they would sing the tune from memory. Some years later, I took it as a recognition that the words deserve better consideration, when the Episcopalians in the United States published as poems the words of their 1982 hymnal, in a fat little paperback entitled *Poems of Grace*. They did not expect anyone actually to sing from a book containing no music, but they offered this book of 631 pages as 'a source of beauty, a guide in meditation, and most importantly, a means of prayer'.[53]

So let the text be printed in full. Let there be verse numbers in any congregational hymnal, not just to allow the minister to shorten the hymn, but also to expound and comment on it, and let the original indentation be faithfully observed. It is part of the hymn, and helps to clarify the meaning and emphasize the rhyme scheme. Funeral directors, who have to produce Orders of Service in a hurry, are often offenders here, but it can be a lazy short-cut for anyone who uses a word-processor which will automatically centre each line. For myself, I try to insist on my indentation, while allowing capitalization and punctuation to follow the house style of the publishers. For example, it is my practice, following the Prayer Book, to use a capital N to begin the word Name when this is the Name of God or of Jesus Christ, but not to capitalize pronouns of deity. I am always pleased when this is followed by hymnal editors, but I do not insist; they have enough trouble in trying to ensure a proper consistency of usage without having to take such preferences into account. Again, to my eye the page looks better and is more easily understood without too great a sprinkling of capital letters. I do not use them at the start of a line where grammar does not require them. Some, indeed, have their proper place. The capitalization of 'church' for example, is I think generally agreed: upper case for the universal Church; lower case for anything less, apart from proper names, such as Methodist Church. It is my practice to give the Bible, and the word Scripture, capital letters, but not when they form adjectives. 'Word' is more difficult, and I have settled on an initial capital to distinguish Christ, the incarnate Word, from all other uses, even the word of Scripture or the word of the gospel. Again, I think it helps towards clarity of meaning to reserve the upper-case G for the four Gospels. For quotes in this book, in the interests of consistency, I begin each line of verse with a capital letter, unless it is my own.

Punctuation, too, as with capital letters, can have a strong visual effect on the printed page. I have been working over the years to try to reduce my use of stops and to eliminate the dash. T. S. Eliot found the use of the dash a symptom of weakness, 'like [Matthew] Arnold's irritating use of italicized words';[54] while John Betjeman in a letter of 1958 offered what must surely be a counsel of perfection, saying that 'a really natural poem should need no punctuation; it should punctuate itself by the natural cadence of its words'.[55] Certainly there are poems that attempt this, though no hymns that I am aware of; the poet e.e. cummings forgoes not only punctuation but capital letters as well, and some of Emily Dickinson's verse is unpunctuated. For myself, I do not find in either case that it makes understanding easier. There are plenty of instances where the reverse is true, and only the punctuation shows the sense. Henry Bett gave as an example the sentence 'The Mayor says the Inspector is a fool'. Unpunctuated, it expresses the Mayor's opinion of the Inspector, but add a couple of commas and their roles are reversed: 'The Mayor, says the Inspector, is a fool.'[56] Chapter 2 of this book showed how important is the punctuation in certain hymns by Mrs Alexander, John Keble, and Edward Caswall.

These last few paragraphs have been about the form of the text on the printed page; but increasingly, it seems, congregations have to take their hymns from a screen. The Church of Scotland in a Report of 2001 listed three *concerns* over the exclusive use of overhead projection. First, that 'to be able to thumb through a hymn book'—to take it home and have it beside the Bible, perhaps at the bedside—'is to have access to a treasury of spiritual wisdom'. Second, the fact that the screen tends to show only a single verse at a time, and sometimes less than a verse, means that worshippers cannot easily grasp the whole, cannot look back on what they have just sung, and have no idea how many verses remain or what they are about. Third, there were misgivings concerning 'something very like a centralisation of power'; worshippers are denied even the chance to know what texts are available.[57] These are real concerns which go well beyond the Scottish Church; they deserve serious consideration by all local churches using or contemplating the video-screen. In fairness, I am glad to place on record that some of the churches known to me who sing largely from the screen seem to be growing, flourishing, and multiplying, with a vibrant sense of committed worship. Nevertheless, some misgivings remain, and I admire the practice which I sometimes meet where the Service, complete with hymns, is found both on the screen and on a printed Order. Those who follow the printed version can not only take it home afterwards, but during worship can see what comes next. I sometimes think of a family Service which I attended on holiday in Yorkshire with my young family. We were all welcomed, and told that the first song would give us a chance to greet our neighbours in the pew; and then the opening few lines appeared on the screen. As best I remember, they went something like this:

>   Give a little nod to the head beside you,
>   Give a little nod, give a little nod...

Under the enthusiastic direction of the worship leader, we turned to the person next to us, and gave a reserved kind of nod by way of greeting. The screen changed as if by magic:

> Give a little shake to the hand beside you,
> Give a little shake, give a little shake...

A trifle sheepishly, we did so; and then came:

> Put a little hand on the knee beside you,
> Put a little hand, put a little hand...

By this time I was very glad to be sitting between my wife and daughter—especially as there was no way of guessing what the screen might ask of us next. It has stayed in my memory both as a source of gentle amusement, but also as a reminder of one reason why the hymn book suits me better than the screen. If the hymn writer has 'gruelled' at form as well as content, the work deserves better than piecemeal presentation, where all you have sung vanishes at once into limbo, and what you will be asked to sing comes as a surprise, whose meaning will only be grasped when you are halfway through singing it.

* * *

This chapter, like the last, has been about a happy marriage—or, if you prefer, twin sisters—known by a variety of names. These include, as we have seen, 'artistic impression and technical merit', 'feelings and skill', 'vision and execution'. Austin Lovelace, whom I knew as a veteran of the American Hymn Society, likened their partnership to 'soul and body',[58] as did C. S. Lewis: 'In poetry the words are the body and the "theme" or "content" is the soul.'[59] William Wordsworth wrote of 'poetic spirit and the power of expression',[60] while Dr Johnson refers to 'Ball and Powder',[61] Philip Larkin to 'Knife and Fork',[62] Kenneth Clark to 'Intuition and Intellect' ('the Blot and the Diagram') and therefore related to the two halves of the brain;[63] while from his long experience as a lyricist for the stage Stephen Sondheim wrote of Art as 'skill in the service of passion'.[64] Such a variety of names and metaphors indicates how universal is the experience. 'Content and form', for the hymn writer as for any artist or creator, belong together. It is only in harmonious partnership that they can hope to achieve that elusive aim of 'an authentic emotion controlled by an assured art'.

ETERNAL GOD, BEFORE WHOSE FACE WE STAND

ETERNAL GOD, before whose face we stand,
your earthly children, fashioned by your hand,
hear and behold us, for to you alone
all hearts are open, all our longings known:
> so for our world and for ourselves we pray
> the gift of peace, O Lord, in this our day.

We come with grief, with thankfulness and pride,
to hold in honour those who served and died;
we bring our hurt, our loneliness and loss,
to him who hung forsaken on the cross;
> who, for our peace, our pains and sorrows bore,
> and with the Father lives for evermore.

O Prince of peace, who gave for us your life,
look down with pity on our sin and strife.
May this remembrance move our hearts to build
a peace enduring, and a hope fulfilled,
> when every flag of tyranny is furled
> and wars at last shall cease in all the world.

From earth's long tale of suffering here below
we pray the fragile flower of peace may grow,
till cloud and darkness vanish from our skies
to see the Sun of Righteousness arise.
> When night is past and peace shall banish pain,
> all shall be well, in God's eternal reign.

© Timothy Dudley-Smith in Europe and Africa. © Hope Publishing Company in the United States of America and the rest of the world. Reproduced by permission of Oxford University Press. All rights reserved.

CHAPTER 7

Meaning and Language

> He would as soon have thought of carrying an odour in a net as of attempting to convey the intangibilities of his feeling in the coarse meshes of language.*
>
> Thomas Hardy of Gabriel Oak, 1874

THIS RATHER PORTENTOUS CHAPTER HEADING might suggest a learned discussion of semantics and linguistics: nothing could be further from the truth. My acquaintance with these, in any formal sense, is like Walter Bagehot's verdict on the public schools of his day, that 'though it could not be claimed that they succeeded in teaching their pupils Greek and Latin, they left on their minds the indelible impression that there were such languages'.[1] Yet a writer of any kind must inevitably acquire some practical interest in the relationship between meaning as it exists in the author's mind and the language which is the means of expressing this. It is certainly so of the writer of hymns, and in fact it is a version of the 'marriage' we met in chapter 6 between content and form. C. Day-Lewis, in a Preface to a collection of his poems, wrote of how 'we [we poets] are concerned always with the techniques of putting words together so that they *give* experience... for me, at least, strict verse-forms are discoverers of meaning'.[2] There are here both differences and similarities between the hymn and the poem. Robert Frost, in conversation, was of the opinion that 'a poet doesn't want to know too much, not while he's writing, anyway. The knowing can come later.' And equally, 'I don't think a thing has to be obvious before it's said, but it ought to be obvious when it's said.'[3] Both these apply in part to the writing of hymns. Of course, there must be a controlling sense of what a hymn should say; but, at least in my experience, some of the content may not be there at the beginning, but appear to the writer only as the text develops. Equally, we do not want baffling obscurity (Frost had been asked about Eliot's poetry) and yet something should lie below the surface, a hint of meaning which may only become apparent to a particular singer at a particular time.

Indeed in poetry, and in part at least in hymnody, the various meanings a text may come to have are not by any means always plain to the writer of it. In 1884, Lewis Carroll was asked by some children what was the meaning of *The Hunting of the Snark* and in reply gave them this universal truth: 'Words mean more than we mean to express when we use them: so a whole book ought to mean a good deal more than the writer meant.'[4]

To take an extreme example, Coleridge scribbled on the manuscript of his 'Kubla Khan' that 'these are very fine lines, tho' I say it, that should not: but, hang me, if I know or ever did know the meaning of them, tho' my own composition'. His biographer adds that for the first time he was recognizing that poetry may be written not under conscious control.⁵ Coleridge was even then familiar with laudanum, which may be part of the explanation; but the experience is not uncommon. When W. B. Yeats had got to know his London publisher, Harold Macmillan, he would sometimes be confronted by a question as to the exact meaning of something in his poetry:

> There has never been an imaginative writer not a charlatan who has not been pleased by his publisher's interest in his work, and Yeats was delighted rather than annoyed by queries. He would sit down, pore over the doubtful line, seek and seek in his memory for a clue to the meaning that either his youthful ardour or some ancient misprint had clouded.⁶

By contrast, Robert Browning in the years of fame was once asked to explain an obscure passage in one of his poems. 'Upon my word, I don't know what it means', was his response; 'I advise you to ask the Browning Society—they'll tell you all about it.'⁷ The same can be true of hymns. In Newman's 'Lead, kindly light' there has been much speculation about the angel faces of the final lines:

> And with the morn those angel faces smile
> Which I have loved long since, and lost awhile.

This has been variously interpreted as the lost 'faces' of fancy and hope and youthful confidence; or perhaps, more simply, of faith and assurance; or, more literally, of lost friends, perhaps children, though I have never seen an identification of them attempted. William Alexander, Archbishop of Armagh and husband of the hymn writer Cecil Frances, offers—who knows on what grounds?—a clear-cut solution:

> The pure and imaginative child had believed himself to be perpetually in the society of Angels whose faces he came to know. But as he grew older and advanced towards manhood, like Wordsworth's clouds of glory, the Angel vision fell from him to his great grief. It is the restoration of this which he had lost, and not the sight of beloved dead to which he refers.⁸

Alexander's daughter, who wrote his biography, might have been less ready to quote this had she consulted Julian's great dictionary, published a few years before her book. There Julian himself, after offering five possible suggestions, largely hinted at above, quotes in full a letter from Newman, dated 1879, forty-six years after the lines were written:

> I think it was Keble who, when asked it [to elucidate a poem] in his own case, answered that poets were not bound to be critics, or to give a sense of what they had written, and though I am not, like him, a poet, at least I may plead that I am not bound to *remember* my own meaning, whatever it was, at the end of almost fifty years.⁹

He goes on to talk of 'the expression, not of truth, but of imagination and sentiment', and to plead transient states of mind in home-sickness or sea-sickness. Owen Chadwick notes that though Newman was always one for emending his own poems, 'a great tinkerer with his texts',¹⁰ he never touched this one, apart from the title. Hymnal editors, though, have sometimes done so since.

There are other references in hymns whose exact meaning will now never be known for certain. Charles Wesley, in his famous hymn 'And can it be', includes the lines:

> In vain the first-born seraph tries
> To sound the depths of love divine.

It is, I think, the only obscurity in the hymn and again various interpretations have been offered. I see it as an allusion to 1 Peter 1.12, which speaks of the good news of the gospel as 'things into which angels long to look'—but this leaves much unexplained. William Cowper, whose style was so original in its day as notably plain and direct, used to puzzle me with this verse from one of his best-known hymns, 'God moves in a mysterious way':

> Deep in unfathomable mines
>   Of never-failing skill
> He treasures up his bright designs,
>   And works his sovereign will.

It is a deservedly popular hymn, and it would be fascinating to know what is in the minds of the worshippers who sing this verse. I have come to think that we are misled by the metaphor of 'mining', which leads us—me, at least—to picture miners deep beneath the earth at work with picks and shovels. This is a scene vividly described in Job, chapter 28, which must surely have been Cowper's inspiration. Silver, gold, iron, and copper all come from the mine, but not 'wisdom', so why does the verse place God's 'treasury' underground? What has helped me to a less puzzling interpretation is the use of the noun 'mine' in a saying such as 'He is a mine of information.' This does not call to my mind simply the visual image of the tin-miner or collier, but also of a capacious store which is, I find, the primary figurative sense given to the word in the OED. We could then paraphrase Cowper's lines as expressing how God's providence, the subject of the hymn, includes an inexhaustible 'store' of divine wisdom, working his will for our good as Paul describes it in Romans 8.28. How far this is in fact what Cowper meant we shall never know, but it appeals to me in singing the hymn. If some reader of this book has a better interpretation, it would be a kindness to share it with me.

It was John Ellerton's belief that because hymns are forms of worship, it was not enough that they should *suggest* devotion; they must be capable of *expressing* it.[11] That last (the italics are original) is a useful description. It was echoed some seventy years later by Percy Dearmer, who suggested that the purpose of a hymn was to *express* and not *define*.[12] Such lack of definition is not, to my mind, to diminish the great facts of our faith 'set forth in the Holy Scriptures' which is the birthright of every Christian. We have come a long way since the Rheims New Testament of 1582, whose Preface speaks of 'better times' when poor ploughmen could

sing the hymns and psalms, either in known or unknown languages, as they heard them in the holy Church, though they could neither read nor know the sense, meaning and mysteries of the same...[13]

It had been William Tyndale's passion, fifty years before, to see 'a boy that driveth the plough' able to know and understand the Bible in his own tongue. Nevertheless, there can be in hymnody a proper reluctance to define boundaries too sharply, as a consequence of the diverse nature of any parish congregation. Something of this thought can never be far from the mind of someone struggling for words to put into the mouths of worshippers; but it has twice been brought vividly home to me in my own hymn writing. The first occasion was a request from the then Chaplain of the Great Ormond

Street Hospital in London, known throughout the world as a centre of excellence in the care of sick children. A Service was being planned for the rededication of the hospital chapel of St Christopher, which would form the central part of a TV documentary about the work of the hospital. Would I write a special hymn for the occasion? My response to almost all such requests is to say that I cannot promise, but that I will try; and to ask for necessary background information, and the assurance that if a final text is not thought suitable I shall be told so frankly and the text set aside.

In his original letter the Chaplain described the hospital to me as a place where many are far from home; where children are in pain, and parents torn between anxiety and hope; where death has to be faced, not always as an enemy; and where healing is struggled for by dedication and devotion, by science (often at the frontiers of knowledge), and by prayer. Part of the Chaplain's response to my request for further information, 'a brief', was as follows:

The occasion is obviously a joyful one. Within it, however, we need a reflective hymn which, while avoiding Trinitarian language, touches on the themes of human vulnerability and dependency, recognizes the place of the child, and acknowledges the contemporary scientific world view. Provided that the tune which begins to run through your mind (if that is how the process works) is fairly familiar, I would be content to leave the metre to you. There you are. It's pretty straightforward really!

My first thought was that I could not with integrity work to such a brief. My texts are firmly Christian and I have never come to terms with multi-faith hymnody. But then I reflected that I had in fact written a good many psalm paraphrases, some with no specifically New Testament reference. So the hymn was written and duly sung to DARWALL'S 148TH. In his letter afterwards the Chaplain spoke of 'putting yourself in the shoes of others... acknowledging the shadow side... an appropriate expression of joy'. Here then is the text. As you read it, put yourself for a moment 'in the shoes' of the sick children, anxious parents, doctors, and nurses at the Service of Rededication of their beautifully refurbished chapel:

> O LORD, whose saving Name
> is life and health and rest,
> to whom the children came
> and in your arms were blest,
> we seek your face;
>   your love be shown,
>   your presence known,
> within this place.
>
> That love be ours to share
> with tenderness and skill,
> with science, faith and prayer,
> to work your sovereign will;
> we praise you, Lord,
>   for banished pain,
>   for strength again,
> for health restored.

When deepest shadows fall
  to quench life's fading spark,
be near us when we call,
    walk with us through the dark,
      our Light and Way,
        by grief and loss
        and bitter cross,
  to endless day.

In God our hope is set,
  beneath whose rule alone
is peace from fear and fret,
  and strength beyond our own.
    His kingdom stands,
      and those this day
      for whom we pray
    are in his hands.

Join every heart to bring
  our praise to God above,
whom children's voices sing
  and whom unseen we love.
    O God of grace,
      for evermore
      your blessings pour
    upon this place.[14]

Another occasion when I had to think especially hard about 'putting myself in the shoes' of a variety of different worshippers was in attempting to write a hymn for Mothering Sunday, a day to be firmly distinguished from the secular and much more recent 'Mothers' Day' beloved by the manufacturers of greetings cards. Mothering Sunday, though not recognized by the Book of Common Prayer, has long been observed on the Fourth Sunday in Lent, and is so named in *Common Worship*. It is a day and a subject not plentifully supplied with hymns, and it was suggested that I might write one. Such a text must take account of the very differing personal backgrounds, emotions, needs, and circumstances of those who may be invited to sing together. There will be many in church whose mothers are dead; some indeed who have grown up motherless, and some who remember a mother who abused or abandoned them. One cannot ask everyone, not even every child, in a large congregation to thank God unreservedly for their own mother: memories may be poignant for a host of reasons. Equally, if the hymn is sung in an all-age family Service, it must try to avoid giving pain to those who are alone in the world, lacking any human family or perhaps estranged from them, and understandably finding their church family unable to satisfy in quite the same way the empty place in their hearts and lives. Yet for most worshippers the hymn must surely express thankfulness for all that motherhood at its best is found to be.

After some searching, it was that final phrase which seemed to supply the key, so that the hymn is written in general terms, thankful 'for God's good gift of mothers', in a way that I hope does not cause pain, or make any worshipper feel excluded.[15] It *expresses*, but does not *define* for any individual, what God intends in his gift of motherhood, in a way that can be universally recognized. This factor of recognition was never far from the mind of Robert Frost. 'In literature,' he wrote, 'it is our business to give people the thing that will make them say, "Oh yes, I know what you mean". It is never to tell them something they don't know, but something they know and hadn't thought of saying. It must be something they recognize.' He went on to say that his hope was 'to tell people what they haven't as yet realized they were about to say for themselves'.[16] In hymnody, where familiarity can be double-edged, both opening and closing the doors of meaning, this realization may spring from what is hardly more than a hint, a clue; and in consequence is a different kind of recognition according to age and circumstance, achieving definition from the singer, not the writer. C. E. Montague chose to illustrate this deliberate lack of precision by describing how Corot used to go out very early on misty summer mornings in order to paint, knocking off work at about nine o'clock. 'He used to say, "Everything can be seen now. And so there's nothing to see." He felt that... as soon as the elements of a landscape began to emerge from the first tender vapours enough to take definite shape, they lost part of their expressive value.'[17] Similarly, when Philip Larkin was asked about the apparent 'simplicity' of his poems in the BBC programme 'Desert Island Discs', he responded:

I think that a poem should be understood at first reading line by line, but I don't think it should be exhausted at that first reading. I hope that what I write gives the reader [we might substitute 'singer'] something when they read it first, enough in fact to make them read it again and so on *ad infinitum*.[18]

If a hymn is in the repertoire of a congregation, the likelihood is that the worshipper *will* meet it again and again, as Larkin hoped for his poetry. One of the tests of a text is whether it still has something to offer, whether by familiarity or perhaps by some new insight, when it has been sung many times before. If the hymn is to survive such repetition, there must be some ordered pattern of thought, some structure to the content. The verses should follow one another in a natural sequence, so that on analysis a framework can be discovered around which the hymn has been built. Worshippers may well know nothing of this, but its value remains. Such an analysis was made by J. R. Watson of the structure of Ellerton's 'The day thou gavest, Lord, is ended', looking in turn at the construction of the line, of the verses individually, and of the whole, which he compares to a bridge with three spans based on an abutment on either side.[19] Thirty years earlier R. Newton Flew wrote a small book entitled *The Hymns of Charles Wesley: a study of their structure*,[20] indicating, for example, the three divisions of the familiar 'Love divine, all loves excelling' when seen as Wesley wrote it: a prayer for the Holy Spirit; for the return of Christ; and for the completion of God's new creation. He shows how, as was Charles' usual practice, these three are stated or suggested in the first verse: 'Come... visit... enter... dwell... crown'. These are then worked out more fully in succeeding verses, so that a pattern of ordered thought emerges which, consciously or not, supports the worshippers in making the content and meaning increasingly their own.

To all this, of course, the tune and the act of singing add a new dimension. I believe that it was Beaumarchais in *The Barber of Seville* who first suggested that 'what is not worth saying is sung', but the idea was deployed to great effect by Kenneth Clark in his programme 'The Pursuit of Happiness', part of his ground-breaking 1969 BBC TV series *Civilization*. Talking about opera, he described it, next to Gothic architecture, as 'one of the strangest inventions of modern man' and went on to ask:

What on earth has given opera its prestige in western civilization?... chiefly, I think, because it *is* irrational. 'What is too silly to be said may be sung'—well, yes; but what is too subtle to be said, or too deeply felt, or too revealing or too mysterious—these things can also be sung and only be sung.[21]

It is improbable that Kenneth Clark was here thinking about hymns, but this is surely true of them. Not, I hope, that they are too silly, though I could suggest a few contenders for that crown, but that there is mystery and subtlety and emotion in those movements of the heart to which our hymns, at their best, can help to give meaning and expression. It is neatly summed up in these words of Basil Willey, though he was writing of nineteenth-century poetry rather than of hymns:

Meaning in poetry, as we all know, is far more complex than meaning in logical statement; it operates through image, symbol, rhythm, suggestion and association, and therefore calls forth from us a far more complete response—'complete' in that the emotions, imagination and sensibility are involved as well as the intelligence.[22]

It is a high ideal: 'Ah, but a man's reach should exceed his grasp, or what's a heaven for?'[23]

When the *New English Bible, New Testament* was published in 1961, it was suggested that it offered the word of Scripture in 'timeless English', though the actual Preface spoke only of 'a contemporary idiom'. This must have been in C. S. Lewis's mind a year or two later when he was writing *Letters to Malcolm*. In the very first 'letter' he talks about the language of worship:

If you have a vernacular liturgy you must have a changing liturgy; otherwise it will finally be vernacular only in name. The ideal of 'timeless English' is sheer nonsense. No living language can be timeless. You might as well ask for a motionless river.[24]

Lewis, a professional to his finger-tips, had strong views on language in poetry, some of which he expressed in a review of the 1940 *Oxford Book of Christian Verse*. 'The subject of our poetry is high beyond all height' he wrote:

We shall not try pitifully to scale that height with the carnal beauties of poetic diction... Strong sense, rigid sincerity, genuine English, and the firmness of the metre shall be the only beauties of our sacred poetry... We may, as in Cowper's *Castaway*, be standing on the brink of hell: that is no reason why our grammar, our scansion, or the shape of our lyric should be modified. The heart may be broken but the head is clear. It is the method of Watts and the Wesleys at their best, of Cowper nearly always.[25]

But does not so high a theme as is proper to hymnody demand, perhaps not 'the carnal beauties of poetic diction', but a language of its own? Bridges thought so: 'his own translations were a deliberate attempt to distance hymn language from the discourse of everyday life'.[26] There is a case for this. Hymns find their place within public worship, often liturgical worship, where our address to God is most natural when it has in mind the two extremes of intimacy and majesty, as in the prayer that Jesus taught us, where we begin with 'Father' but move to Kingdom, Power, and eternal Glory.

These two, intimacy and majesty, are to be found together in the openings of a number of our Collects, as we are continually reminded from the Prayer Book when we use the third Collect, for Grace, at Morning Prayer. It begins, 'O Lord, our heavenly

Father', and continues, 'Almighty and everlasting God...' summing up these two ways in which to approach him. Though there is room for both of them in our hymnody, some of the actual language of intimacy—not, of course, the recognition of Fatherhood—is in general more suited to private devotion, while hieratic language, a special form of speech for our address to God, cannot be out of place in public worship as conveying reverence, a proper sense of awe at the mystery of what lies beyond our human understanding, of God as 'a consuming fire' (Hebrews 12.29), and of that gulf which separates the human from the divine. Hieratic language has a very respectable history, not least in hymnody. I sometimes feel that texts such as Richard Jones' 'God of concrete, God of steel', brave and pioneering in their day, are now less sung because on the one hand technology has moved on, and on the other they lose touch with the tradition. Ronald Knox, who did not feel 'Bible English' a model to be imitated, nevertheless spoke of 'a hieratic language, deeply embedded in the English mind and perhaps indispensable to the ordinary Englishman's religion'. In the same essay he wrote of how hieratic language need not be Elizabethan English, even in our liturgy. Admittedly, he was prepared to retain the older forms when he was translating the Bible, but he died more than half a century ago and his New Testament was published in 1945. 'If we are to write modern English,' he explained, ' "thou" hast to go, with all the verbal forms appropriate to it, except in translation designed for liturgical use.' He goes on to say that if spiritual writing is to have a direct challenge today, 'it must convey its message under the unlovely American formula, "This means you!" The effect is lost, somehow, if we substitute the locution, "This meaneth thee".'[27]

All my life I have regarded 'thee' and 'thou' as hieratic, the proper and respectful way to address Almighty God, and reserved almost exclusively for that purpose. It was with something of a shock that I heard Neil MacGregor in a recent broadcast explain that in Shakespeare's time, English used 'thee' and 'you' as the French still use *tu* and *vous* to distinguish between the respectful and the familiar—but 'thee' was the familiar, 'you' the mark of deference and respect. Shakespeare was still living when the Authorized Version was published; so perhaps we should look more closely at what in Scripture and in traditional hymnody these alternative pronouns signify. There appears to have been a complete reversal of usage, so that Isaac Watts, for example, less than a century later, seems to use 'thou' as the proper address to the divine, and would have felt, surely, that 'you' was altogether too familiar. Think of his line, 'from everlasting thou art God'. To our ears, 'you are' would lose any sense of majesty and awe. And so it continued, down to our own day, so that those uneasy about such changes would quote a line that sounds like 'Yoo Hoos almighty word' (from John Marriott's nineteenth-century hymn on the Holy Trinity) as a kind of *reductio ad absurdum*.

I can still remember how strange I found the loss of thee and thou in religious verse. The short lyrics which I was writing in my twenties were all in that form,[28] as indeed were a number of my early hymns. 'Faithful vigil ended', based on the Nunc Dimittis, is one example. It was written in 1967, the word 'thy' coming five times in four short verses. By the time I put together my early self-published collection in 1981 there were two distinct versions, and a note explained how, 'Following the NEB, my original version of this hymn retained the use of "thy"; but there is now an alternative version using "your"...revised in response to editorial requests, at Bramerton, February 1981.'[29] The phrase 'in response to editorial requests' was, I am pretty sure, a way of explaining this departure from my principle that once a text is in print, only the most urgent necessity justifies further alteration. It was the editors of *Hymns for Today's Church* who, in 1982, persuaded me that I should allow the alternative version. My 1984 collection, *Lift Every Heart*, therefore printed both versions side by side, but *A House of Praise*, 2003, relegated the earlier version to a mention as a 'permitted variation', for by this time only the later version was appearing in hymnals. By then 'you' language was well established as the norm for new writing. Such changes often demand considerable forbearance if they are to be welcomed by those who love what they have grown up with. T. S. Eliot, for example, who served on the commission to revise the psalter which was at work from 1958 until final publication in 1964, was remembered as one 'who seldom spoke except to plead for the retention of an old phrase'.[30] Similarly, P. D. James famously contributed to the *Sunday Telegraph* an article entitled 'Bad Language in Church', explaining how, to one who had loved the Prayer Book and the Authorized Version from childhood, their attempted revision and apparent neglect seemed 'part of that denigration of our language and our culture which in some quarters has become so fashionable'.[31]

Is there then a distinct language suitable for hymnody? It certainly used to be thought that poetry had a right to its own vocabulary. Charles Wesley wrote of

> Those amaranthine bowers,
> Inalienably ours...[32]

but it is hard to imagine that 'amaranthine' was a word he often used outside his verse; it here means fadeless, immortal. It does not seem to have been in Shakespeare's vocabulary, but Milton used it. Cowper in his long poem *The Task* pays homage to Milton, and himself uses 'amaranthine' only thirteen lines later. Perhaps it was in recollection of Milton that Charles used it here, in one of nineteen *Hymns occasioned by the earthquake of 8 March, 1750*. Today this seems an extreme case, but Henry Bett defends the use of 'the rarer word, the more elevated and the more impassioned' as having 'a natural right to be used in the expression of the rarer moods, the more elevated thoughts and the more impassioned feelings'.[33] To go to the other extreme, consider the lines:

> Up God's deathless way to glory,
>   Where God's holy seraphs burn,
> Enoch travelled by translation,
>   With no ticket to return.[34]

They come, admittedly, from what Percy Dearmer described as 'one of the less ambitious communities' of faith! Perhaps these two examples illustrate what Dr Johnson had in mind when he declared that 'words too familiar or too remote defeat the purpose of a poet':

From those sounds which we hear on small or coarse occasions, we do not easily receive strong impressions or delightful images; and words to which we are nearly strangers, whenever they occur, draw that attention to themselves which they should transmit to things.[35]

Dante Gabriel Rossetti, so we are told, kept lists of 'stunning words for poetry',[36] and I have to confess that in a rather different way I do something of the same. The words I list as they occur to me (for otherwise I should forget them) are of a kind which

I think Dr Johnson would approve: not too obvious, and yet not strange; they are not like Rossetti's 'virelay', 'citole', or 'shent'. One example would be 'tempest-tossed'. I know this could fall under John Wesley's disapproval of 'pretty compound epithets', but it comes in *Romeo and Juliet* and in the witches' curse in the first act of *Macbeth*:

> Though his barque cannot be lost
> Yet it shall be tempest-tossed...

Julian of Norwich was using it some 200 years earlier, and John Newton has it more than once in his *Olney Hymns*, and Cowper in his poem 'On the receipt of my Mother's picture'. But what made me mark it down for future use (and I have indeed used it more than once in a hymn text) was the evocative verse by Emma Lazarus, inscribed on New York's Statue of Liberty:

> Give me your tired, your poor,
> Your huddled masses yearning to breathe free,
> The wretched refuse of your teeming shore,
> Send these, the homeless, tempest-tossed, to me:
> I lift my lamp beside the golden door.

A hymn text, as is true of all literature, is raised above the commonplace by language which conveys a feeling of colour in its imagery. Kenneth Clark noted how Edith Sitwell, in her strange poetry, used a number of words 'which had a special, and almost magical, meaning for her'. He gives as examples 'the golden words of life'—honey, amber, wheat, the lion, the sun; and the white words of death, 'dust and the bone, frost and snow'.[37] This is to take the word 'colour' in a more literal sense than I intend. It can, of course, work in that way: how pedestrian would be Mrs Alexander's line, 'There is a green hill far away', without that splash of colour, or Watts' image of 'his dying crimson, like a robe'. But I chiefly mean here by 'colour' the sort of vocabulary found in a hymn such as 'Be thou my vision', where a 'colourful' richness of language is skilfully woven into the text by author and translators and conveyed in the titles : 'Lord of my heart', 'Great Father', 'Strong Tower', 'High King of heaven', 'Heaven's bright sun', 'Heart of my own heart', 'Ruler of all'. Without using the word, the text manages to convey majesty, to combine intimacy with transcendence, and to conjure up the same sense of visual richness and significant imagery that we find in apocalyptic writing. The significance is important: Michael Ramsey, in a talk to ordinands at Durham, urged them to be ready for new experiments in worship:

but do not, by sophisticated attempts to be contemporary at all costs, blunt the force which lies in the universal imagery of the Bible: bread, water, light, darkness, wind, fire, hunger, thirst, eat, drink, walk.[38]

Ramsey's examples, without exception, are in fact metaphors used in the Gospels by Jesus himself. I expect that was his intention.

Consider yet another happy marriage, that between sound and sense. It is one of the glories of language that, at its best, the sound contributes to the meaning. At its most extreme, this is onomatopoeia, found in single words like 'clang', 'tinkle', or 'cuckoo'; but more usually in phrases which allow the effect to be developed. An example often given is in the song Tennyson added to *The Princess* where:

> Sweet is every sound...
> The moan of doves in immemorial elms,
> And murmuring of innumerable bees.

The doves and the bees are brought vividly before our imagination by sound as well as sense. To my ear, this is seldom done better than by Walter de la Mare in one of his most anthologized poems, 'The Listeners', which begins ' "Is there anybody there?" said the Traveller'. In the line

> And a bird flew up out of the turret

I can hear the flutter of wings disturbed by the Traveller's knock on the door, a repeated knocking which again is not only described but heard in the line

> And he smote upon the door again a second time.

If the effect escapes you, try joining all the words, as though with hyphens, to make one continuous sound, and then repeating the lines aloud. The whole poem is an example of how sound, language, and meaning combine to make a whole; in this case, so the poet told Laurence Whistler, about *a* man encountering *a* universe.[39] Not surprisingly, Eliot had a phrase to describe this: the 'auditory imagination', which he knew as 'the feeling for syllable and rhythm, penetrating far below the conscious levels of thought...'.[40] Clearly this matter of sound and sense is especially important in hymnody, designed not so much to be read silently alone as to be sung aloud together. It may not be in the forefront of the hymn writer's mind, but it must not be far away. Its origin may well lie far back in some early poetic influence or sensibility; hence the importance of reading verse for those who seek to write it. Christina Rossetti, still in most of the hymn books, composed these lines before she had learned to write:

> Cecilia never went to school
> Without her gladiator.

She had no idea what a gladiator was, but was informed, so her biographer says, 'by pure liking for the sounds, and perhaps also by the fact that the rest of the family were always using long words she did not know'.[41]

She is not, of course, alone in this. Alison Cunningham, nurse to the infant Robert Louis Stevenson ('the angel of my infant life'), would read aloud to him, as many nurses do to their young charges. Because of her, a later critic would say that 'The hearing of words was the first and perhaps the strongest influence on his imagination. Now he was writing to make his readers hear...'[42] In a remarkable essay Stevenson noted how certain letter combinations seemed to crop up in writing which haunted the memory, giving as his example the conjunction of P, V, and F, and quoting Milton's line, 'I cannot praise a fugitive and cloistered virtue.'[43] Henry Bett explored this further, though not always, to my mind, totally convincingly. We can all hear in the letter D the ominous approach of darkness, despair, death—'the thudding of clods on a coffin' as Bett calls it. Similarly, L reminds us of life, light, love, and when combined with S of what is slow, sleepy, slouching. The letter H to him suggests effort, as in haul, heave, hurry.[44] It is a fascinating insight, but rather beyond my present purpose. Nevertheless, though I do not consciously strive for it, I am always half-pleased, half-amused when

PVF appears by chance in a text of mine, as it does in the concluding lines of 'No longer now, as once we were'.

Dylan Thomas was another who used to say that the first poems he knew were nursery rhymes, and that 'what the words stood for, symbolized, or meant, was of very secondary importance; what mattered was the *sound* of them as I heard them for the first time on the lips of the remote and incomprehensible grown-ups'.[45] Robert Frost, too, learned 'from hearing his mother read aloud to him . . . to place primary emphasis in his own poetry on the actual *sound* of the spoken word'.[46] Joseph Conrad, who made himself master of an English which was not his mother-tongue, was convinced that 'he who wants to persuade should put his trust, not in the right argument, but in the right word. The power of sound has always been greater than the power of sense . . .'[47] This seems to have been Eliot's view, affirming that 'Between the two extremes of *incantation* and *meaning* we are today [1957] more easily seduced by the music of the exhilaratingly meaningless, than contented with intelligence and wisdom set forth in pedestrian measures.'[48] This is to go where the hymn writer cannot follow. Ronald Knox, himself both hymn writer and editor, praised Hilaire Belloc (who was neither, as far as I know) as showing in his verse a mastery of cadence, 'by which I mean not a mere manipulation of sounds, with a music effect, quite divorced from the sense of what you are saying, and sometimes compelling you to say it unconvincingly—you get it *ad nauseam* in Swinburne'.[49] William Cowper similarly, almost two centuries before, had assured his printer 'that I always write as smoothly as I can; but that I never did, never will, sacrifice the spirit or sense of a passage to the sound of it'.[50] Indeed, Cowper in his hymns seems always to convey an awareness that he is touching the sacred.

More relevant to the hymn writer than onomatopoeia is alliteration, the repetition of letters and their sounds, as in the hackneyed phrase 'alliteration's artful aid'. Overdone, it can be treacherous. E. H. Plumptre almost overworked it in the fourth verse of his 'Thy hand, O God, has guided':

> Through many a day of darkness,
> > Through many a scene of strife,
> The faithful few fought bravely,
> > To guard the nation's life.

The letter D controls the opening line, and S the second. F is not only the rhyming letter of lines two and four, but a triple consecutive alliteration in line three. It would only have needed 'fiercely' to replace 'bravely' to tip the whole into something more like comic verse or 'The Drawing Room Reciter'. Ronald Knox, as we have seen, found Swinburne's use of the device unable to stand much analysis of meaning, but the sound is almost an incantation. Who else would write 'To the low last edge of the long lone land' or 'The wind that wanders, the weeds wind-shaken', both from his poem 'A Forsaken Garden'? I like to compare the lushness of such a poem with Housman's line in the last verse of No. XXIII in *A Shropshire Lad:*

> They carry back bright to the coiner the mintage of man

where the two initial Bs, Cs, and Ms, and the three short internal As, exemplify—to me, at least—the art that conceals art: the line I have chosen is by no means an isolated instance. As that line illustrates, alliteration is found not only in the first letter of a word.

The line quoted above from Milton, with its P, V, and F, comes from a famous sentence in his *Areopagitica*:

I cannot praise a fugitive and cloistered virtue, unexercised and unbreathed, that never sallies out and sees her adversary, but slinks out of the race, where that immortal garland is to be run for, not without dust and heat...

The letter S, as so often, is prominent; but the last five words all end in dentals, emphasizing conclusion, as in 'shut'. In the nature of things, the letter S is hard-worked in any writing, especially when dealing with plurals. Perhaps because of this, many poets try to avoid it—or at least to keep it within bounds; though C. S. Lewis has pointed out that 'Shakespeare does not share our modern dislike of sibilants (he will "summon" remembrance to "sessions of sweet silent thought")...'.[51] Tennyson may not have been quite among the moderns that Lewis had in mind, but he is well known for a style which ran naturally and usually very finely to alliteration, and therefore was troubled by the way sibilants kept cropping up. 'Why, when I spout my lines first,' he is recorded as saying, 'they come out so alliteratively that I have sometimes no end of trouble to get rid of the alliterations.' When it came to the letter S, he called this process 'kicking out the geese'.[52] Perhaps it was Tennyson's example that Robert Graves had in mind when as an undergraduate he published a book which included the prophecy that on his death bed he would have an important message to deliver. 'The art of poetry,' he declared, 'consists of knowing exactly how to manipulate the letter S.'[53]

Assonance is alliteration's more retiring sister, content to achieve her effects without drawing attention to them as alliteration is prone to do. It consists very largely in the repetition of vowel sounds, and therefore is found more often in the middle of words than at either end. Tennyson was a master of its subtleties, and used it to convey mood. In his poem 'Crossing the Bar', chosen by some editors to include in hymnals, he is using 'when I put out to sea' as a metaphor for death and the hereafter, and (to my ear) uses assonance to emphasize that 'out' at the start of the final verse,

> For tho' from out our bourne of Time and Place...

by placing it in a fourfold assonance of 'ough' (concealed in print by the elision), 'out', and a repeated 'our', made less obvious by slight differences of pronunciation. 'Out' is what matters; the putting *out* to sea, to the unknown that lies ahead. Again, in Bishop Heber's epiphany hymn, 'Brightest and best of the Sons of the morning', the sense of rhythm and movement owes much to the feminine rhymes and the alliterations : Brightest/best, dawn/darkness, cold/cradle, dew/drops, low/lies, angels/adore, Maker/Monarch—all from the first two verses. But assonance comes into its own in verse 3:

> Say, shall we yield him, in costly devotion,
>   Odours of Edom, and offerings divine,
> Gems of the mountain, and pearls of the ocean,
>   Myrrh from the forest and gold from the mine?

This provides an alternation between the short and the long 'o' in each of the lines: short–long in line 1, long–short–short in line 2, short–short–long in line 3, short–short–long–short in line 4. Three of these 'o' sounds at the start of words add the more obvious alliteration to the almost unnoticed assonance. I am not suggesting that this pattern was a deliberate construct of the writer; but in the choices the mind makes when clothing thought with language these things somehow emerge almost of themselves. Charles Wesley, perhaps deliberately, perhaps with no conscious planning, uses assonance to add melody, smoothness, and emphasis. In his line,

> Jesus, to sinners still the same...[54]

there is the alliterative 's'; but also the repeated short 'i', just as in

> 'Tis mystery all! th' Immortal dies![55]

But to look for assonance in the great hymn writers is generally to find it. For my last example look at Cowper's line:

> Redeeming love has been my theme...[56]

Is it just familiarity that makes one feel that 'Redeeming love has been my song' has not the same effect, the same easy flow, having lost the repetition of 'eem' and 'eme'?

There are innumerable other points, most of them with technical names, which attend the writing of poetry, and so of hymns. Opinions differ, for example, about *inversion*, the disturbing of the natural order of the words. It is not quite inevitable—think of the first verse of 'There is a green hill far away'—but seems to be a mark of much hymnody, so widespread that it is hardly noticed as we sing: 'Came he to a world forlorn' might be one example; 'He on his throne shall rest' would be another. Often it comes about because of the exigencies of rhyme (as in these examples, chosen almost at random) or metre. There are plenty of instances of it in my own texts. Sometimes, though, inversion is the making of a verse. If Cowper had written:

> God moves in a mysterious way
> To perform his wonders,

he would, of course, have lost his rhyme, but also some of that sense of greatness and mystery that his line manages to convey, and by which it has become a familiar quotation to many who have no knowledge of its source. When Bertie Wooster quotes it of Jeeves, there is no sign that he knew it was from a hymn, though Jeeves would have known. To see inversion that no editor would be likely to accept in today's hymn writing, where better to go than some of the Scottish paraphrases (as in Martin Browning's parody, already quoted), or other early psalm versions? William Kethe's sturdy rendering of Psalm 100, which gives its name to the tune OLD HUNDREDTH, is well over 400 years old. Here is verse 3:

> O enter then his gates with praise,
>   Approach with joy his courts unto;
> Praise, laud, and bless his name always,
>   For it is seemly so to do.[57]

The inversions in the even lines are so familiar that we hardly notice them. Indeed, they add to our sense that hymn singing can bridge the Christian centuries. But they could not be imitated today.

Hymn writers, perhaps more than most poets, must have an eye to *enjambment*. The word is from the French for 'to stride', and so to encroach, and the OED gives no example before the 1830s; it may therefore be a word unknown to Watts, or the Wesleys, or the Olney hymn writers. It is used now to describe the carrying over into the next line of verse what by sense or syntax belongs to the line above. Where this is avoided, the couplet is described as 'closed' and the lines as 'end-stopped'. A familiar example of *enjambment* might be Keble's lines from 'New every morning is the love':

> Room to deny ourselves, a road
> To bring us daily nearer God.

This is perhaps less than happy; and indeed the word *enjambment* seems often to carry an overtone of imperfection—indeed, of encroachment. In my own text, 'Name of all majesty', I feel it is now too late to make changes; but were I writing it today, I would try to avoid the enjambment in the lines:

> So with the ransomed, we
> praise him eternally...

not least because I once heard a disastrous attempt on TV 'Songs of Praise' to sing these words as if the 'we' were part of the later line. I think it is fair to suggest that in hymn writing (I am not here thinking of lyric poetry) enjambment usually suggests a lack of that 'smoothness' which was Charles Wesley's aim. With John, mainly in his translations, it seems to have been perfectly acceptable. Indeed, he has been described as 'unique among English hymn writers in making a habit of it'.[58] In poetry it may be different, since most poetry in modern times is written to be read, silently or aloud, by an individual, and not for congregational singing. When William Wordsworth wrote to his patron and friend, Lord Lonsdale, to say that he had at last despatched the manuscript of the first two books of his translation of Virgil's *Aeneid* he explained:

I have run the Couplets freely into each other, much more even than Dryden has done. This variety seemed to me to be called for, if anything of the movement of the Virgilian versification be transferable to our rhymed poetry... long Narratives in couplets with the sense closed at the end of each, are to me very wearisome.[59]

This was in 1824, and it seems likely that though describing enjambment, the word was not then in use.

Wordsworth is no doubt right as regards 'long Narratives', but the reverse is usually true for hymns where, at least in common metres, the sense is best conveyed complete within the line. Take as one of many possible examples Charles Wesley's 'Soldiers of Christ, arise'. I quote here the original final verse, but the same is largely true throughout the hymn:

> From strength to strength go on,
> Wrestle, and fight, and pray,
> Tread all the powers of darkness down,
> And win the well-fought day;
> Still let the Spirit cry
> In all his soldiers, 'Come,'
> Till Christ the Lord descends from high,
> And takes the conquerors home.

Perhaps Wesley learned to appreciate this skill from Isaac Watts. In one of his most highly regarded hymns Watts uses commas to continue his meaning in line after line:

> O God, our help in ages past,
>   Our hope for years to come,
> Our shelter from the stormy blast,
>   And our eternal home.

All this is by way of his address to God; we have yet to reach a main verb. The full stop at the end derives from Watts himself who evidently felt that the verse, as an apostrophe to Almighty God, could stand alone. Modern editors replace the stop with a semicolon, allowing the sentence to continue and be completed in the next verse. One of the few places in the hymn as we sing it today (shortened from the original nine verses) where a line is incomplete within itself is:

> ...Dies at the opening day.

This takes its sense and syntax from the line above:

> They fly, forgotten, as a dream...

It is a skill found in many poets, though perhaps hymn writers need it more. A. E. Housman, for example, exercises it on page after page:

> Their shoulders held the sky suspended;
>   They stood, and earth's foundations stay;
> What God abandoned, these defended,
>   And saved the sum of things for pay.[60]

So does John Betjeman, in lines which also lack a main verb:

> Sand in the sandwiches, wasps in the tea,
> Sun on our bathing-dresses heavy with the wet,
> Squelch of the bladder-wrack waiting for the sea,
> Fleas round the tamarisk, an early cigarette.[61]

But to be complete within the line is not, and should not be, a universal characteristic of lyric poetry, as is amply demonstrated by a dip into most anthologies.

Less technical but more noticeable is the use of *repetition* in verse. Sometimes it is simply a tour de force, as in Poe's poem 'The Raven', where each verse concludes with 'more'—nothing more, evermore, nevermore—the last coming as the closing word of the final eleven stanzas. Many Easter hymns break into repeated 'Alleluias', but Fred Pratt Green in his text 'When in our music God is glorified' manages to weave the final Alleluia of all six verses into the sense and syntax, as, for example, in verse 2:

> How often, making music, we have found
> A new dimension in the world of sound,
> As worship moved us to a more profound
> Alleluia!

Chapter 3 noted the tendency of some of today's worship songs, and indeed worship leaders, to overwork repetition; but this is nothing new. Ian Bradley has drawn attention to John Wesley's aversion to certain kinds of repetition which he confided to his journal for 9 August 1768:

When we came to Neath, I was a little surprised to hear I was to preach in the church; of which the Churchwardens had the disposal, the Minister being just dead. I began reading prayers at six. but was greatly disgusted at the manner of singing: 1. Twelve or fourteen persons kept it to themselves, and quite shut out the congregation; 2. These repeated the same words, contrary to all sense and reason, six, eight, or ten times over...[62]

Wesley's assessment of 'contrary to all sense and reason' suggests that he may have Jesus' warning against 'vain repetition' in mind.[63] But in her study of liturgy Cally Hammond offers another view:

Repeating words to God is analogous to saying to a loved one, a spouse, parent, partner, child, 'I love you'—the repetitions do not add semantic content but they still apply layers of meaning the more they are iterated, like the antonym of swear words: words as *actions*. In such a context, repetition enriches the relationship, rather than cheapening it.[64]

There, surely is the test; and whether repetition truly enriches or cheapens the relationship will depend on both the content and context of what is being repeated.

Hymn writing can offer many examples of where deliberate repetition enhances the text. When we sing 'Dear Lord and Father of mankind' to REPTON part of the charm, surely, lies in the repetition of the final lines. If I am writing in that metre, I make it my aim to see that the last line of each verse adds its own emphasis to the meaning when the tune requires it to be sung twice over. Nor need such repetition be only of the final line. The American poet Richard Wilbur uses it to great effect by repeating line 4 as an identical line 5 in his Christmas text, 'A stable lamp is lighted'. Here is the second verse which shows the origin of the repeated line, echoing Luke 19.40:

> This Child through David's city
> Shall ride in triumph by;
> The palm shall strew its branches,
> And every stone shall cry.
> And every stone shall cry,
> Though heavy, dull and dumb,
> And lie within the roadway
> To pave God's kingdom come.

Had this been written in eight four-line stanzas, the final line of each verse would form the opening line of the next; and this is indeed a pattern sometimes adopted. I used it back in 1975 for a short hymn of praise,[65] and said in my note that the form owed something, though with a difference, to the French villanelle. In the eighteenth century John Byrom, who gave us 'Christian awake, salute the happy morn', used this form for his meditative hymn, 'My spirit longs for thee', which is still in hymn books today. This was first published in a collection of his poems some ten years after his death, but it was a further 200 years before it found a place in *Hymns Ancient & Modern:*

> My spirit longs for thee
> Within my troubled breast
> Though I unworthy be
> Of so divine a guest.

> Of so divine a guest
>   Unworthy though I be,
> Yet has my heart no rest
>   Unless it comes from thee.
>
> Unless it comes from thee,
>   In vain I look around;
> In all that I can see
>   No rest is to be found.
>
> No rest is to be found
>   But in thy blessèd love:
> O let my wish be crowned,
>   And send it from above!

Another early use of repetition, rather different, comes in Samuel Crossman's 'My song is love unknown'. This dates from a century earlier than Byrom's hymn above, but again was included in *Hymns Ancient & Modern* only in the revised edition of 1950. Crossman, unlike Byrom, conceals his use of repetition so modestly that it serves its purpose of emphasis but never obtrudes. We see it in this opening verse:

> My song is love unknown,
>   My Saviour's love to me,
> Love to the loveless shown,
>   That they might lovely be.
> O who am I,
>   That for my sake
>   My Lord should take
> Frail flesh and die?

Here Crossman uses the words love (twice), loveless and lovely in the first four lines. In verse 2 we have:

> But O, my Friend,
> My friend indeed . .

while verse 5 begins by repeating the close of verse 4: 'And 'gainst him rise./They rise...'. The final verse gives us 'Never was love...never was grief...', but it is in verse 6 that the most daring repetition occurs, of a kind which, in lesser hands, would be counted a flaw:

> In life, no house, no home
>   My Lord on earth might have;
> In death, no friendly tomb
>   But what a stranger gave.
> What may I say?
>   Heaven was his home;
>   But mine the tomb
> Wherein he lay.

The identical rhyme-endings, home/tomb, are used first in lines 1 and 3, and then again in lines 6 and 7. Because of the metrical variations (in DLM, for instance, it would be unacceptable) and the fact that 'home' is first earthly, then heavenly, while 'tomb' is first Christ's and then mine, the emphasis is made discreetly stronger by the repetition.

I used to regret that such a marvellous hymn stopped short of affirming Christ's resurrection after this repeated 'tomb'. But of course it is there, clear but easily overlooked, in the final verse where we sing

> This is my Friend...

and in singing 'is', we affirm that Jesus rose and lives.

Sometimes repetition extends to a whole verse, so that the hymn concludes by coming full circle. I never think of this without recalling a Sunday morning Service in the little church of Ruan Minor on the Lizard Peninsula. I was standing in for the Rector so that he could have an August holiday, and the Service seemed to have been going on for rather a long time. I felt this especially for the children in the congregation, my own and those of other holidaymakers. When we arrived at the final hymn I saw it was lengthy, and announced that we would sing just the first and last verses. A voice came from the organ bench, not without some satisfaction: 'They're both the same!'—as indeed they were.

The last of these devices which merits a mention here is the *chiasmus*, from the Greek for 'placing crosswise'. It is a term from the old study of logic and grammar, and seen at its simplest in rhymes like:

> Old King Cole [a] was a merry old soul[b]
> And a merry old soul[b] was he [a].

The phrases I have marked as [a] match each other crosswise, as do those marked [b]. Henry Lyte uses a chiasmus to begin his great hymn 'Abide with me':

> Abide with me; fast falls the eventide;
> The darkness deepens; Lord, with me abide!

The second line echoes the first, but reversed or crossed over. The same is used memorably by Isaac Watts in 'When I survey the wondrous cross':

> Then am I dead to all the globe,
>   And all the globe is dead to me.

As we might expect, Charles Wesley excels with a double chiasmus in four simple lines. Bernard Manning, who takes a couple of pages to expound it asks, 'Have you noticed the fingerprints of the accomplished classical scholar?'[66] Here is Wesley's verse, from 'Jesu, Lover of my soul':

> Just and holy is thy name,
>   I am all unrighteousness;
> False and full of sin I am,
>   Thou art full of truth and grace.

We have the contrasting crossover of 'Saviour/sinner' in lines 1 and 2, followed *by* 'sinner/Saviour' in lines 3 and 4. But Manning points out a further chiasmus within each of two pairs of lines. In 1 with 4 we have 'just and holy' paired with 'truth and grace' and 'Thy name' with 'thou'. In lines 2 and 3, the 'I am' is similarly paired; as is 'unrighteousness' with 'false and full of sin'. No wonder that Wesley's hymns so often carry within them the sense of something perfectly satisfying, fitting, and complete.

* * *

Rhyme and metre must wait for chapter 8, with a glance at metaphor in chapter 9. But perhaps I have said enough for my purpose here to show that in hymnody the 'happy marriage' of meaning and language usually depends on some understanding of both, and must attend to sound as well as sense. I admitted at the start of this chapter that my own knowledge of some of these numerous forms, tropes, and techniques is only that of the interested amateur. Were I to forget this, there are books on my shelves—dictionaries of poetic terms—which would soon cut me down to size. One of them includes, for example, a list of 'grammatical constructions that are technically incorrect but have become traditional devices'. I confess that I do not now remember, if indeed I have ever known, what many of the words mean: brachylogia, hypozeuxis, mesozeugma, syzygy, and a dozen more—and this is only one of more than thirty such lists.[67] But once again we can turn to Housman for comfort and counsel. In a letter to a young American, written when I was barely three months old, he advises: 'Do not read books about versification: no poet ever learned it that way. If you are going to be a poet, it will come to you naturally and you will pick up all you need from reading poetry.'[68]

GLORY TO GOD, AND PRAISE

GLORY TO GOD, and praise:
    exalt his holy Name!
the Ancient of eternal Days
    from age to age the same.
The whole created earth
    proclaims his sovereign power,
whose love has brought us from our birth
    to serve this present hour.

Glory to God the Son,
    who laid aside his crown:
by wood and nails his work was done
    who came in mercy down.
The hands that made the hills
    took chisel, saw and plane,
and hallowed all our human skills
    of heart and hand and brain.

Glory to God on high
    whose Spirit gives us breath.
Our life in him shall never die,
    his love has conquered death.
May we his presence know:
    descend in power, we pray!
O Wind of God from heaven blow
    about our world today.

Glory to God who reigns
    all thrones and powers above,
whose arm the sum of things sustains
    in righteousness and love.
When earthly days are done
    and shadows fade and flee,
then still to Father, Spirit, Son,
    our endless praise shall be!

© Timothy Dudley-Smith in Europe and Africa. © Hope Publishing Company in the United States of America and the rest of the world. Reproduced by permission of Oxford University Press. All rights reserved.

CHAPTER 8

Rhyme and Metre

> What still compels attention to Marvell's work is the ease with which he manages the fundamental paradox of verse—the conflict of natural word usage with rhyme and metre.*
>
> Philip Larkin on Andrew Marvell, 1978

BY THE TIME THAT PHILIP LARKIN wrote the essay on Andrew Marvell just quoted, the fount of his poetic imagination had almost ceased to flow. Soon after the publication of *High Windows*, his last book of verse, he confessed to his friend Barbara Pym that 'the notion of expressing sentiments in short lines having similar sounds at the ends seems as remote as mangoes on the moon'.[1] Put as vividly as that, one can catch a glimpse of just how odd a convention can seem the use of metre and rhyme. Yet, for most of us, it carries associations going right back to the roots of childhood: Miss Muffet on her tuffet, Bo Beep and her sheep, Jack Horner in his corner. Noël Coward, whom we shall meet again, said that there was no time he could remember when he was not fascinated by this 'going together' of rhyme. He adds, thinking of nursery rhymes,

'I can distinctly remember being exasperated when any of these whimsical effusions were slipshod in rhyming or scansion. One particularly was liable to send me into a fury. This was 'Little Tommy Tucker':

> 'Little Tommy Tucker
> Sings for his supper,
> What shall he have
> But brown bread and butter.'

That 'Tuck' and that 'Sup' and that 'But' rasped my sensibilities...[2]

Rhyme and metre have had a long run in the living tradition of English poetry. Today it seems they are rather out of fashion. But Larkin, for all his sense that they had become 'remote', worked hard at both in much of his own poetry. In November 1964 an interviewer asked him whether he felt constricted by traditional forms. Larkin replied, 'I think one would have to be very sure of oneself to dispense with the help that metre and rhyme give and I doubt if I could really operate without them.'[3]

This is certainly true of traditional hymnody, though there are familiar hymn texts which dispense with rhyme. 'O come, all ye faithful' is one example often cited, a translation from a number of sources, and translators have more than enough to contend with if they are to be faithful to their original. Modern worship songs often dispense with rhyme, a more sensible solution than some of the inadequate attempts at rhyme which is what many offer. An example here might be Sebastian Temple's 'Make me a channel of your peace', from the Franciscan Community on Los Angeles. This is not only unrhymed but also irregular in metre, so that the *Companion* to the United Reformed hymn book, *Rejoice and Sing,* speaks of 'an undignified scramble to accommodate the varying number of syllables'.

It has long been known that form and metre together appeal to a deep-seated part of our human nature. Perhaps it goes beyond human nature to the structure of creation, since Dr Roger Payne, who in the 1960s first recorded the songs of the hump-backed whale, reported that they included something akin to rhyme! Certainly order and pattern, of which rhyme and metre are one expression, are found everywhere in the natural world from the planets in their courses to the petals of a daisy. Robert Frost put his finger on it when he was asked about the response of children to rhythm in poetry, and said that it was 'because their hearts beat, and they see the waves'.[4] Karen Blixen on her African farm found her young native field-workers fascinated when she introduced them to verse, even nonsense verse:

They waited eagerly for the rhyme, and laughed at it when it came... they begged: 'Speak again. Speak like rain.' Why they should feel verse to be like rain I do not know. It must have been, however, an expression of applause, since in Africa rain is always longed for and welcomed.[5]

Rhyme is described in the dictionaries in terms of 'the harmony or identity of sound value'. We value it as satisfying our need for form, indeed as making form recognizable. This is an experience well known to mathematics. G. H. Hardy, writing of Pythagoras and Euclid, claimed for their theorems 'a very high degree of unexpectedness, combined with inevitability and economy'.[6] These are three qualities which can lift verse above the commonplace, and for which hymn writers also strive. It was Larkin again who described this in terms of making everything 'come together and cohere'.[7] In Christopher Idle's illuminating metaphor, rhyme is the bow in the ribbon that holds the box together. The young C. S. Lewis, burning to be a poet, wrote as a teenager that 'the thing I really want is to move easily in shackles'.[8] Much later he described rhyme not in terms of restriction and difficulty but of the pleasure that comes from 'a need and the answer of it, following so quickly they make a single sensation'.[9] It was, I believe, just this experience which made Tennyson's friend Arthur Hallam speak of rhyme as making 'a constant appeal to Memory and Hope'.[10] The start of a rhyming couplet looks forward in expectation, awaiting a resolution, until the second line ties the bow in the ribbon with a reminder of where we began. We have somehow reached an inevitable destination.

I believe, therefore, that we would be poorer without a rhyming hymn book. We should miss the sense of satisfaction, completion, and fulfilment that rhyme helps to convey; and without the 'shackles' of rhyme there would be less of the careful craftsmanship which strives towards a fusion of sound and meaning until the form of expression most aptly conveys the thing expressed. In hymnody, this goes beyond the reaches of the mind to touch the world of the spirit, and for this high purpose we should neglect nothing that can contribute. Certainly a true poet may not need rhyme, as a true painter may not need representational form. But just as I would be a little wary of abstracts done by an artist who cannot draw, so we may rightly have our doubts about facile poems or hymns which evade the rewards and difficulties of rhyme.

A further very practical reason why rhyme is of value to our hymns is that it plays a large part in securing them in our memory. Advertisers have long known this, and indeed have enlisted well-known rhymes, already lodged in the memory, to sell their wares. The Opies give a number of examples in their dictionary of nursery rhymes, such as:

> Mary, Mary, quite contrary
> How does your romance go?
> A boy, a girl, a Bravington ring,
> And bridesmaids all in a row.[11]

But beyond even these practical reasons, rhyme has an aesthetic appeal which perhaps we only notice in its absence. If you are a lover of poetry, look away now while I lay violent hands on one of John Keats' most famous lyrics to make my point. Suppose his *Ode to a Nightingale* went like this:

> Thou wast not born for death, immortal Bird!
>   No hungry generations tread thee down;
> The voice I hear this passing night was sent
>   In ancient days to emperor and fool...

I hardly think I need say more.

Rhyme, then, satisfies our deep-seated need for form. But not all rhymes are equal and, as the infant Noël Coward discovered, an inadequate rhyme can be a source of irritation rather than fulfilment. When Stephen Sondheim came to publish a collection of lyrics from some of his best-known musicals, he introduced them with an essay on 'Rhyme and its Reasons' which included a useful classification of three familiar types of rhyme. First he placed *true* (or *perfect*) rhyme, then *near* (or *false*) rhymes, and then *identities*. An example of true rhyme taken almost at random from the hymn book might be:

> Lead us, heavenly Father, lead us
>   O'er the world's tempestuous sea;
> Guard us, guide us, keep us, feed us,
>   For we have no help but thee;
> Yet possessing every blessing,
>   If our God our Father be.

Sea/thee/be, are perfect rhymes in spite of differences in spelling. So are lead us/feed us, and possessing/blessing, where the accent falls on the penultimate syllable, and which are known as feminine rhymes—'perhaps,' says Sondheim, 'because the fall-off after the accent gives it a bit of added grace'.[12] False rhymes come in many shapes and sizes. Here is a type frequently met with, taken from the old Scottish psalter:

> When I look up into the heavens,
>   Which thine own fingers framed,
> Unto the moon, and to the stars,
>   Which were by thee ordained...

It seeks to rhyme M and N sounds, and these will never make a true rhyme. Charles Wesley loved to rhyme, and did so with art, skill, and abandon. In lesser hands, we might find fault with power/conqueror, endued/God, done/alone, joined/mind, all taken from the first few verses of 'Soldiers of Christ arise'. But older texts should be criticized with circumspection. Students of Wesley's writings have shown how words have changed their pronunciation over the years.[13] The classic case is 'join' which, in the eighteenth century, did indeed rhyme with 'mine'. On their annual Covenant Sunday the Methodists sing Charles Wesley's hymn:

> Come, let us use the grace divine,
>   And all, with one accord,
> In a perpetual cov'nant join
>   Ourselves to Christ the Lord.

It is only since Charles's day that this has ceased to be a true rhyme. To take another example, I was humbled to discover, having felt that blundered/hundred was a false rhyme in Tennyson's 'The Charge of the Light Brigade', that in his day 'hundred' was indeed pronounced 'hunderd'. Gwen Raverat, writing of her Uncle William (eldest son of Charles Darwin), remembered that he always said *hunderd* for hundred: 'I would go a hunderd miles to see a really fine tree.'[14] But much false rhyme in our hymn books cannot offer this excuse. The writers of some worship songs seem not unlike Benedick in *Much Ado about Nothing*, who in a poem to Beatrice could find no rhyme to 'lady' except 'baby', and concluded 'I was not born under a rhyming planet.'

For the rhyme he calls an *identity* Sondheim cites as an example the words motion/ promotion. In my view, a couplet remains an identity if the sounds are the same, even though the spelling may differ:

> Yet she on earth hath union
>   With God the Three in One,
> And mystic sweet communion
>   With those whose rest is won...

Union/Communion is a true feminine rhyme because 'union' is preceded by that 'th' of 'hath'; one/won, however, is an identity, though it does not appear so on the page. Simply by way of illustration consider how the author, Samuel Stone, would have given us a true rhyme if he had concluded with 'whose race is run' or 'whose work is done'.

Sondheim's second category he calls *near rhymes* or *false rhymes*, and it is humbling to see how often these can be found in the hymn book, but how seldom in the verse of the professional entertainer. Coward's sensibilities were rasped, he says, by tuck/sup/but. Mine tend to be disturbed by plurals rhymed with singulars, such as bring/sings; confusion between N and M, giving sin/him, for example; or rhyming schemes which are not consistent from verse to verse. Unless it is for some good reason, I believe that the verses of a hymn should aim at symmetry, not least in their pattern of rhyme. I have to admit, however, that Isaac Watts, in his hymn 'Come, dearest Lord', changes his rhyme scheme from *abab* in verses 1 and 2 to *aabb* in verse 3. I am sure he knew perfectly well what he was doing and could have continued *abab* had he wished. I guess he would have said, rightly in my view, that a middle or final verse can differ from the rest without spoiling the symmetry of the hymn.

There are, of course, special cases. 'Eye rhymes' are those which appear as rhymes on the printed page, but are pronounced differently. I confess I allow myself a few of these: Lord/word is one example hallowed by long use, as is love/move/prove and so on. 'Heaven' is a word which every hymn writer has to come to terms with. Of course, it can be placed within the line so that no rhyme is needed; but there are a limited number of pure rhymes. 'Leaven' is the most obvious; and 'seven' and 'eleven' perfectly permissible, but for the most part these would become words obviously dragged in to make the rhyme, and it is always a fault to let the exigencies of rhyme or metre seem to dictate the sense. In common with most of the hymn books, I am at ease with heaven/given/forgiven/riven/even and so on. George MacDonald employed eye rhyme, sometimes known as 'courtesy rhyme' when he published what he called 'The Shortest and Sweetest of Songs':

> Come
> Home.[15]

Eye rhymes are more suited to private reading, a largely visual experience, rather than to speaking or singing; but where we have become accustomed to them, as in Lord/word, for example, they slip by without disturbing any but the most fastidious, and I do not count them as faults to be avoided. There are ample distinguished precedents.

Robert Frost had a sharply critical eye when it came to rhyme which was too obviously contrived. He described to an interviewer how when a poem was sent to him, he would notice first if it used rhyme, adding, 'The rhymes come in pairs, don't they? And nine times out of ten with an ordinary writer, one of two of the terms is better than the other... I want to be unable to tell which of those he thought of first.'[16]

Sondheim's subtitle for his collection, *Finishing the Hat*, included the words, 'with attendant comments... grudges, whines and anecdotes'. He spends several paragraphs on 'X', standing for 'one of pop music's most successful lyricists', and quotes him as saying, 'I hate all true rhymes... if the craft gets in the way of the feelings, then I'll take the feelings any day'. Sondheim stigmatizes this as a defence of laziness:

The notion that good rhymes and the expression of emotion are contradictory qualities, that neatness equals lifelessness, is... 'the refuge of the destitute'. Claiming that true rhyme is the enemy of substance is the sustaining excuse of lyricists who are unable to rhyme well with any consistency.[17]

I quote this, hiding behind Sondheim, because it expresses what I feel about the words of some hymns and worship songs, but rebuke myself for feeling, since charity and humility are more important than consistency. But Sondheim certainly speaks for me when he affirms that 'there is something about the conscious use of form in any art that says to the customer, "This is worth saying".' In Sondheim's view a perfect rhyme 'snaps the word, and with it the thought, vigorously into place, rendering it easily intelligible; a near rhyme blurs it'. But this is an ideal, not always reached. John Betjeman wrote once to two Etonians who had sent him the draft of a poem for his comments: 'Tower and hour,' he wrote, 'are not to my nice ear, true rhymes...'.[18] He himself rhymes tower with flower, power, and shower, which are unexceptionable; but in his light-hearted song 'Longfellow's Visit to Venice' there is the couplet:

> Here the youthful Giorgione gazed upon the domes and towers,
> And interpreted his era in a way which pleases ours.

I have no problem with such a rhyme, but I think he was a little hard on the Etonians. Even Housman has what Professor G. B. A. Fletcher called 'inexact rhymes', and Grant Richards, his publisher, lists them in a memoir for all to see. Most of them are of the kind already mentioned as hallowed in verse and hymnody by long poetic licence, but there are also morning/returning, trader/nadir, Africa/away, and a few others.[19]

Other types of rhyme also find their place in our hymn books. Triple rhyme is the term used to describe couplets such as victorious/glorious. More common is the use of multiple rhymes: Charlotte Elliott, for example, uses threefold rhyme in her hymn of 1834 offering a response to the call of the gospel:

> Just as I am, without one plea
> But that thy blood was shed for me,
> And that thou bidd'st me come to thee,
>   O Lamb of God, I come!

Percy Dearmer does the same, seventy years later, in 'Jesus, good above all other'. John Marriott, twenty years before Charlotte Elliott, combined threefold rhyme with two pairs of rhymes in each of his four verses of 'Thou, whose almighty word/Chaos and darkness heard'. Internal rhyme is found less frequently, but sometimes to great effect. Phillips Brooks' 'O little town of Bethlehem' owes something of its charm to those third and sixth lines:

> Above thy deep and dreamless sleep...

and in the same verse,

> The hopes and fears of all the years...

Robert Bridges manages to combine threefold with internal rhyme in the final couplet of each verse of his fine text, 'Thee will I love, my God and King', written for his own *Yattendon Hymnal* in 1899 to a tune he wished to use from the Genevan Psalter. Verse 1 ends as follows:

> And on thy throne, unseen, unknown
> Reignest alone in glory seated.

Just as a weed can be defined as a flower in the wrong place, so it is possible to have unwanted rhymes, where the word that sense demands rhymes with another in a way that is unintended, jars on the ear, or spoils the symmetry of construction. Sometimes, indeed, a possible rhyme is rejected by the writer in order to underline what he or she is seeking to convey. I recall writing on behalf of an editorial committee to a distinguished hymn writer asking him to look again at a false rhyme in a verse of his which we hoped to use. He did not wish to make a change—a position I respect—on the grounds that his choice had been deliberate, a dissonance in keeping with the theme of the verse. Tennyson, we are told, did something of the same when working on 'The Lotus-Eaters' with its theme of languor:

> 'Courage' he said, and pointed towards the land,
> 'This mounting wave will roll us shoreward soon.'
> In the afternoon they came unto a land
> In which it seemèd always afternoon.

Long afterwards, he explained that he had first written 'strand', but 'the no-rhyme of "land" and "land" seemed lazier',[20] in keeping with the mood he was seeking to convey.

If rhyme is so important in our hymnody, are there means which will help to achieve it? I suppose the most obvious is the rhyming dictionary, but it should not be the first recourse. Jimmy Webb, the American song writer, offers this advice which he attributes to Oscar Hammerstein:

A rhyming dictionary...should be used as a supplement to one's own ingenuity, and not a substitute for it. I do not open mine until I have exhausted my own memory and invention of rhymes for a word.[21]

Webb adds that it is hard to argue with this. I was lucky enough, many years ago, to find a second-hand copy of an American *Aid to Rhyme*,[22] which has the advantage that every verso page is blank, for one's own notes and additions. My copy is now nearly worn out but most of that comes, not from hymn writing, but from the days when I was regularly writing comic verse. Certainly I use it when at work on a hymn text, just as I do a thesaurus; but I find their chief usefulness is negative, and lies in telling me that there is no suitable rhyme for the word I am seeking, or no synonym with the metrical value I need. This makes it a good deal easier to abandon the couplet, or even the verse, which is before me in draft, and start afresh. I am always thankful for that early apprenticeship in light or comic verse, since it is here that much can be learnt about rhyme. W. S. Gilbert had the gift of rhyming in a way of which Robert Frost would have approved, so that each of a pair of rhyming words is entirely appropriate in its context, and is indeed the word which fits best, even if no rhyme were involved. Wordsworth, in a letter of 1827, wrote of 'an adroitness which can proceed from nothing but practice'.[23] C. S. Lewis as a teenager wrote to his friend Arthur Greeves, who was also struggling to write, saying 'What you want is practice, practice, practice',[24] and it remains good advice. One of Robert Louis Stevenson's many biographers says of him:

His loyalty to his craft lay in the fact that he regarded it as just that, not as a spontaneous expression of genius, or as a happy facility with words, but as a craft to be practised and improved and made to work.[25]

Sometimes, particularly with light verse, the finished product appears at first sight so natural and easy that one feels that anyone might have written it. I am helped to understand this (it is, of course, a total misconception) by two simple ideas. The first is the analogy with snooker, when a professional on a winning streak pots ball after ball in shots which by any standard do not seem particularly difficult. The secret lies, of course, not in the easy pot being made now, but in the shot before which left the balls so well placed. It is a little like that with rhyme. It appears most natural when it has been prepared for, perhaps right at the start of an eight-line verse; and most contrived if it has to be tacked on to the end of a couplet where no preparation has been made to receive it. A good example seems to me Flecker's couplet in the long poem, 'The Road to Samarkand' which concludes his play *Hassan*.[26] The Chief Grocer is recounting some of the exotic merchandise which his camels are carrying:

> We have rose-candy, we have spikenard,
>   Mastic and terebinth and oil and spice...

Flecker is planning to rhyme the word 'jarred' with 'spikenard'—and somehow to make that word seem natural, and indeed inevitable in the context. So he continues:

> And such sweet jams meticulously jarred
> As God's Own Prophet eats in Paradise.

The remarkable rhyme, 'jarred', works because of two factors. First, the mention of 'jams' earlier in the line has prepared us for it. In association with jam, jars do not seem out of place. But secondly, we are so lost in admiration for the adverb 'meticulously' that 'jarred' slips past unobtrusively.

The second idea is one I learned from Robert Frost, who described his craft in many interviews and lectures. His advice was to try to make the rhyming word part of a phrase, rather than having to stand alone.[27] By way of illustration, think of Captain Corcoran singing by moonlight on the deck of *H. M. S. Pinafore:*

> Fair moon, to thee I sing,
> Bright regent of the heavens,
> Say, why is everything
> Either at sixes or at sevens.

The difficult rhyme to 'heavens' slips securely into place because is it contained within a phrase. Try to rewrite that line with just a single unsupported word to end it, and you will see what I mean, and credit Gilbert with an art that conceals art. Some years ago the Methodist Publishing House invited me to write for them a hymn celebrating the opening and dedication of new premises, on the theme of 'Publishing Salvation'.[28] I found that I wanted to incorporate a phrase from a well-known prayer, so as to make the second half of a verse read like this:

> who speak where many listen,
> who write what many read.

The word 'listen' offers few suitable rhymes. Irving Berlin in 'White Christmas' gives us 'glisten', natural enough in his context but no use to me. 'Christen', perhaps? But that word, standing alone, would seem a little precious and far-fetched or, worse, simply put in to make up the rhyme. However, if the reader or singer can be *prepared*, so that the word falls naturally as part of an extended phrase, 'Christen' may well be appropriate. So we have:

> Baptize, O Lord, and christen
> their culture and their creed...

('Baptize' at the start of the line prepares the way, and alliteration, too, can help smooth the flow)

> who speak where many listen,
> who write what many read.

It is a salutary business for those who write hymns to look at the craftsmanship that goes into the best of show business. In an extended review of *Finishing the Hat*, Sondheim's collection of his earlier lyrics, I once tried to show how much hymn writers can learn from what appears at first sight an unlikely source.[29] Among the qualities to be admired were his meticulous attention to detail. All writers, I imagine, have at some time asked themselves as they lay down their pen, 'Will it do?', and if the question needs to be asked, there can be only one answer: back to work. Sondheim writes also of how, in his craft, less is more: 'lyrics are an unforgivingly compact form'. Even so, he is adamant that content must not be sacrificed to form, and that it is the writer's task to wrestle at compression and concision until a way is found which does justice to what the work seeks to communicate. Finally, as befits someone working for the stage, he stresses the need for the lyricist always to be conscious that he is putting words into other people's mouths; which is an exact description of the hymn writer. Interestingly, Sondheim is not an admirer of the work of Noël Coward, but it is to a song of Coward's that I turn from time to time as a reminder of what can be done by way of the craftsmanship of rhyme in a sentimental patriotic song.

Noël Coward himself described more than once how he came to write the song 'London Pride', inspired by a moment during the war when he was standing amid the debris on the platform of a London railway station after a night of bombing, watching the Londoners go about their business as if nothing untoward had happened.[30] The song was finished, he said, in a couple of days, words and music, and consists of three stanzas each of some twenty-one lines, though some lines contain only two words. Here is the middle verse:

> London Pride has been handed down to us.
> London Pride is a flower that's free.
> London Pride means our own dear town to us,
> And our pride it for ever will be.
> Hey, lady,
> When the day is dawning
> See the policeman yawning
> On his lonely beat.
> Gay lady,
> Mayfair in the morning,
> Hear your footsteps echo in the empty street.
> Early rain
> And the pavement's glistening,
> All Park Lane
> In a shimmering gown.
> Nothing could ever break or harm
> The charm of London town.
>
> *Interlude* In our city darkened now, street and square and crescent,
> We can feel our living past in our shadowed present,
> Ghosts beside our starlit Thames
> Who lived and loved and died
> Keep throughout the ages London Pride.[31]

London Pride © NC Aventales AG, 1941 by permission of
Alan Brodie Representation Ltd. www.alenbrodie.com

Only two lines in all twenty-six have no partner in rhyme. There is internal rhyme (harm/charm), threefold rhyme (dawning/yawning/morning), triple rhymes in 'down to us' and 'Hey, lady', feminine rhymes (crescent/present) and five pairs of simple rhymes, but not all spaced as simple couplets. The other verses are entirely comparable. I am not suggesting that it is a form which could be copied in our hymnals; but does it not make some of our hymns, which seem content with no more than *abcb*, look a little like poor relations when it comes to rhyme? James Montgomery thought so, and wrote:

It is a great temptation to the indolence of hymnwriters that the quatrain measures have so often been used by Dr Watts without rhyme in the first and third lines. He himself confessed that this was a defect; and though some of his most beautiful hymns act upon this model, if the thing itself is not a fault, it is the cause of half the faults that may be found in inferior compositions—negligence, feebleness, and prosing.[32]

W. H. Auden reflected on some of the ways in which rhyme and metre perform different functions in serious poetry as against comic verse:

In serious poetry thought, emotion, event, must always appear to dictate the diction, meter and rhyme in which they are embodied; vice versa, in comic poetry it is the words, meter, rhyme which must appear to create the thoughts, emotions, and events they require.[33]

Hymnody, strangely enough, seems in this to stand somewhere between the two, where the form, metre, and rhyme both embody the meaning, but also help to create it. If this is so, we must look again at what Montgomery is saying in the quotation above. He sets there a high standard—some would say unnecessarily high, even impossibly high. But for whom are we writing? If indeed it is for the Church, and the Lord of the Church, how can we set our sights too high?

* * *

Rhyme, however desirable, is not essential to all hymnody, but it is hard to imagine hymns devoid of rhythm, which is expressed as metre. Because rhythm seems to be part of the created order, it again appeals to the uncharted depths of our nature; but rhythm alone, perhaps because it is so primitive, so atavistic, does not take us far in worship. Eliot imagined the beginning of poetry 'with a savage beating a drum in a jungle', and went on to add that 'hyperbolically one might say that the poet is *older* than other human beings'.[34] Coleridge writes of how metre quickens attention, much as rhyme does, 'by the quick reciprocations of curiosity still gratified and still re-excited, which are too slight indeed to be at any one moment objects of distinct consciousness, yet become considerable in their aggregate influence'.[35] He goes on to compare the sense of something amiss when a fault in metre jars upon us with that of 'leaping in the dark from the last step of a staircase, when we had prepared our muscles for a leap of three or four'. But just as rhymes which were true when they were written can become false with a change in pronunciation—join being 'jine' in Wesley's day was one example—so too there can be a change in accentuation which makes the metre appear faulty to a later age. To cite Wesley again, in his 'Hymn Before Work' he gives us:

> The task thy wisdom hath assigned
> O let me cheerfully fulfil,
> In all my works thy presence find,
> And prove thine acceptable will.

The word 'acceptable' was so stressed in Wesley's day that this final line was in perfect metre. Later editors, beginning with the original edition of *Hymns Ancient & Modern*, have recognized the change in pronunciation over the years, and substituted the familiar line:

And prove thy good and perfect will.

Books on prosody, the craft of versification, can make the subject appear dry, technically baffling, and woefully complex. I find it hard in practice to pay much attention to the theoretical distinction between anapaestic and dactylic, for example, or what would be a good example of a tetrameter. It was Coleridge again, in an age that set more store by this sort of thing than we today (perhaps because a classical education was more general) who gave us this mnemonic, 'Metrical Feet: Lesson for a Boy' written for his son Hartley in 1806, though not published until 1834:

> Trochee trips from long to short.
> From long to long in solemn sort
> Slow spondee stalks; slow foot yet ill able
> Ever to come up with the dactyl trisyllable.
> Iambics march from short to long.
> With a leap and a bound the swift anapaests throng.[36]

It continues in this vein for another twelve lines, a tour-de-force, especially in its original form, spattered with accents and long/short symbols. I confess that for myself I tend to work by ear, and seldom have recourse to any structural device more sophisticated than a count of syllables, and repeated trials of any draft against a possible tune. A definition of metre which offers a simpler explanation might be this, from a basic linguistic course:

Stripped of all subtleties, conventional English metre is nothing more than rhythmic parallelism: a patterning of the succession of stressed and unstressed syllables with greater regularity than is necessary for spoken English in general... the patterns of rhythm organize themselves into lines, which in turn enter into further structures of parallelism: couplets, stanzas, etc.[37]

All this might have come as a surprise to Peter Quince the carpenter, Nick Bottom the weaver, Tom Snout, and the rest as they rehearsed their amateur theatricals in Act 5 of *A Midsummer Night's Dream*.[38] They are worried that the ladies will not like sword-play, and Robin Starveling speaks for them all in wondering how they can manage if they omit the killing. Bottom has the answer: 'Write me a prologue, and let the prologue seem to say we will do no harm with our swords, and that Pyramus is not killed...This will put them out of fear.' Quince agrees, and says that such a prologue should be written in 'eight and six'. Bottom says: 'No, make it two more: let it be written in eight and eight.' What these figures refer to is what we would call common metre, namely 86 86, and long metre, 88 88. These are still found in all our hymn books, and their names exactly describe them. Among the 120 or so different metres in the most recent edition of *Hymns Ancient & Modern* more tunes are listed in common metre (CM) than in any other, and long metre (LM) is not far behind. Isaac Watts, in his 450 or so hymns, uses mainly CM, LM, or short metre (SM), which is 66 86. Examples of these, all by Watts, would be 'O God (or, in Watts' original, 'Our God...), our help in ages past' (CM); 'When I survey the wondrous cross' (LM); and 'How beauteous are their feet/Who stand on Sion's hill' (SM). When at length, with a flourish of trumpets, Peter Quince is allowed to deliver his Prologue, it is not in CM or LM, but in 10 10 10 10. We know this in our hymn books as the metre of ELLERS, to which we sing 'Saviour, again to thy dear name we raise'.

If Watts limits himself in his metrical choices, Charles Wesley has been called the hundred metres champion. 'Because there was music in his soul, lilting, rapturous, divine music,' writes Frank Baker (the foremost Wesley scholar of his generation), 'he could not be confined to the humdrum in verse.'[39] It is a fact that he wrote his hymns in at least one hundred different metres, said to be more than any other English poet, even though in some instances the differences are slight. I confess that I have not attempted to test this assertion against W. H. Auden who, one biographer says, 'liked to boast that he had written in every known metre and was always searching for new forms'.[40] Usually, in the metrical index of any hymnbook, there will be a final class of 'irregular' metres. These include texts where the scansion differs from verse to verse, and texts written to a metre otherwise unknown. I find I have contributed to both these categories. The first I can excuse on the grounds that (at least in most instances) I was writing verse with no thought that it might make a hymn; or else that I was beginner who had yet to learn. An example would be my passiontide hymn from 1968, 'A purple robe/a crown of thorn'. The syllable count is equal in each of the five verses and at the time I thought that was all that mattered; there was no tune available to me against which I could test the words. So, without my being really aware of it, the middle verse differs in its stresses from the others in such a way that only the skill of David Wilson, the composer of the tune, makes it possible to sing it as a hymn. An example of a truly irregular metre is the tune RECTORY MEADOW by Erik Routley. He was staying the night with us in our home, 'Rectory Meadow' in Norfolk, and I showed him a carol I had written for our Christmas card, 'O Prince of peace/whose promised birth'. Rather like 'The House that Jack built', each verse is one line longer than the verse before. Erik wrote a tune which he called after the name of our home, sent it to me in manuscript, and allowed text and tune to appear together in hymnals, the tune listed, of course, as 'Irregular'.[41]

There is really no limit to texts and tunes that adopt a pattern or metre unknown to any hymn book. To see how this might be so, in theory at least, look at the work of Ogden Nash. Here is the start of his poem 'This is Going to Hurt Just a Little Bit':

> One thing I like less than most things is sitting in a dentist chair with my mouth wide open
> And that I will never have to do it again is a hope that I am against hope hopen.
> Because some tortures are physical and some are mental,
> But the one that is both is dental...[42]

I suppose one would have to classify the metre of those four lines (the poem continues with equal bravado) as 22 23 14 9; and index them under 'Irregular'. A hymn which began with a syllable-count of 22 23 14 9 would surely defeat most congregations, even in plainsong!

Metre, then, is a major part of form, and because form and content cannot be independent of each other, metre should help the hymn communicate what it seeks to say. 'Miltonic grandeur' will need a metre more expansive than CM to convey its true effect; narrative will often be served by LM, though what Watts called 'proper metre' lends itself to great effect in Crossman's hymn 'My song is love unknown'. It is easy to overlook the effect of metre in hymnody, because it is always combined with music, and we find it is the tune, of which metre is only part, that enhances the mood or theme. Consider the difference between Bach's PASSION CHORALE, set to 'O sacred head, sore wounded' and ANTIOCH (CM extended) to Watts' 'Joy to the world, the Lord is come!' These effects are seldom quite so obvious; and my own use of metre is as often by instinct as by design. For many a poet, this is not so; there is a careful and deliberate choice. Think of a collection like Stevenson's *A Child's Garden of Verses*;[43] 'Marching Song' (XXII) to SM is a good example; one can almost hear the fife and drum:

> Mary Jane commands the party,
>   Peter leads the rear;
> Feet in time, alert and hearty,
>   Each a Grenadier!

By contrast, these next two metres convey quite a different sense of movement. First, 'The Swing' (XXXIII):

> How do you like to go up in a swing,
>   Up in the air so blue?
> Oh, I do think it the pleasantest thing
>   Ever a child can do.

That is in 10 6 10 6, a lilting measure which fits the sensation. Equally, in its own rather breathless way, Stevenson's use of an irregular but highly effective rhythm magically evokes the experience in 'From a Railway Carriage' (XXXVII):

> Faster than fairies, faster than witches,
> Bridges and houses, hedges and ditches;
> All charging along like troops in a battle,
> All through the meadows the horses and cattle:
> All the sights of the hill and the plain
> Fly as thick as driving rain;
> And ever again, in the wink of an eye,
> Painted stations whistle by.

Is not this what Wordsworth was describing in his Preface to *Lyrical Ballads*? He writes: 'The music of harmonious metrical language, the sense of difficulty overcome... an indistinct perception perpetually renewed of language closely resembling that of real life... imperceptibly make up a complex feeling of delight.'[44] And it has long been recognized, though it is beyond my power to analyse, that this 'harmonious metrical language' is formed, not by simple quantities or syllable-counts, but also by duration, the length of the syllable, and by stress. Stress is indeed one of the challenges of metre in hymnody. Because of the demands of the tune, opportunities for any kind of variation in stress are very limited if they are not to be distracting, and yet it is variation in stress that contributes to the charm of English poetry. It is one reason why long hymns can become wearisome, monotonously restricted to an identical beat.

The distinguished neurologist, Oliver Sacks, probably best known to the lay mind as the author of *The Man who Mistook his Wife for a Hat*, has written of the power of music in all societies to bind people together into community. He explains:

This binding is accomplished by rhythm—not only heard but internalized, identically, in all who are present. Rhythm turns listeners into participants, makes listening active and motoric, and synchronizes the brains and minds (and, since emotion is always intertwined with music, the 'hearts') of all who participate.

He goes on to write of how we are so constituted that music can be 'played in the mind':

Our auditory system, our nervous systems are indeed exquisitely tuned for music. How much of this is due to the intrinsic characteristics of music itself—its complex sonic patterns woven in time, its logic, its momentum, its unbreakable sequences, its insistent rhythms and repetitions... we do not yet know.[45]

Nor, as worshippers, do we need to know; it is enough to experience. Rhyme and metre, at least in my estimation, are worthy marriage partners to content and form. Take a moment before you end this chapter to ponder the opening verse of this hymn by Joseph Addison. It was written three centuries ago, a metrical version of part of Psalm 19, and first published in *The Spectator*. All four marriage partners, content, form, rhyme, and metre, join to support that earlier couple, meaning and language, to give a sense of completion, resolution, inevitability even, in words of praise to the Creator which we are glad to make our own:

> The spacious firmament on high,
> With all the blue ethereal sky,
> And spangled heavens, a shining frame,
> Their great Original proclaim.
> The unwearied sun from day to day
> Does his Creator's power display,
> And publishes to every land
> The work of an almighty hand.

GOD WHO FORMED THE MIGHTY OCEAN

GOD WHO FORMED the mighty ocean,
    loosed the winds upon their ways,
gave the circling planets motion
    in their round of ceaseless praise,
hear our thanks for those who love us,
    for the hour that gave us birth,
heirs of starry skies above us
    and the seas of all the earth.

Hold within your care unsleeping
    all who face tempestuous seas,
harvests from the waters reaping,
    God be thanked for such as these.
Earth is rich beyond all measure,
    may we prize her gifts the more,
we who find our work or pleasure
    on the seas or by the shore.

Guard, when stormy waves are breaking,
    those who cross the oceans wide;
share with them their watchful waking,
    be with them through wind and tide.
Christ our Saviour, friend unfailing,
    as the seas of life we roam,
chart our course and guide our sailing
    safe to harbour and to home.

© Timothy Dudley-Smith in Europe and Africa. © Hope Publishing Company in the United States of America and the rest of the world. Reproduced by permission of Oxford University Press. All rights reserved.

CHAPTER 9

Creativity and Criticism

> I began writing hymns at the age of six, but I am afraid, from what I can remember, that my efforts were deeply indebted to previous authors. From hymnology it was a short step to nature poetry, to the grand drama, to all that one does write at eight years old.*
>
> R. A. Knox, 1918

'SURELY,' wrote Walter de la Mare, 'Cornwall's unreality is the nearest thing to the idea of a terrestrial paradise.' It was to him, his biographer tells us, a landscape 'as nearly as possible a parable of inward solitude'.[1] I was not aware of this during the 1970s and 1980s, when most of my hymns were written in Cornwall, but the thought has resonated with me since. I was writing in Cornwall for two reasons. First, it was difficult to make space in a working ministry, so that hymn writing was very much a holiday occupation. Second, we were fortunate enough to buy a house of our own in 1968. As a clergyman's family we lived in a tied house which went with the job, so with the money my mother left me we were delighted to be able to buy a 'holiday' house in Cornwall, which would also be a foot on the housing ladder against retirement. 'Seacroft' was a very ordinary house in the village of Ruan Minor, just above the fishing community of Cadgwith on the Lizard. There, for the next twenty years or so, we had a family holiday each summer, and throughout those years I used to take a couple of hours each day to work at hymn writing. It would begin over a solitary early breakfast, breaking off for beach expeditions, picnics, cliff walks, exploration, the real business of the holiday, but returning at odd moments to whatever I was working on. It was here I began to use a manuscript book rather than odd scraps of paper; and though the early record is not clear, by the time we sold 'Seacroft' to buy a retirement house, I think about half of my texts were written there. I was pleased to discover later, therefore, that Walter de la Mare's creative instincts flourished when he was 'west of the Tamar'. For me, to be among the beaches and cliffs, the seas and skies of Cornwall, the ancient timeless landscape of the West, combined with freedom from all the workaday preoccupations of home, seemed to make for a release of often pent-up creative energy. During this time I discovered a saying of Robert Frost's which became a sort of talisman for me, as I sat with a new page open in my manuscript book: 'There are the days you can and the days you can't and both are training towards the future days you can.'[2] Because, while the holiday lasted, there was always tomorrow, I was content to spend two hours achieving a first line and crossing it out again, without feeling that it was time wasted.

The first thing we learn about Almighty God is that he is a creator. Soon after, we are told that we are made 'in his image' so that we should not be surprised to find how strong in humanity is the urge to create. This is not always a matter of utility. Tennyson's Uncle Charles, on hearing that his twenty-four-year-old nephew had made a book of poems (*Poems*, 1833), 'wished that he had made something useful like a wheelbarrow.'[3] We do, of course, make wheelbarrows and very useful they are; but we also procreate children, we shape our environment, we probe creatively into the mysteries of the natural world, and we create art, music, literature, poetry—and hymns of praise to the glories of our creator God, the God and Father of our Lord Jesus Christ. In much of this creativity there can be distinguished an element of 'inspiration', which seems to spring, at least in part, from somewhere other than the conscious mind; together with an element of 'craftsmanship' in which highly conscious mental faculties draw on memory, training, and experience to give such inspiration communicable form. Christina Rossetti thought of them as 'genuine lyric cry' in contrast to 'skilled labour';[4] and poets, when they write about these things, often come down more firmly on one side or the other, as their own experience suggests. For myself, I believe that they are not totally distinct, but interdependent and often closely related.

The 'skilled labour' is mostly within our own control. Although the result may fall short of our ideal we can always persevere, 'gruelling' in Walter de la Mare's word, as time and ability permit. Sometimes, in my experience, there is a kind of barrier of frustration, perhaps not unlike the 'pain barrier' athletes have to overcome, when one is faced with a growing conviction that this text is never going to come right and had better be abandoned. Often it is abandoned, only to be taken up again the next day as perhaps containing, after all, the seed of some way forward. I have learned almost to expect this frustrating 'barrier' and to tell myself that I have been here before, and that sooner or later, light will break in. I recall how Philip Larkin wrote of one of his best-known poems, 'I've spent nearly all evening trying to finish this poem ["The Whitsun Weddings"]: I've never known anything resist me so.'[5] It is a matter of setting oneself to go on and not give up, and may, I think, be what Coleridge was describing when he wrote of composition as 'no voluntary business: the very necessity of doing it robs me of the power of doing it'.[6] Nevertheless, we can set our teeth and go on working. 'Inspiration', on the other hand, is not at our command; 'gruelling' may develop it, but will not produce it. Inspiration seems to have, so to say, a life of its own, as many practitioners testify. The Christian will remember, too, that the third Person of the Holy Trinity is a Creator Spirit. When Henry Chadwick was chairing the meetings of the editorial committee for *Common Praise*, he would begin by leading us in the ancient Latin hymn (we used Bishop Cosin's seventeenth-century translation) known as the *Veni Creator*:

> Come, Holy Ghost, our souls inspire,
> And lighten with celestial fire...

Who is to say that the Spirit of God may not be at work in the subconscious as well as in the conscious mind?

Of John Ellerton, to turn to another hymn writer, his biographer writes, 'It seems to be in the very nature of the poetic faculty...to have, like an intermittent spring, its seasons of comparative rest varied by bursts of irresistible activity.'[7] Nor is this intermittent quality confined to poetry. David Ogilvie, one of the most successful practitioners of his generation in creative advertising, wrote of how he 'developed techniques for keeping open the telephone line to my unconscious, in case that disorderly repository has anything to tell me'.[8] He would walk, listen to music, work in the garden, and take long hot baths, explaining that 'While thus employed in doing nothing, I receive a constant stream of telegrams from my unconscious, and these become the raw material for my advertisements.' In short, time is what is needed. Larkin wrote of how a poem came 'dangerously quickly'.[9] This would certainly apply to those confirmation hymns which A. C. Benson wrote in the train from London to Horsted Keynes, but there is no universal truth here. The poem—indeed, in some collections, the hymn—which Hallam Tennyson called the crown of his father's life's work, 'Crossing the Bar', was written during the short homeward voyage from Lymington to Yarmouth in the Isle of Wight. As they crossed the Solent in the gathering darkness, Tennyson saw an outward-bound steamer dropping the pilot by the Needles; and on the inside of a used envelope (so some accounts say) jotted down the poem. It was Autumn; he had recently turned eighty; and the poem was a metaphor for what must lie ahead.[10]

More recently, R. S. Thomas, in one of his 'autobiographies', has described the sudden appearance of a poem. To him, time and silence were 'the main prerequisites of the creative mind':

It was a perfect morning today. After breakfast as usual went down the Ty'n Parc lane and saw the dew hanging from the branches, and heard the redpoll and the siskin going past. And without warning and without effort a little poem formed in my mind... God has to do with this subject, too. In talking about how a poem will come easily and effortlessly, one must remember the possibility of being mistaken, of deceiving oneself. Not every poem that comes like this is good. Some believe that this is how they should come, and that if you have to labour, it indicates a lack of inspiration. But there are too many examples to the contrary.[11]

Musicians and mathematicians know this experience. Beethoven told a fellow-musician how his ideas seemed to arise unevoked, whether spontaneously or unspontaneously:

I could grasp them with my hands in the open air, in the woods, while walking, in the stillness of the night, at early morning, stimulated by those moods which poets turn into words, into tones with me, which resound, roar and rage until at last they stand before me in the form of notes...[12]

In something of the same way Arthur Koestler quotes from a lecture by Henri Poincaré about mathematical discovery. Poincaré described how ideas had sometimes come to him after drinking black coffee, after a sleepless night, or even when getting into a bus or walking along the street. He concluded: 'Most striking at first is this appearance of sudden illumination, a manifest sign of long, unconscious prior work. The role of this unconscious work in mathematical invention appears to me incontestable...'.[13] The unconscious is not to be hurried and can sometimes take a very long time. 'Crossing the Bar' was completed almost at once; by contrast, the opening line of Tennyson's poem 'The Revenge' ('At Florés in the Azores Sir Richard Grenville lay') remained in draft on his desk for years, but at last was finished 'in a day or two'.[14] Thomas Hardy's poem, 'In Time of "The Breaking of the Nations"' ('Only a man harrowing clods/In a slow silent walk'), was inspired by a memory of how, walking in Cornwall, he heard news of the defeat of the French. That was in 1870; the poem was written 45 years later.[15] Robert Frost kept a folder marked 'Unfinished Poems' to which he would return from time to time. Some would stay there for more than twenty years before completion and publication.[16] Nor is it only poets who do this. John Constable would produce finished paintings from sketches made twenty years before.[17] To compare great things with small, I myself can remember sitting in one of the very earliest Deanery Synod meetings after Synodical structures came to the Church of England in 1970. A line for a passiontide hymn came into my head and I jotted it down: 'brighter than rubies in the young spring grass'. It was more than twenty years later that I found a place for it in a hymn text; but on the advice of my mentor, Derek Kidner, I put it away for further work. Only in 2010 did it appear, slightly modified, in one of my collections.[18]

Inspiration, then, can come in very different ways. We have seen Baring-Gould dashing off 'Onward, Christian soldiers' in what he remembered as 'ten minutes'. The blind George Matheson would be another example. 'O love that wilt not let me go', almost the only one of his hundred or so poems still in mainstream hymnals, was not written as a hymn. Ian Bradley tells how in the summer of 1881 Matheson was alone for the day in his large manse in some turmoil of mind, 'with just the sound of the sea for company', while the rest of the household were at a family wedding. George Matheson later called this poem 'the quickest composition I ever achieved. It was done in three minutes. It seemed to me at the time as if someone was dictating the thought to me and also giving the expression...'.[19] John Newton, many of whose hymns are still a valued part of our common stock, often wrote for a particular occasion. It might be to accompany a sermon, or to be sung at the weekly prayer gathering at Olney. He was a busy pastor, both in person and by correspondence, but he spent time on his hymns. Bruce Hindmarsh makes just this point in a recent study of the man and his work, drawing on Newton's diary:

There is good evidence...that Newton laboured over his hymns and sought to achieve the very best craftsmanship he could according to his principles...it was not the case that any doggerel would do. He did not simply dash off verse on the run. In December 1773 he remarked, 'Making hymns now and then, which is with me generally a work of time.'[20]

Next summer he returned to this theme, writing: 'I usually make a hymn weekly & sometimes it cost[s] me so much thought and study that I hardly do anything else.'

I have come to believe that in spite of all this variety, there is at least one factor that poets, including hymn writers, have in common: the discovery of a starting point. It is what C. Day-Lewis wrote of as the *donnée*, something 'given'.[21] It is symbolized for me by the story of the young J. R. R. Tolkien sitting at his desk marking exam papers, early in the 1930s. 'Suddenly,' according to Michael White's reconstructed account, 'his eye is drawn to the carpet...he notices a tiny hole in it and stares at it for long moments, daydreaming.' Taking a clean sheet, he began, 'In a hole in the ground there lived a hobbit.'[22] It was the first that he, or indeed anyone, knew of hobbits. The blank sheet at least is authentic: Tolkien himself described it and added 'One writes such a story out of the leaf-mould of the mind.'[23] It is the hole in the carpet, whatever its authenticity, that illustrates the unsought starting point, something given, a *donnée*. I remember, too, how the young W. B. Yeats was once walking along Fleet Street in London, homesick for Ireland. A little fountain in a shop-window reminded him of the splashing of lake water and so gave birth to one of his most famous poems, 'The Lake Isle of Innisfree'; it is still possible to hear Yeats himself tell the story, in a recording in the

British Library. For me, the *donnée* is more likely to come from hearing or reading a passage of Scripture. But it may be a single word, sometimes even a tune, sometimes what is literally 'a given' in the sense of a commission, a particular request. In the days when I largely wrote on holiday, I began to keep a page in my notebook of 'starting points' because they are difficult to recapture once the moment has passed.

After the initial 'inspiration' and the first draft comes the painstaking business of revision; indeed, it has been going on in the mind before anything appears on paper. For some poets there seems less need to depend upon a draft; it all takes place on the tablet of the memory. A. E. Housman, when he described in his famous lecture how he came to write his poems, spoke of 'a line or two...sometimes a whole stanza' flowing into his mind on his afternoon walk.[24] Wordsworth, too, was almost reluctant to commit to paper the lines that he carried in his head, until, in his own words, 'I feel an impulse to precipitate my verse.'[25] Peter Levi says of Tennyson that 'the process of composition had already taken place before he wrote down his poems. The last minute dithering and polishing was only the visible continuation of a process that had been going on in his head.'[26]

What Levi calls dithering and polishing describes a process of revision about which the views of poets differ sharply. Here is Isaac Watts in 1709 describing how he came to revise the second edition of his *Hymns and Spiritual Songs:*

The method I took was, to collect all the remarks together, that several friends had made by word or letter, and got a friend or two together, and spent a whole day in perusing and considering their remarks; I agreed to their judgments I think in all things; in the whole there are near half a hundred lines altered, I hope always for the better...[27]

This exemplifies the writing of hymns, as against the work of the poet, as 'a functional art'. Watts wished to offer his hymns to the judgement of the church so that they might appear in the form most serviceable for purposes of congregational worship. But before satisfying other people, which must for Watts have been a particularly self-denying practice, it is necessary to satisfy oneself. Auden used to say, echoing Paul Valéry, that a poem is never finished, 'only abandoned'; though he added that it must not be abandoned too soon.[28] There is something admirable about this divine discontent; the same feeling that perfection would always remain just beyond his grasp, which led him to throw his early manuscript poems into a pond. A poet's dissatisfaction with earlier work may not spring entirely from the sense that he has since improved his technique, but from the fact that we ourselves change. For hymn writers, rooted in the Scriptures and seeking words for the worship of the unchanging God, the changes the years bring to ourselves make little difference to the dogmatic content of our texts, though one hopes that the form and the lessons of experience mature with practice. For the poets, expressing more of their own hearts and minds, the urge to revise is necessarily stronger. Wordsworth is a good example:

For Wordsworth, a poem was never finished; as he changed, so he wanted the poem to change, to conform with the man he had become. He found it hard to let go of his work and only reluctantly would he give it to the world.[29]

But this is very different from the revisions that mark a work in progress. Because we have his notebooks, it is often possible to look over A. E. Housman's shoulder and see him choosing and rejecting epithets in search of the exact word or phrase. The verse, perhaps, will have formed itself in his mind during an afternoon's walk, but not to his entire satisfaction, so that the process of revision may continue for some time. In his poem 'Be still, my soul' (*A Shropshire Lad*, XLVIII) there is the line:

> All thoughts to rive the heart are here, and all are vain...

Housman's brother Laurence in his *Memoir* tells us that 'rive' was reached 'by no fewer than eight alternatives: vex, plague, tear, wrench, rend, wring, break, and pierce'.[30] In one of his most famous poems, 'In summertime on Bredon' ('Bredon Hill', *A Shropshire Lad*, XXI) the second verse speaks of the landscape spread out before the two lovers, the 'coloured counties'. The word 'coloured', selected with precision, is evocative as well as descriptive. His brother asked him once,

> whether, as a rule, his so happily-chosen adjectives had come to him spontaneously or after labour and with difficulty; and I gave as an instance 'coloured counties', a phrase which had become famous. 'Now that you should have picked that out', he said, 'is interesting. When I wrote the poem I put down, just to fill up for the time, a quite ordinary adjective, which didn't satisfy me; others followed. Then with the poem in my head I went to bed and dreamed, and in my dream I hit on the word "painted"; when I woke up I saw that "painted" wouldn't do, but it gave me "coloured" as the right word.'[31]

The notebooks show that among the other adjectives tried and rejected—and these were just the ones written down—were sunny, pleasant, chequered, and patterned.[32]

But once Housman arrived at a form of words which satisfied him, it was set in stone. No further alteration or revision was even contemplated. I believe that this is a good rule for a hymn writer. Those who sing hymns have, it seems to me, a right to expect that these will be in the same form in different books. This is not as simple as it sounds. By 1889, Charles Wesley's 'Jesu, lover of my soul' had been in print for 160 years, and a zealous researcher from the Wesley Historical Society identified 154 variant versions in different books.[33] In our own day, if you look up 'Jesus, lover of my soul' in the index of one hymnal of the 1990s, you will find a worship song written jointly by three Australians! 'If there is one thing that makes me froth' wrote P. G. Wodehouse,

> it is these fellows changing a couple of lines in a lyric and then calling themselves part-authors... it is so maddening, that tinkering with lyrics. Any ass can do it once he has got the lyric in front of him. I'll do one now. The lyric:
>
> > Daisy, Daisy,
> > Give me your answer, do.
> > I'm half crazy
> > All for the love of you.

My version (entitling me to half the publishing rights)

> Maizie, Maizie,
> Can't one and one make two?
> I'll go crazy
> If I don't marry you.[34]

Moreover, the alteration of hymn texts is subject to the law of unintended consequences. Consider these lines by Robert Bridges, as they left his pen:

> Pride of man and earthly glory,
> Sword and crown betray his trust;
> What with care and toil he buildeth,
> Tower and temple, fall to dust...

I can only suppose that it is in the rather doctrinaire interests of 'inclusive language' that recent hymnals have changed that first line to read 'Human pride and earthly glory'. But what does this do to the following pronouns? Once 'man' has gone from the opening line, 'he' and 'his' are left orphans. One can understand the feelings of the hymn writer who submitted his work to the first chairman of *Hymns Ancient & Modern*, Sir Henry Baker. His texts were published, but much altered. He declared that now he knew what A&M really meant: 'Asked for, and mutilated'.[35]

One of the problems with freedom to revise, such as the poet has, but the hymn writer (so I believe) usually does not, is that second thoughts, once a lyric has settled into shape, are not always for the better. 'Stupid ass,' wrote Larkin of Auden in a private letter, 'he's been mucking about with them again...',[36] and there are plenty of instances of published poems undergoing numerous revisions, only to return to their original form. C. S. Lewis noted this of Milton in a letter to his friend Arthur Greeves:

> I have been nailed down ever since term ended to a very hard, tho' quite interesting task: a study of the different versions of *Comus*. You know that Milton's MS is extant & we can trace all his corrections... he often crossed out a phrase, put something else, crossed that out, & then returned to the original phrase. Just like ourselves in fact![37]

The process seems to me not unlike that of a sculptor modelling a head in clay. If the work is unfinished at the end of the day, it can be covered with a damp cloth, and further touches added later.

But once time has passed and the clay has hardened, it is quite a different story. This was, it seems, true of Keats, who always found it difficult to restart a poem which had 'gone cold' on him.[38] Charlotte Brontë's experience was similar. 'I can go on working indefatigably at the corrections of a work before it leaves my hands,' she wrote, but after that 'it becomes next to impossible to alter or amend.'[39] Jane Austen would agree; a memoir of her speaks about her 'invincible distrust of her own judgment' and how she would only release her work when 'time and many perusals had satisfied her that the charm of recent composition was dissolved'.[40] That last is a telling phrase, 'the charm of recent composition', and can delude an author into thinking the text is completed when there is still work to do. It is to me, therefore, an obligation to go on contemplating and revising a new text for as long as it takes before the clay hardens or the draft 'goes cold' on me: I remind myself, 'What kills an author is complacency.'[41] But, equally, once I regard a text as finished only the most urgent necessity will persuade me to change it. It can happen, of course. There is a distinct charm in Watts's verse from Psalm 133:

> 'Tis like the Oyl on Aaron shed,
> Which choice perfumes compose,
> Down softly from his Reverend Head
> It trickled to his toes.

One is almost disappointed to see his 1707 revision:

> 'Tis like the Oil descending sweet
> On Aaron's reverend Head,
> And gently flowing to his feet
> Thro' all his Garments spread.[42]

There is in most of us a strong sense that creation should be original. For a critic to label a new work 'derivative' is usually derogatory. Yet, at least to those who work with words, there can be legitimate and conscious 'borrowing' as well as the accidental drawing on phrases lodged in the memory from earlier reading, but with no realization that they are not original. 'As to remembering whether a line is by me or by someone else,' wrote Vita Sackville-West in a letter to her husband, Harold Nicolson,

you know very well that I never could. The first shock of this realisation came when I very laboriously hammered out a line, choosing every word most carefully, and arrived at: 'Men are but children of a larger growth.' Since then I have been cautious.[43]

Harold Nicolson was presumably meant to recognize that the entire line is part of Dryden's *Alexander's Feast*, written in 1697. Sir Walter Scott apologized for such inevitable unconscious borrowing in his General Preface to the 1829 collected edition of his Waverley novels, claiming them as 'entirely the composition of the author...with the exception, always, of avowed quotations and such unpremeditated and involuntary plagiarisms as can scarce be guarded against by anyone who has read and written a great deal'.[44]

Tennyson, who was sensitive to any suggestion of plagiarism, replied curtly to a correspondent who had claimed to find in his work an unacknowledged source from a Chinese poet: 'I thank you for your book...No man can write a single passage to which a parallel one may not be found somewhere in the literature of the world.'[45] One could say something of the same about hymns, and various studies have been done, tracing the unfamiliar earlier antecedents of lines which are still sung widely today. Henry Bett places Charles Wesley's line 'Armed with that adamant and gold' beside Milton's description of Satan as 'armed in adamant and gold'; and his couplet

> With thee conversing, we forget
> All time, and toil, and care...

with Eve's praise to Adam, again from *Paradise Lost*, 'With thee conversing, I forget all time...'.[46] Milton also provided Cowper with one of his best-known concluding lines to verse four of 'Jesus, where're thy people meet':

> Here may we prove the power of prayer,
> To strengthen faith and sweeten care,
> To teach our faint desires to rise,
> And bring all heaven before our eyes.

That final line was used by Milton in *Il Penseroso*, first printed in 1645, nearly a century before Cowper was born. Erik Routley, who noted this, thought it could not be accidental, but was 'one of the most striking instances of quotation of one poet by another'.[47] To my mind it is less striking than Charles Wesley's adaptation of Dryden's 'Song of Venus' from his opera *King Arthur* of 1791, but this may be because Dryden clearly provides the opening of one of Charles's most hard-worked hymns, 'Love divine, all loves excelling'. Dryden has:

> Fairest isle, all isles excelling,
> Seat of pleasure and of loves,
> Venus here will choose her dwelling
> And forsake her Cyprian groves.

The similarity is not only in the first line, where 'love' replaces 'isle' but in the rhyme identical with Dryden's in lines one and three.[48] Professor Watson has noted that a later, but equally familiar hymn, Ellerton's 'The day thou gavest, Lord, is ended', takes its opening line from an anonymous verse in *Church Poetry* published twenty-five years before. Some of its imagery, too, seems to be borrowed from a hymn by James Montgomery, a generation earlier. Montgomery wrote:

> Soon as the light of morning broke
>   O'er island, continent, or deep,
> Thy far-spread family awoke,
>   Sabbath all round the world to keep.

And here is Ellerton:

> As o'er each continent and island
>   The dawn leads on another day,
> The voice of prayer is never silent,
>   Nor dies the strain of praise away.
>
> The sun that bids us rest is waking
>   Our brethren 'neath the western sky,
> And hour by hour fresh lips are making
>   Thy wondrous doings heard on high.[49]

Whether or not Ellerton was drawing on a memory, conscious or unconscious, of *Church Poetry* or of Montgomery's lines, he clothed the thought of unceasing praise as the earth turns on its axis with a simplicity of form for which generations of worshippers have cause to be thankful. In fact, such 'echoes' or 'borrowings' abound in hymnody. A phrase such as 'each returning day' was Cowper's in the 1750s before it was Keble's in the 1820s. And must not Samuel Stennett's line, 'Sweet fields arrayed in living green' from the 1770s or 1780s, owe something to Watts' famous image, said to have been inspired by the view across the Solent, published in 1707:

> Sweet fields beyond the swelling flood
>   Stand dressed in living green...?

Such echoes or similarities have widely different roots. Sometimes they must have been deliberate, as when I incorporated the opening line of R. F. Littledale's translation from Bianco da Siena, 'Come down, O Love Divine' into a text written in the 1990s.[50] This is not plagiarism but allusion, and the difference is simply this: that the writer hopes his allusion will be recognized, but that his plagiarism will not.[51] I only know of one instance in poetry of deliberate and undoubted plagiarism, when at the age of twelve that *enfant terrible*, Dylan Thomas, sold to the *Western Mail* for ten shillings a poem by another writer which had appeared in the *Boys' Own* paper four years before.[52] A much more recent instance, not quite of plagiarism, since it could hardly escape notice, but of borrowing on an extensive scale, might be found in the two adjacent hymns in a popular collection of the 1990s. The first by S. J. Stone is familiar to almost anyone who has ever sung a hymn:

> The church's one foundation
> Is Jesus Christ her Lord;
> She is his new creation
> By water and the word...

Turn the page, however, and we find:

> The church's one foundation
> Is Jesus Christ the Lord
> And on that revelation
> Each one of us is call'd...

Nor do the rhymes improve in the succeeding verses. Stone's writing is long out of the protection of copyright, but his work, so I believe, still deserves respect. Perhaps, indeed, the writer of that second version sees his 'borrowing' in this way as paying Samuel Stone a compliment. Coleridge might have thought this: 'I regard truth as a divine Ventriloquist', he said. 'I care not from whose mouth the sounds are supposed to proceed, if only the words are audible and intelligible.'[53] Indeed, for friends to quote from one another's verses, as Wordsworth and Coleridge did, was seen in his day as 'a conventional means of mutual acknowledgment'.[54]

Perhaps this applies across the generations, too. When Charles Wesley wrote,

> Kindle a flame of sacred love
> On the mean altar of my heart...

he was either a victim of that lapse of memory which can plague us all, or else—and surely more likely—he was paying deliberate homage to Dr Watts's lines:

> Kindle a flame of sacred love
> In these cold hearts of ours.[55]

There are many similar instances recorded, and probably more to be discovered. Thomas Kelly's hymn 'The head that once was crowned with thorns' takes its first line, in that exact form, from a poem of John Bunyan's published 130 years earlier. Charles Wesley's fine conclusion to 'Love divine',

> Lost in wonder, love and praise

was first coined and published by Joseph Addison in the *Spectator* in 1712, when Charles was seven or eight years old. It would be pleasant to think that Toplady, that rather pugnacious hymn writer, intended a compliment to Shakespeare in his hymn, 'Rock of Ages, cleft for me'. As we have seen, one line of the hymn, long since emended, went 'When my eye-strings break in death'. Was this a nod towards *Cymbeline*, where Innogen has the line 'I would have broke mine eye-strings, cracked them...'? Probably not. It seems to have been an expression in common use; the dictionary cites almost a dozen references in the centuries when Shakespeare and Toplady were at work.

What I have here illustrated from hymnody is a thread that runs through all literature. Robert Burton in his *The Anatomy of Melancholy* (1621) was writing that 'we can say nothing but what hath been said... our poets steal from Homer'. When W. S. Gilbert's wandering minstrel describes himself as 'a thing of shreds and patches' he is drawing on Hamlet's portrayal of his uncle as 'a king of shreds and patches'; and when in Bunthorne's song in *Patience* we have the reference to a 'vegetable love', that phrase goes back at least to Andrew Marvell. We owe it to T. S. Eliot that we can be comfortable when 'echoing', 'alluding', or 'borrowing' from the work of others. He asserted boldly that 'immature poets imitate; mature poets steal; bad poets deface what they take, and good poets make it into something better, or at least different'. In saying this, he was himself 'borrowing' from an essay by George Saintsbury:

The charge of plagiarism is usually an excessively idle one; for when a man of genius steals, he always makes the theft his own; and when a man steals without genius, the thefts are mere fairy gold which turns to leaves and pebbles under his hand. [56]

Perhaps Francis Thompson summed it up in his reminder that Mercury was the patron saint of both thieves and poets![57]

Much creativity is dependent on metaphor, not least in hymnody, where it is concerned with matters of the spirit; and metaphor in turn is a function of imagination. In his book on preaching, John Stott wrote of how

we human beings find it very difficult to handle abstract concepts; we need to convert them either into symbols (as in mathematics) or into pictures. For the power of imagination is one of God's best and most distinctive gifts to mankind.

He goes on to quote from Professor Macneile Dixon's book, *The Human Situation*, which names metaphor, figurative expression, as 'the most powerful force in the making of history... The human mind is not, as philosophers would have you think, a debating hall but a picture gallery... Metaphor is the essence of religion and poetry.'[58] Indeed, Owen Barfield called it 'the conspicuous point of contact between meaning and language',[59] and without it we could hardly communicate. To be creative in words, metaphor comes into its own. C. S. Lewis, spurred on by his friendship with Barfield, had thought much about this. In one of his earlier books he illustrates the way in which we use words from the concrete world of action as metaphors which enable us to talk about things that lie outside the realm of our five senses. Someone *grasps* an argument; we *see* the point; we *follow* the discussion. 'But,' he adds, 'it is a serious mistake to think that metaphor is an optional thing which poets and orators may put into their work as a decoration and plain speakers can do without.'[60]

Metaphor is so regular a part of our hymnody that it passes unnoticed, as indeed it should. 'Awake, my soul, and with the sun/Thy daily stage of duty run' sings Thomas Ken; but does the soul in fact 'sleep' or 'wake' day by day? Does it 'run'? Does the sun do so? These are metaphors, and therefore they make his meaning not only plain but vivid to our imagination. In his early days as a Christian apologist C. S. Lewis was defending such usage against the misconceptions of the too-literal-minded:

There is no need to be worried by facetious people who try to make the Christian hope of 'heaven' ridiculous by saying they do not want 'to spend eternity playing harps'. The answer to such people is that if they cannot understand books written for grown-ups, they should not talk about them.[61]

He goes on to explain how such scriptural imagery is 'a merely symbolic attempt to express the inexpressible', illustrating this from music, crowns, and gold. 'People who take these symbols literally,' he adds, 'might as well think that when Christ told us to be like doves, He meant that we were to lay eggs.' With this in mind, consider the last verse of Whittier's hymn 'Dear Lord and Father of mankind':

> Breathe through the heats of our desire
>   Thy coolness and thy balm;
> Let sense be dumb, let flesh retire;
> Speak through the earthquake, wind and fire,
>   O still small voice of calm.

'Breathe' is a metaphor from human respiration; 'heats', 'coolness', 'balm' are metaphors from physical temperature; 'sense' as a general term has no voice that we should bid it be dumb, and 'retire' is a metaphor of motion. Lines four and five are drawn directly from the biblical imagery of 1 Kings 19.11, 12, when the Lord met with Elijah. But when, in the hymn, we ask God to speak to us 'through' the earthquake, which at first glance is specifically *not* how he spoke to Elijah, I think he is not saying 'by means of' but 'above the sound of'. Even so, the earthquake he has in mind is not anything that would be recorded on a seismograph: it is a metaphor—so I understand it—for being willing to hear what God may have to say to us. Kenneth Clark wrote of metaphor as 'one of the chief endowments of the English mind'.[62] Setting aside the fact that J. G. Whittier was an American, Clark's statement attributes to a single country what is far more generally true: in Basil Willey's words, 'something ultimate, some unanalysable fact about the fabric of our minds'.[63] It is within just such 'fabric of our minds' (there is another metaphor) that all creativity is born.

* * *

Creativity and criticism are interdependent, in hymnody as 'a functional art' at least as much as in any other. C. Day-Lewis expressed this with clarity and conviction in writing about his own art of poetry:

The making of a poem and the questioning of it during composition, the creative and the critical, are two inseparable modes of the one process: every line—even those peremptory 'given' lines that come out of the blue—has to be judged finally by the poem as a whole.[64]

The hymn writer is in the special position of writing what others may be required to affirm in public, with little or no choice in the matter, beyond that of keeping silent while the congregation sings around them. Not everyone would feel that they could emulate Mrs Christopher Wordsworth, wife of the Bishop of Lincoln, himself a prolific hymn writer. A. C. Benson tells how it was known that the bishop disliked the line 'and only man is vile' in Heber's missionary hymn, 'From Greenland's icy mountains'. Benson's mother, sitting next to Mrs Wordsworth in church, 'saw the Bishop, with a very undisguised smile, bending down to listen to Mrs Wordsworth singing the hymn, and substituting for the obnoxious words a line which hardly satisfies the required antithesis—"and all the pastures smile" '.[65] Perhaps this assertion of independent taste was a characteristic of those formidable Victorian ladies. Charles Darwin's eldest daughter Henrietta, Gwen Raverat's 'Aunt Etty', was one who always applied the full measure of her drastic common sense to all the more imaginative passages of the poets.... One of her most engaging habits was to alter the phrase in a poem to suit herself... I remember that Wordsworth's *The wind comes to me from the fields of sleep* did not please her. What does it means, anyhow? Sleep does not grow in fields. I said, why not try *fields of sheep*. This was not well received.[66]

Browning, not surprisingly, fared even worse; and there was a family version of Wordsworth's *Tintern Revisited*, entitled *Tintern Revisited and Improved*.

In something of the same way, no hymn writer can expect to satisfy all the congregation all the time. There will always be those who take exception to certain expressions for quite the wrong reasons. But the necessity of continuous self-criticism bears more hardly, perhaps, on him or her than on most poets, and self-criticism is notoriously deceitful. The great Dr Johnson admitted as much when, so Boswell tells us, he talked of making verses, and observed: 'The great difficulty is to know when you have made good ones.' On another occasion he spoke of a man who wrote verses, 'but who literally had no other notion of a verse, but that it consisted of ten syllables...As he wrote a great number of verses he sometimes by chance made good ones, though he did not know it.'[67] John Newton, who died two centuries ago but whose hymns we regularly sing today, was a wonderful mentor, in person or by letter, to many who sought his help. There is extant a whole series of letters to a young protégé, John Ryland, who at one time was trying his hand at writing hymns. Newton offered encouragement, but saw no point in not being frank with his criticism:

Your writings, though too inaccurate and hasty, bear evident marks of genius, and I think if you allowed yourself more time, and could have revised your poems with a severer eye of criticism (as you disclaimed any assistance from a friend) you were capable of making us a very acceptable present. But I have thought you are not entitled to much of that commendation which Mr Waller speaks of when he says,

> Poets lose half the praise they should have got
> Could it be known what they discreetly blot...

If you will, you can make your lines smooth and your rhymes true, and avoid improper expressions which you have sometimes used, merely for the number or sound of the syllables.[68]

In this matter of self-criticism, Wesley and Watts present a contrast. Both were careful revisers, and, like any creator, cherished their literary children. John Wesley was notoriously jealous to preserve unaltered his brother's work once it had left his, John's, editorial pen. As we have seen, he wrote, in the celebrated Preface to the 1780 *A Collection of Hymns for the Use of the People called Methodists*:

Many gentlemen have done my brother and me (though without naming us) the honour to reprint many of our hymns. Now they are perfectly welcome so to do, provided they print them just as they are. But I desire that they would not attempt to mend them—for really they are not able. None of them is able to mend either the sense or the verse. Therefore I must beg of them one of these two favours: either to let them stand just as they are, to take them for better, for worse; or to add the true reading in the margin, or at the bottom of the page, that we no longer be accountable either for the nonsense or for the doggerel of other men.

Isaac Watts, on the other hand, in the Preface to his *Hymns and Spiritual Songs*, dating from the year that Charles Wesley was born, gives a kind of *carte blanche* to any would-be revisers, nonsense or doggerel notwithstanding:

If any expressions occur to the reader, that savour of an opinion different from his own, yet he may observe, these are generally such as are capable of an extensive sense, and may be used with a charitable latitude. I think it is most agreeable that what is provided for public singing, should give to sincere consciences as little disturbance as possible. However, where any unpleasing word is found, he that leads the worship may substitute a better; for (blessed be God) we are not confined to the words of any man in our public solemnities.

It is a good maxim, at least as far as hymnody is concerned, that every poet needs a critic. Dorothy Wordsworth, writing to a friend in 1793, confided how she 'regretted exceedingly' that 'Brother William', who in his early twenties had just published two thin books of poems,

> did not submit the works to the Inspection of some Friend before their Publication, & he also joins with me in this Regret. Their faults are such as a young Poet was most likely to fall into & least likely to discover, & what the Suggestions of a Friend would easily have made him see & at once correct.[69]

I have referred already to my own good fortune in having Derek Kidner as just such a friend and critic through all my early years of learning to write hymns. There must be quite a number (since it is surprising to find how many people do write a hymn now and again) who wish they could enjoy a similar benefit; and I am glad to say that, at least in some measure, they may. They can look over the shoulder of Erik Routley, a highly accomplished hymn writer and musician, as well as a student, lecturer, and indeed expert in the history and practice of hymnody, while he mentors a beginner in the art.

This is because Adrienne Tindall, a mature student with a passion for hymns and hymn writing, published in 1997 her extensive correspondence with Erik, following attendance at some of his workshops and lectures. In the letters, Mrs Tindall submits texts and tunes, and Erik sends back his encouragement, comments, and criticisms. He shared with her, as teacher to pupil, his long experience and his own convictions, sometimes idiosyncratic but full of wisdom. He advises her, for instance, not to try to write both text and tune: ' I don't think this works', he says of the example sent to him. 'You must be aware, with your knowledge of history, how rarely this happens in hymnody. Luther is one of the very few examples and he didn't always bring it off.' He reminds her that he thinks of hymns 'as being sung to God...I do want them to be *hymns*, not sermons or exhortations'. Gently he criticizes rhyme, scansion, meaning, form; but is careful to add, 'Keep up the good work; you're developing an easier and more relaxed style and that is all to the good.' Towards the end of the correspondence he mentions the name of John Wilson, Director of Music at Charterhouse from 1947 to 1965 before moving on to the Royal College of Music. Routley describes him to his pupil Adrienne as 'my master in all things hymnological...nowadays no reputable hymnal editor goes to work without consulting him'.[70] We do not outgrow the need for another mind to advise us on our work.

Criticism is, of course, a sensitive business. Erik Routley was careful to mix firmness and frankness with encouragement. I have said elsewhere that it was Derek Kidner's encouragement that gave me confidence to continue. But there is a part of all of us, I think, which resonates with what John Betjeman confessed once in the *Spectator*: 'I have come to dread all but undiluted praise and friendly constructive criticism from people who write poetry themselves...my verses are my children...They are part of me and attacks on them I take as personal.'[71] Betjeman is by no means the only one. Rose Macaulay felt the same: 'We all have a feeling for the children of our brain: even if we don't think them particularly good children, we don't like to see them slighted.'[72] Philip Larkin might have responded to this with a telling quote about critics, which he attributed to Ernest Hemingway: 'If you believe them when they say you're good, you have to believe them when they say you're bad.'[73] Tennyson in his younger days suffered at the hands of the critics, but there is something touching in the unashamed innocence with which he later came to uphold the merits of his own work. Here is one biographer's picture of him in old age among his guests. It was Elizabeth Barrett Browning, Robert's wife, who saved the evening,

> by asking Tennyson to read to them from the volume of *Maud*. He sat on the sofa facing her, his back supported by a cushion, his left hand pulling a foot up under him as he read, his right hand holding the book close to his near-sighted eyes, for he was not wearing spectacles... he would frequently stop to say ingenuously, 'There's a wonderful touch!' or 'That's very tender.' During the softer passages the tears coursed down his cheeks.[74]

Apart from the tears, Tennyson is surely not alone. It is not unnatural that authors should appreciate the merits of their work but such paternal affection only increases the need for the judgement of others. Few poets, perhaps, have been as careful as Housman to maintain the exact text of what was once in print: his letters to Grant Richards, his publisher, are full of complaints about misplaced commas in new editions. Yet he himself made at least two changes in poems which had been in print for twenty-five years: coming from him, a remarkable example of self-criticism.[75] Equally surprising is his request, when putting together *Last Poems*, for advice from friends. To J. W. Mackail, academic and poet, Housman wrote asking him to note 'anything that strikes you as falling below my average, or as open to exception for any other reason'. Characteristically, he adds: 'You need not be afraid of stifling a masterpiece through a temporary aberration of judgment, as I am consulting one or two other people, and shall not give effect to a single opinion unless it coincides with my own private suspicions.'[76]

Editors, too, act as critics. There is an implied criticism simply in the acceptance or rejection of a hymn for a particular hymnal. Dean Plumptre, author of 'Thy hand, O God has guided/Thy flock from age to age', must surely have been incensed by the determination of the editors of *Hymns Ancient & Modern* to omit one verse from what he had sent them. It contained the lines:

> God bless our merry England,
>   God bless our Church and Queen,
> God bless our great Archbishop,
>   The best there's ever been.[77]

When Archbishop George Carey consulted me about hymns suitable to be sung at his enthronement in Canterbury Cathedral, I was tempted to suggest that at last this stanza had come into its own! But surely in due time the author must have lived to be thankful to the editors; and this is certainly true of the Wesleys. Here is Henry Bett again:

> It is only when you go through the original volumes of Charles Wesley's verse, and note the way in which his brother chose the best of the hymns, and then omitted from these the weaker stanzas, until out of a long string of verses of very varied quality there often emerges a hymn of sustained excellence, which is a complete lyric in itself—it is only after such a study that one realizes the excellence of John Wesley's editorial work.[78]

Dr Bett gives several instances of how, on the extant MS evidence, John criticized—and editorially emended—some of his brother's work. Against Charles's line,

> Thou dids't in love thy servant leave,

there appears 'Never—JW'; just as, against the lines,

> And all our rapturous happiness
> In hasty sorrow ends,

we find, 'Not always—JW'. When you remember what was said above about the work of writers being their 'literary children' I am lost in admiration at Charles's humility in thus submitting the work in which he was an acknowledged master to the judgement of another, even to one who was himself a hymn writer as well as an elder brother. Charles knew that his was 'a functional art', where he was writing, not to please himself alone, but to be of usefulness to the Christian fellowship.

What is needed, once again, is a happy marriage. Let creativity find expression, and criticism shape it to meet the needs and standards of the day, and let both be satisfied with nothing less than the best they can achieve. When Hensley Henson was Bishop of Durham, the story goes, a visitor stopped by a tank of goldfish in the entrance hall. 'Bishop,' he asked, 'why are these small black fish (they were the immature ones) called goldfish?' 'Because,' came the instant reply, 'we are what we aspire to become.'[79] Creation and criticism, similarly, are both to do with aspiration, the reaching towards an ever-elusive goal. But it may not always be so. Let Isaac Watts close this chapter with his glimpse of the beatific vision, when perhaps both shall be counted 'nobler powers':

> I'll praise my Maker with my breath,
> And when my voice is lost in death,
>   Praise shall employ my nobler powers:
> My days of praise shall ne'er be past,
> While life, and thought, and being last,
>   Or immortality endures.

WE HAVE A DREAM

WE HAVE A DREAM, who are the heirs,
        through centuries of praise,
of all whose worship, work and prayers
        have hallowed former days;
upon their faithfulness we build
        for futures none can see,
a dream of purposes fulfilled
        in all that is to be.

We have a dream of listening hearts
        where Jesus' voice is heard,
a church where God himself imparts
        the treasures of his word;
a pilgrim church whose longing eyes
        are set on things above,
a church united by the ties
        of fellowship and love.

We have a dream to serve, and care
        for all who know distress;
the world our parish, and our prayer
        the search for holiness:
a church sustained by broken bread,
        the cup of wine outpoured,
a church for whom his blood was shed
        who reigns as risen Lord.

We have a dream, a goal, an aim,
    a charge that Jesus gave,
to share the blessings of his Name
    with those he died to save.
Help us to heed the Master's call,
    the Spirit's power renew,
for God is with us, best of all,
    to make our dreams come true.

© Timothy Dudley-Smith in Europe and Africa. © Hope Publishing Company in the United States of America and the rest of the world. Reproduced by permission of Oxford University Press. All rights reserved.

CHAPTER 10

What of the Future?

> I, too, have thought many years on this subject, and am more and more convinced that the *age* of hymns has passed. Happy those who can use the ancient Latin ones...*
>
> John Mason Neale, 1839

SUNDAY BY SUNDAY many Church of England congregations join in what are called 'acclamations'. These form a threefold affirmation in the most solemn part of the Service of Holy Communion:

> Christ has died:
> Christ is risen:
> Christ will come again.

The Gospels and the New Testament letters describe in some detail all three of these momentous events, decisive turning points in the history of humankind. Two are matters of historical record, but the third lies in the future. The Lord Jesus himself told his disciples to prepare for this 'second advent', his return in glory at the end of the age. But what, very specifically, we are *not* told is when this will be. Jesus declared that he himself did not know. In his days on earth he told his followers that 'of that day or that hour no one knows, not even the angels in heaven, nor the Son, but only the Father'.[1] They must therefore be on the watch, 'for in such an hour as ye think not, the Son of Man cometh'.[2]

When I hear those words, I remember a story told by D. L. Moody of the Scottish divine, Robert Murray McCheyne, preacher, pastor, author, and hymn writer. McCheyne was sitting one evening among a circle of friends; I picture them silhouetted in the light of the fire. During a lull in the conversation—godly talk, I have no doubt—McCheyne turned to the man nearest to him and asked quietly, 'Do you think Christ will return tonight?' The friend, perhaps a little startled, replied, 'I think not.' McCheyne went round the little group asking each the same question and getting the same reply, 'I think not.' Then with deep solemnity he reminded them of the Lord's warning: 'In such an hour as ye think not, the Son of Man cometh.' What we confidently talk of as the future may be shorter than we think.

But if we assume that there is a future, is there a future for hymnody? You have only to look at the epigraph that begins this chapter to see how mistaken predictions can be. Few were better placed than Erik Routley to read the signs of the times in the world of church music and hymnody: he found them 'favourable'. Yet when Dr Lionel Dakers as Director of the Royal School of Church Music came to add a chapter, after Routley's death, to his *Short History of English Church Music*, he commented on 'how different things are now from what Erik Routley forecast, the more remarkable in that he was so visionary a person'.[3] It is a salutary warning against over-confidence; and yet it cannot be a mistake to try to arrive at some assessment of what the future may hold for our heritage of hymnody. It seems to me that there are at least four possibilities.

Some, like J. M. Neale in his day, do not think there is a future for hymnody. When in 1984 David Edwards published the last of his trilogy on *Christian England* he ended the story at November 1914 because he could only see then 'an England which was no longer Christian in any substantial sense'.[4] In a similarly bleak vein we find people who confidently predict, sadly or gleefully according to their standpoint, that the tradition of hymn singing in religious cultures such as ours will soon be a thing of the past. Tennyson, as we have seen, wondered (perhaps not very seriously) whether the day would come when churchgoing would lack all participation, beyond sitting in silence and listening to the organ.[5] He may yet be right. As we see Christian faith and Christian values ignored, trivialized, or marginalized by so much of our press and political life, will the singing of the hymns that generations have known and loved still remain a credible expression of a disregarded faith? Perhaps in the long sweep of history it will not be like that. There have always been prophets of doom, sometimes among the church's most loyal members. It was the devout Henry Liddon who in the mid-nineteenth century described Christian work in the University of Oxford as 'combing the hair of a corpse'.[6] Alister McGrath, writing with a world vision in our own twenty-first century, tells a different story:

> Religion was meant to have disappeared years ago. For more than a century, leading sociologists, anthropologists and psychologists have declared that their children would see the dawn of a new era in which the 'God delusion' would be left behind for good. Back in the 1960s, we were told that religion was fading away, to be replaced by a secular world...[7]

He explains that he was an atheist back in the late 1960s, and remembered looking forward to the demise of religion 'with a certain grim pleasure...the future was bright— and godless'. But this is not how it turned out: 'Religion has made a comeback... It seems strange to think that it was only a generation ago that its death was foretold with such confidence...Not only was God not "dead"—as the German philosopher Nietzsche prematurely proclaimed—he never seems to have been more alive.'

Were we to lose hymn singing from our worship, it would (to me, at least) be an unimaginable change, but it would by no means be unprecedented. Since the days when I was ordained, how many robed choirs have vanished from our churches? I can remember as a curate sitting across the darkened chancel one Sunday evening when the choir had gone on strike; the churchwardens had turned off the chancel lights, perhaps to mitigate the nakedness of the choir stalls, but no doubt also to save on the electricity bill. My eyes met those of my vicar opposite me as we found ourselves singing,

> Three in One and One in Three,
> Dimly here we worship thee...

but I do not think it ever occurred to me that the day might come when the choir would be gone for good. Again, Frank Field, interviewed by the *Church Times* in 2008 in his role as chairman of the Cathedrals Fabric Commission, predicted that their choral tradition, because of its cost, could not last another thirty years.[8] To take another example, the singing of the psalms has been part of the worship of Almighty God for three thousand years. Even in translation, I am told, their nature has produced remarkable consistent patterns of musical settings. Plainsong, Anglican chant, and the much more recent Gelineau settings, are all said to echo the pattern of the original Hebrew. Tom Wright calls the Psalms 'the steady, sustained subcurrent of healthy Christian living. They shaped the praying and vocation even of Jesus himself.'[9] Yet, as we noted earlier, in countless churches the singing of the psalms seems to have been abandoned, and only a few vestiges retained in such metrical versions as 'The King of love my Shepherd is' or 'Through all the changing scene of life'. If this can happen to the psalms, it can happen to hymns.

I confess that I do not think it will. Part of my reason can be found in a small notice which appeared in a supplement to *The Times*[10] a few Christmasses ago under the heading of 'Events' happening in the week in question. It read in part:

Nine Lessons and Carols for Godless People
£25-£27.50
A night of music and comedy to celebrate the rational and scientific... guests include the author Richard Dawkins. A humanist choir will perform.

Could anything be more indicative of the place of singing and celebration, even in the psyches of those who have only the secular and the rational to celebrate, and need a humanist choir to help them? If such a novel event meets a popular demand, it is hard to think that those who have everything to celebrate, on Christmas Day and every day, will allow the inheritance of centuries to die.

A second and perhaps more likely possibility is that hymns will develop in ways which we do not yet see. I could not have imagined, for example, looking back again to the days of my curacy, that what the Sunday School sang as children's choruses would influence, at least in lyrics, the future hymnody of adult congregations. Of course, it is possible to trace development in all the hymns we sing. Addison's polished phrases are very different from Tate and Brady. Jan Struther, Albert Bayly, Fred Kaan, and many moderns (of whom Sydney Carter—'I danced in the morning'—might be an extreme instance) are different again, reflecting their generation. As an example of what I am groping for, in suggesting that hymnody may develop in ways which we do not now see, consider the style of writing which characterizes Thomas Troeger. He was formerly a Presbyterian minister and is now an Episcopalian. He has degrees in both literature and theology and is an accomplished musician. He brings these gifts to a style that for many years now has been extending the boundaries of traditional hymn writing.[11] Often his vivid imagery and striking vocabulary seem to be turning the hymn into something new. Newness is not always in favour with editors or congregations, but Troeger has been doing this with considerable acceptance in his native North America since at least the start of the 1980s. English editors have been more cautious, wondering with some justification, whether his colourful and creative approach will suit their constituencies. There are, however, texts of his in the *Hymns Ancient & Modern* collections, *Common Praise*, 2000, and *Ancient & Modern*, 2013; as well as in the Scottish *Church Hymnary*, 2005, and in the Methodist *Singing the Faith*, 2011; though none includes more than two or three of his texts. To show what I mean by his new approach, consider these opening lines:

> Above the moon earth rises,
> A sunlit, mossy stone...

They could only have been written late in the twentieth century, when we had grown familiar with the contours of planet earth viewed from the moon; and seen, as no previous generation could have seen, the moss-like appearance of much of its surface. Troeger's texts published in British hymnals tend to be among his more traditional; others seem so innovative as at times to present a discontinuity with the hymns of the past. 'Startled by a holy humming' or 'Silence! Frenzied, unclean spirit' or 'If Christ is charged with madness' are sufficiently unfamiliar in expression as to make hymnal editors think twice. It may be that as far as this country is concerned, Troeger is simply ahead of his time. It is some fifty years since Erik Routley wrote about what might be the future of the hymn:

> If, as I myself firmly believe, the new hymns turn out to be carols rather than hymns, earthy, familiar, bold, and by present-day standards unconventional, so much the better. Not only will the new hymns produce a new and daring faith. They will shed new light on the old hymns. We shall not lose the Old Hundredth and 'O worship the King'; but we may start singing them without that glazed expression and that mental stagnation which are now only too familiar.[12]

Perhaps he had been having a bad day, which gave rise to that final line in the quote above; but his sense of the hymns he would not live to see is a not unfair description, for a guess in the dark, of the folk-hymns exemplified by John Bell and others. As regards Thomas Troeger's hymns, the words 'bold' and 'unconventional' certainly fit. Erik was generous to me in the early days of my hymn writing, but I hardly fit the vision set out above. I think I had not then arrived at the sense that my calling is to try to offer something of a bridge between the older hymns and the future. This, indeed, is what the 'hymn explosion' (some say that Erik coined the phrase[13]) may yet prove to be when the dust has finally settled. My friend Christopher Idle tells of talking with a minister who, not without a certain complacency, was assuring him that in *his* church they were inclusive in their choice of hymnody, making sure they offered *both* traditional hymns and modern worship songs. Christopher gently reminded him that there was a third category that he had overlooked, the contemporary hymn. Perhaps all three, and maybe still other kinds of Christian congregational song, will survive to nourish the faith of our great-grandchildren. But it would be foolish to go on attempting to foresee a future which I have already admitted may well hold changes which cannot be foreseen.

A third possibility is that the hymn as we know it will be entirely replaced by the modern worship song; indeed, there are plenty of faithful congregations where this is already so. I have touched on this in an earlier chapter, and lack of musical understanding makes this a field in which I am ill-equipped to trespass. But I believe that the ephemeral worship song, a genre it is easier to recognize than define, carries some of the seeds of its own decay. Performance-orientated music, by its very nature, reflects the culture of the secular music of its day; and he who marries the spirit of the age will be a widower tomorrow. I noted in an earlier chapter how, as the worship song grows more mature, it becomes more like what we have always recognized as a hymn. Graham Kendrick, to his generation the doyen of such song-writing, commented in an interview that 'More and more hymn-like worship songs are being written.'[14] It will take a generation to lose from the church's repertoire the last of the rather vapid and formless ditties that crept in during the 1950s and 1960s, though a good many seem already to have had their day. Monsignor Ronald Knox ('the cleverest boy in Eton's living memory'[15] and himself a hymn writer) discovered this built-in time lag when serving on the committee to revise the old Roman Catholic *Westminster Hymnal*. Evelyn Waugh, his biographer, described something of the process, concluding:

> The new book bears his personal marks clearly; it was issued in 1940 and cordially welcomed by informed critics. Catholic parishes are slow to change their habits. They still sing what the oldest members learned at school. A full generation must pass before the innovations, so patiently debated, are allowed to fulfil their work of enrichment.[16]

In the same way, it is understandable that those who in their formative years were excited by the worship songs then in vogue, will want to perpetuate them now that they edit the hymnals or choose the hymns in church. It is not only the Roman Catholic parishes who like what they already know. I fully expect, therefore, that this rather surprising phenomenon of the charismatic worship song, however unsatisfactory in some of its aspects, is bound to leave a legacy, and for some at least a precious and valued one; but I do not think the future belongs to it.

* * *

These, then, are three possible futures: that the hymn as we know it has had its day and will soon pass into oblivion; alternatively, that traditional hymnody will develop and change, not in the slow winnowing processes of time, but over a generation or two; or perhaps, thirdly, that hymns will largely be replaced by worship songs or their successors. But there is also a fourth possibility: that the hymn, both traditional and contemporary, will be with us and our grandchildren for a long time to come. This is my own view, and before concluding these 'reflections' I offer some reasons for advancing it.

I am not the first to do so. Colin Morris, BBC Head of Religious Broadcasting in the 1980s, gave the address in Westminster Abbey on the fiftieth anniversary of their flagship TV programme, 'Songs of Praise'.[17] He took as his text the question asked of themselves by the Israelites in exile, 'How shall we sing the Lord's song in a strange land?', and offered five reasons why the Lord's song was able to survive and indeed thrive in the 'strange land' of the mass-media; we have considered some of them in earlier chapters. He reminded his hearers, first, that singing has its own mysterious power, and that 'people can often sing what they cannot say'. Singing touches a part of us 'beyond conscious beliefs... because the many layers of meaning music and poetry are able to accommodate not just what we think, but also what we feel.' Indeed, he claimed, 'the programme survives because hymns are the essence of ordinary people's religion... an expression of democracy at the heart of religious authority'. A further reason, he suggested, for the programme's popularity was that it offered a potent combination of the old and the new. This is an exact description, not just of a TV programme but of what we mean by hymnody, which for most of us is a key aspect of 'the Lord's song'. It unites us with those who sang this song before us, and may contribute its own small offering to those as yet unborn.

Colin Morris's fourth reason for the programme's longevity and vitality, in his own startling metaphor, was 'because hymns plant spiritual time-bombs in the mind'. He cited the continuing power of what we sang in childhood; and the way in which hymns, half-forgotten in the rush of life, can come into their own at times of personal or national crisis. And lastly, he affirmed, 'We are able to sing the Lord's song in a strange land because we are exiles and it's the song of home.' 'It gives' ('it' here being the programme, but I offer it as true of all hymnody)—'It gives us melodies to march to and songs to cheer our spirits and orchestrates our celebration when we arrive at journey's end.'

My belief that the hymns we have known will continue to survive and flourish shares much of the thinking of that sermon in the Abbey. But because this is a book of personal 'reflections' let me state or restate them as a personal *credo*, reverting to that earlier metaphor of 'happy marriages'.

* * *

I believe, then, in the future of the hymn as a continuing part of worship, because it represents *a marriage of singing with celebration*. This is a theme which has appeared often in these pages, from the copperbelt in South Africa, or from Baroness Blixen's Kenya; from the successors to the old slave songs in the Southern states, from village congregations, and from great Cathedrals. Contemporary Christian hymnals are published, to my knowledge, in Taiwan and Korea, Latvia and Estonia, China and Japan, as well as in most of the English-speaking countries. Some of these books include in translation hymns which we sing in English churches and chapels, but music is a universal language of praise. It celebrates first and foremost all that God has done for us in Christ—what Henry Lyte summed up, for the individual Christian, in that pregnant four-word line, 'Ransomed, healed, restored, forgiven'; which continues, 'Who like me his praise should sing?' And such singing also celebrates our togetherness, our unity in Christ, as in the German saying (Luther, perhaps?), 'The folks I talk to are my fellow human beings; the ones I sing with are family.'[18] Open the calendar of Christian history at any page you wish, and the chances are you will find celebration and song. It was there in the psalms when Christians were still faithful members of their synagogues; Paul and Silas sang their midnight duets in prison; the younger Pliny's famous letter to the Emperor Trajan reported how the members of this new religion, the second-century Christians, were accustomed 'to meet before daybreak, and to recite a hymn antiphonally to Christ, as to a god...'.[19] Fast-forward some 1,400 years and the story is the same. Here is John Jewel, Bishop of Salisbury, writing in 1560 to his friend Peter Martyr:

Religion is now somewhat more established than it was. The people are everywhere exceedingly inclined to the better part. The practice of joining in church music has very much conduced to this. For as soon as they had once commenced singing in public, in only one little church in London, immediately not only the churches in the neighbourhood, but even the towns far distant, began to vie with each other in the same practice. You may now sometimes see at Paul's Cross, after the service, six thousand persons, young and old, all singing together and praising God.[20]

Derek Kidner sums it up for me in a comment on Psalm 96: 'Where God is, there is singing.'[21] And because humanity bears God's image, the marriage of singing with celebration is a human before it is a Christian phenomenon. A response to rhythm begins, perhaps even in the womb, with the beating heart, soon to be followed by the pounding surf, the marching stride, the galloping hooves. The *Oxford Companion to Music* used to state categorically, I understand, that 'No songless people has ever been discovered.'

My tenth edition is more guarded, but still claims that the art of singing 'has been cultivated in some sort of way amongst all peoples that have attained any considerable degree of ordered life'. Hymns, surely, are as universal as the Christian church. In the light of all this and of what has been said earlier in these pages, and of so much more that might be said, I cannot believe that hymn singing has had its day.

I believe in the future of the hymn, second, because it offers continuity with our Christian past, in *a marriage of the traditional with the contemporary*. In the hymns we sing, more perhaps than in any other part of our worship, we are one with former ages—former centuries—in our devotion. Moreover, we find in our hymn books the work of acknowledged masters from past generations, both men and women. Worship is not, for most of us, such a natural and easy business that we can afford to neglect a proven resource which has nourished piety over many years. In the indexes of almost any hymn book we find such names as Catherine Winkworth and Ralph Vaughan Williams, Milton and Mendelssohn, Herbert and Handel, the Wesleys (John, Charles, and Samuel), Robert Bridges and J. S. Bach. It is unthinkable that such resources should be for long abandoned.

We live in an age of hugely increased mobility, when people change homes and jobs more frequently than did their forebears, and when family breakdown is an all too common experience, so that such roots as there are become more valued. Hymns can root us firmly in the apostolic Christian tradition, giving continuity, authority, and a sense of permanence: we are not adrift, we are not alone. At the same time, neither are we imprisoned in the past. Of the hymns that were sung, even a mere hundred years ago or so, far more have now perished without trace than remain in today's hymnals. The very word 'continuity' implies progress and change, but change that is not severed from its roots. 'Heritage' is perhaps the word to describe a treasure that does not belong to us, though for the moment it is ours to enjoy. But that privilege carries with it the responsibility to care for it, and in our turn to pass it on. This, I believe, is where the traditional has to find room for the contemporary, as it has done in an almost unbroken succession. The Psalmist speaks of 'a new song in my mouth' and every generation should be ready to contribute 'new songs'. With the task of innovating and of preserving goes also the work of discarding. Our heritage of hymns is a resource for worship which expresses not what is 'top of the Christian pops' at the moment, but the considered mind of the church, the worshipping family, winnowing, welcoming, relinquishing the outmoded, right up to the present day. Hymnal editors may think that their work is to shape the kind of hymnody the churches sing; and there is some truth in that. But if their new hymnal is to find a market, it must also express that mysterious 'mind' which is the unorganized but real consensus among worshippers.

Next, I believe in the future of the hymn because it offers *a marriage of poetry and piety*. It was John Wesley who coupled them together in his famous Preface which was quoted in chapter 2. He is very firm in stating that the spirit of piety 'is of infinitely more moment' than the spirit of poetry, but at the same time he points out that the latter, while not of first importance, comes a good second:

May I be permitted to add a few words with regard to the poetry? Then I will speak to those who are judges thereof, with all freedom and unreserve. To these I may say, without offence: (1). In all these hymns there is no doggerel, no botches, nothing put in to patch up the rhyme, no feeble expletives. (2). Here is nothing turgid or bombast on the one hand, nor low and creeping on the other. (3). Here are no *cant* expressions, no words without meaning. Those who impute this to us know not what they say. We talk common sense (whether they understand it or not) both in verse and prose, and use no word but in a fixed and determinate sense. (4). Here are (allow me to say) both the purity, the strength, and the elegance of the English language—and at the same time the utmost simplicity and plainness, suited to every capacity. Lastly, I desire men of taste to judge—these are the only competent judges—whether there is not in some of the following verses the true spirit of poetry... What is of infinitely more moment than the spirit of poetry is the spirit of piety. And I trust all persons of real judgment will find this breathing through the whole *Collection*... When poetry thus keeps its place, as the handmaid of piety, it shall attain, not a poor perishable wreath, but a crown that fadeth not away.

Opinions differ greatly as to the merits of hymns regarded as poetry, or indeed if they are truly poetry at all as poets use the term; Wordsworth was right to call it 'a word of very disputed meaning'.[22] James Montgomery, a hymn writer whose work we sing today, felt that 'hymns had been written by all kinds of persons except poets'.[23] Donald Davie, poet and critic, has written of 'our resistance to considering hymns as poetry'.[24] Bernard Manning trumps all arguments when he declares:

I think it is improper to criticize hymns as if they were ordinary verses: to say of any hymn it is 'not poetry' or it is 'poor poetry' is to say nothing. A hymn—a good hymn—is not necessarily poetry of any sort, good or bad: just as poetry, good or bad, is not necessarily a hymn.[25]

My own preference is to think of hymn texts as *verse*, which begs the question—the really rather unimportant question—of whether it is right to dignify them with the name of poetry. I am fortified in this opinion by John Newton's perception that hymn writing 'may be more successfully or at least more easily attained by a versifier than a poet',[26] though I believe that it can well be informed and nourished by an enjoyment of the poets. When the celebrated *Oxford Book of English Verse* was in preparation, there was much discussion over what to call it. 'Q', the editor (Arthur Quiller-Couch), offered among other suggestions the title *The Pageant of English Poetry*.[27] If he saw no real distinction between what we should call verse and what we should call poetry, I am happy to settle for 'verse' for myself and 'poetry' (at his best) for Charles Wesley. To me he exemplifies just what his brother described: the marriage of poetry and piety in a way that has moved and satisfied worshippers ever since, and will, I contend, continue to do so.

I believe, finally, in the future of hymnody because at its best it represents *a marriage of truth and experience.* Many years ago I remember visiting Exeter Cathedral as a tourist. We pushed open a heavy door, as I recall it, to be confronted with a notice of welcome. I could not find it on a more recent visit, but it so struck me at the time that I copied it down. It read:

> To thirty generations of Devon folk
> in this home of their souls,
> the Word of God has been preached,
> the Sacraments administered,
> and the Way of Eternal Life made plain.

I have come to see in that simple but moving statement a parallel with the ministry of hymns. They too, at their best, offer biblical truth; and was it not Augustine who compared a sacrament to a 'visible word'? Sacraments dramatize the word of God through their imagery. Can we not say that hymns, while not 'visible' words, are yet musical, melodic, metrical words, by which the word of Christ is carried on wings of song to the hidden places of spirit and of heart? And we shall not have sung many hymns before we are reminded that we are pilgrim followers of Christ the Way, the way of eternal life.

In such a marriage, truth is the essential partner to experience: real, revealed, rational, and redemptive truth, in Dr Packer's alliteration,[28] and in hymnody, as we have seen, Scripture is both the starting point and the authenticating touchstone. For today's worshippers, this is both more necessary and more difficult than in the past:

> John Wesley was right when he claimed for his brother's verse that it was 'Scriptural', in the sense that almost every metaphor or striking turn of phrase can be traced to a biblical origin... Wesley enjoyed, as Pope did or Johnson, a sort of extra poetic dimension. He could expect his congregation to know Scripture as Johnson and Pope could expect their readers to know Virgil and Horace.[29]

We can only expect that knowledge today, when daily Bible reading in the home is the exception rather than the rule, from a kind of 'inner circle' of worshippers. The hymn must therefore express biblical truth in a way that does not presuppose familiarity with the source. Yet, in J. R. Watson's phrase, the biblical stories and elements must be 'kept as they are': that is, he explains, 'hymns cannot be allowed to contradict the Bible, invent their own narratives, or deny the teachings of the Apostle Paul'.[30] When I sit down to work at a hymn, my mind sometimes goes back to January 1981, when I was consecrated Bishop of Thetford beneath the great dome of St Paul's Cathedral. In the course of the Service Archbishop Robert Runcie held aloft a copy of the Bible before handing it to me with these words: 'Receive this Book; here are the words of eternal life. Take them for your guide and declare them to the world.'

In writing hymns, I still aim to fulfil that commission. I covet for myself the words of Isaac Watts in his Preface to *Hymns and Spiritual Songs* in 1707:

> The second part consists of hymns whose form is of mere human composure; but I hope the sense and materials will always appear divine. I might have brought some text or other, and applied it to the margin of every verse, if this method had been as useful as it was easy.

'Biblical', while an essential attribute, is not a kind of magic talisman that can ensure a hymn's effectiveness. That requires experience to partner truth. Donald Hustad described once how his daughter Donna came home from Children's Church happily singing a little Bible chorus. 'I asked her what the song meant. "Don't be silly, Daddy," she said, "It doesn't mean a thing; it's just a song".'[31] More serious than that is the experience of the new convert who found himself singing words which did not match his experience. 'When I became a Christian,' he is supposed to have said, 'I stopped telling lies and started singing them.'[32] More disturbing still is the assessment of Fred Pratt Green, Methodist and hymn writer, who some thirty years ago suggested that 'we have been singing the Charles Wesley hymns in the Methodist Church now for many years without the experience that created them'.[33] In saying this, perhaps he was putting his finger on what lies behind the falling numbers in Christian congregations. 'The ultimate reason,' Professor Tasker reminds us, 'for the decline of Christian worship' is, and must always be, a failure to recognize or experience the redeeming work of Jesus; for it is not as a social reformer, nor as an ethical teacher, but as a Saviour that he claims and receives the adoration of the faithful.[34]

If Fred Pratt Green's misgivings are true of Methodism, they are not alone. Yet Biblical hymns will, surely, continue to be sung in any church that values Scripture, provided they are firmly based on this happy marriage of truth with experience. When Leonard Wilson, Bishop of Singapore, was the prisoner of the Japanese in the infamous camp at Changi, it was the hymns he knew by heart that helped sustain him through captivity and pain. 'Look, Father, look on his anointed face' were the words that came into his mind, 'And only look on us as found in him'. Such words helped him to see the guards not simply as his torturers, but 'as they were capable of becoming, redeemed by the power of Christ'. Every morning in his cell he would repeat Charles Wesley's morning hymn, 'Christ, whose glory fills the skies', which combined the objective fact of his present experience ('Dark and cheerless is the morn...Joyless is the day's return') with eternal truth ('Christ, the true, the only light') in a way that enabled him to pray,

> Visit then this soul of mine,
> Pierce the gloom of sin and grief...

so that, as he described it, 'the burden of this world was lifted and I was carried into the presence of God'.[35]

Let me end with two further stories, illustrating my conviction that hymns hold so unique a place in the Christian psyche that I am assured of their future. The first is of a phone call from a friend at last discharged from hospital, but with his immune system so impaired that any infection was likely to be terminal. He told me how he and his wife had come across a hymn of mine, 'Safe in the shadow of the Lord', based on Psalm 91; it was printed in an Order of Service from St Paul's Cathedral, where his son-in-law had been the preacher. Night by night in the hospital, my friend told me, he and his wife had read these words together and found comfort, not least from the opening line of verse three:

> From fears and phantoms of the night,
> from foes about my way,
>   I trust in him,
>   I trust in him,
> by darkness as by day.

It was, as you will imagine, a humbling experience to hear this: but what more could a hymn writer ask?

By contrast, this final story comes from North America, from a family quite unknown to me. It concerns a grandmother, so disabled following a stroke that her adult children, visiting her in the nursing home, could not be sure they were even recognized: 'The contrast between such abject impotence and her former vigour of mind and body heightened their feeling of complete powerlessness.' There was a family gathering one New Year's Day, which found them in the afternoon singing hymns round the piano. It occurred to them that their mother might leave the nursing home for a few hours to join them, and some of the men went to fetch her. They placed her wheelchair beside the piano and continued with their singing—'only to find that she was joining in, softly but in time and tune... deep below the frost line, the hymns of faith survived when all else seemed gone'.[36]

Society has its frost line, too. Times of recession and secularization when belief is pushed to the margins can be a kind of local spiritual ice-age. But 'deep below the frost line' I believe that the hymns of faith will survive, 'a functional art', to nourish the worship of future generations, just as they still enrich our own.

ENDNOTES

INTRODUCTION

* Boswell, James, 1791, Vol. 1, p. 189.
1. Morgan, Charles, 1944, pp. 54, 55.
2. Lewis, C. S., 1954, p. 112.
3. Pratt Green, Fred, 1989, p. xxiii.
4. Barry, F. R., 1964, p. 131.
5. Barker, Juliet, 2002, p. 210.
6. Conrad, Joseph, 1919, p. 173.
7. Baker, Frank, 1962, p. xi.
8. Smyth, Charles, 1940, p. 22.
9. Williams, Rowan, 2005, p. viii.
10. Brooks, Cleanth, 1968, p. 66.
11. Dudley-Smith, Timothy, 2003, pp. 212, 228, 249.
12. Baughen, Michael, 1966; 1969; 1973.
13. Dudley-Smith, Timothy, 1981.
14. Thwaite, Anthony, ed., 2001; 2002, p. 26.

CHAPTER 1. WHY HYMNS?

* Watts, Isaac, 1707, Preface.
1. Housman, Henry, 1896, p. 80.
2. Watson, J. R., 1997, p. 8.
3. Raverat, Gwen, 1962, p. 228.
4. Routley, Erik, 1982, p. 1.
5. Routley, Erik, 1952, p. 19.
6. Fletcher, Andrew, 1732.
7. Horne, Sylvester C., 1903, p. 250.
8. Howarth, T. E. B., 1978, p. 173.
9. Betjeman, John, 1960, p. 67.
10. Hopkins, H. A. Evan, 1979, pp. 16, 17.
11. Manning, B. L., 1939, p. 83.
12. Watson, J. R., 1997, p. 44.
13. Jenkyn, Richard, 1997, p. 32.
14. Bridges, Robert, 1935, p. 28.
15. Larkin, Philip, 2001; 2002, p. 212.
16. Amos 5.21–24.
17. John 4.19–23.
18. Temple, William, 1949, p. 64.
19. Wesley, John, 1761.
20. Heaton, Joseph, 1862, p. 52.
21. Creighton, Louise, 1904, p. 488.
22. Kidner, F. D., 1975, p. 344.

CHAPTER 2. WHY NEW HYMNS?

* Lewis, C. S., 1949, p. 20.
1. *Report*, 2001, section 15/1.
2. Mark 14.26.
3. Bettelheim, Bruno, 1976; 1991, p. 12.
4. Davie, Donald, 1933, p. 19.
5. From the Prayer for the Church Militant, BCP Service of Holy Communion.
6. From Robert Bridges' translation, 'All my hope on God is founded'.
7. Watson, J. R., 1997, p. 513.
8. 1 Timothy 6.15f; Revelation 17.14.
9. Manning, B. L., 1942, p. 128.
10. Wyndham Lewis, D. B. and Lee, Charles, 1930; 1963, pp. 4, 8.
11. Alexander, C. F., 1848.
12. Proverbs 22.2.
13. Wallace, Valerie, 1995, p. 70.
14. Hardy, Thomas, 1874; 1995, p. 399.
15. Moore, Henry, 1825, Vol. II, p. 218.
16. Sharpe, Eric, 1982, p. 9.
17. Castle, Brian, 1994, p. 84f.
18. Robertson, Charles, 1990, p. 2.
19. Hindmarsh, D. Bruce, 1996, p. 263.
20. Fletcher, Winston, 2008, p. 62.
21. For example, *Songs of Praise* 565, 692.
22. Janet Wootton, 2010.
23. Acts 13.36.
24. Tennyson, Hallam, 1897, Vol. II, p. 165.
25. Montgomery, James, 1825; 1846, p. xxxiii.
26. Smyth, Charles, 1940, p. 198.
27. Berridge, 1918, p. 168.
28. Austen, Jane, 1818, chapter 5.
29. Eliot, T. S., 1957, p. 51.

CHAPTER 3. WHAT SORT OF HYMNS?

* NRSV.
[1] 2 Timothy 1.6.
[2] 1 Corinthians 14.15.
[3] John 4,23 NEB.
[4] Housman, Henry, 1896, p. 259.
[5] Wright, Tom, 2014, p. 25.
[6] Quoted from Watson, J. R., 1997, p. 44.
[7] Kidner, F. D., 1973, p. 18.
[8] Hardy, Thomas, 1880; 1990, p. 129.
[9] Patrick, Millar, 1949, p. 176.
[10] Stott, J. R. W., 1966, p. 12.
[11] Macaulay, Rose, 1961, p. 100.
[12] Montgomery, James, 1825; 1846, p. vi.
[13] Leaver, Robin, 1975.
[14] Harvey, Paul, ed., 1932., p. 750; citing R. E. Prothero, 1903.
[15] Watts, Isaac, 1772.
[16] Barker, Juliet, 2002, p. 184.
[17] Keble, John, 1839.
[18] Housman, Henry, 1896, p. 80.
[19] Preston, David, 1986; Leckebusch, Martin E., 2006.
[20] Browning, Martin, 1995.
[21] *Songs of Fellowship*, 1991, No. 218.
[22] Cooke, Victoria, 2001, p. 24.
[23] Day, Thomas, 1990, p. 148.
[24] Tozer, A. W., 1959, p. 37; quoted in Lucarini, Dan, 2002.
[25] Ward, Pete, 2005, p. 204.
[26] Jeremiah 31.4, NEB.
[27] Quoted in Wilson-Dickson, Andrew, 1992, p, 62.
[28] Scruton, Roger, 1997, p. 502.
[29] Leach, John, 1995, p. 7.
[30] Lambert, Constant, 1934, chapter 3; cited in the *Oxford Dictionary of Modern Quotations*, 1991.
[31] Ward, Pete, 2005, p. 209.

CHAPTER 4. GOOD AND NOT SO GOOD

* Benson, A. C., 1899, Vol. 1, p. 592.
[1] Tennyson, Hallam, 1897, Vol. II, p. 401.
[2] Rivers, Isabel and Wykes, David L., 2011, p. 1.
[3] Lewis, Warren, 1982, p. 193.
[4] Simeon, Charles, 1832, Vol. I, p. xx1.
[5] Hindmarsh, D. Bruce, 1996, p. 276.
[6] Lewis, C. S., 1954, p. 217.
[7] Housman, Henry, 1896, p. 229.
[8] Manning, B. L., 1942, p. 30.
[9] Sidney, Sir Philip, 1595.
[10] Montgomery, James, 1825; 1846, p. xxiii.
[11] Wesley, Charles, 1741.
[12] Edwards, David L., 1984, Vol. III, p. 61.
[13] Chadwick, Owen, 1990, p. 87.
[14] Reynolds, William J., 1992, p. 40.
[15] Marsh, J. B. T., 1898, No. 65.
[16] Given to me by Dr Lionel Dakers in a photocopy from an unidentified hymnal, as No. 62 to MOZART
[17] *Catholic Hymn Book, The*, 1998, No. 185 to WOLVERCOTE.
[18] Bradley, Ian, 1997, p. 24.
[19] Watson, J. R., 1997, p. 394.
[20] Watson, J. R., 1997, p. 394.
[21] On a postcard to Sir Brian Batsford. See Wilson, A. N., 2006, p. 164.
[22] Brittain, F., 1972, p. 41.
[23] Benson, A. C., 1899, Vol. I, p. 592.
[24] Newsome, David, 1980, p. 127.
[25] Newsome, David, 1980, p. 86.
[26] Newsome, David, 1993, p. 290.
[27] Newsome, David, 1980, p. 86.
[28] Newsome, David, 1980, p. 86.
[29] Benson, A. C., 1907.
[30] Benson, E. F., 1932, p. 71.
[31] Purcell, William, 1957, p. 74.
[32] Watson, J. R., 1997, p. 511, n. 3.
[33] Phillips, Catherine, 1992, p. 198.
[34] Bridges, Robert, 1935, p. 52 n.
[35] Luff, Alan, ed., 2005, p. viii.
[36] Barfield, Owen, 1928, p. 165.
[37] Daniell, David, 1994, p. 344.
[38] Cosnett, Elizabeth, 1990, p. 158.
[39] Frost, David, n. d.
[40] *Church Times*, 27 October 1995, quoting the *Daily Mail*.
[41] E.g. Wren, Brian, 1989.
[42] Routley, Erik, 1982, p. 101.
[43] Pratt Green, Fred, 1982, p. xvii.
[44] Cecil, David, ed., 1940, p. xxxiii.
[45] C. S. Lewis, 1941, p. 97.
[46] Hooper, Walter, ed., 2006, p. 731.
[47] Manning, B. L., 1942, p. 109.
[48] Adey, Lionel, 1988, p. 26.
[49] Lofthouse, W. F., 1953, pp. 349, 345.

CHAPTER 5. WORDS AND MUSIC

* Webb, Jimmy, 1998, p. 70.
1. Citron, Stephen, 1996, p. 3.
2. *The Times*, 22 November 1990, reprinted in Sanders, Andrew, ed., 2007, p. 542.
3. Lewis, C. S. 1942, pp. 12, 18.
4. Chadwick, Henry, 1981, pp. 3, 4.
5. Quiller-Couch, Arthur, 1925, p. 53.
6. Routley, Erik, 1982, p. 1.
7. Murray, Iain, 1990, p. 266.
8. Thwaite, Anthony, ed., 2001; 2002, p. 50.
9. Day-Lewis, C., 1965; 1969, p. 31.
10. Wellesley, Dorothy, ed., 1940; 1964, p. 174.
11. Burnett, Archie, 2007, Vol. I., pp. 458, 501.
12. Richards, Grant, 1941, p. 394.
13. Burnett, Archie, 1997, p. 461.
14. Duncan-Jones, Katherine, 1989.
15. Routley, Erik, 1951, p. 182.
16. Watson, J. R., 1981, p. 4.
17. From 'Dear Lord and Father of mankind'.
18. From 'Light of the minds that know him'.
19. Manning, Bernard L., 1942, p. 60.
20. Rattenbury, J. E., 1941, p. 49.
21. Churchill, W. S., 1948; 2000, p. 450.
22. Milgate, Wesley, 1982; 1985, pp. 8, 9.
23. July 1986.
24. *In Tune with Heaven*, 1992, p. 51.
25. Chadwick, Henry, 1981, p. 16.
26. John 5.8; Acts 3.6.
27. Hosea 14.2; Matthew 9.9f.
28. Stott, J. R. W., 1980, p. 7.
29. Linklater, Eric, 1944, p. 60.
30. Weber, Derek, 1991, p. 154.
31. Lee, Vernon, 1923; reprint 1992, p. 46.
32. McGrath, Alister, 2013, p. 233.
33. Knowles, Elizabeth, ed., 2004, p. 843.
34. Shute, Nevil, 1954, p. 48.
35. Amis, Kingsley, ed., 1978, p. vii.
36. Thwaite, Ann, 1990, p. 249.
37. Routley, Erik, p. 32.
38. Housman, Laurence, 1937, p. 60.
39. Burnett, Archie, ed., 1997, p. 256.
40. Leaver, Robin and Litton, James H., eds, 1985, p. 223.
41. Castle, Brian, 1994, p. 106.
42. Hardy, G. H., 1940, p. 26.
43. Orton, Job, ed., 1755.
44. Battiscombe, Georgina, 1963, p. 107.
45. Marsh, Jan, 1994, p. 26.
46. Julian, John, 1907, p. 1278.
47. Alexander, Eleanor, 1913, p. 222.
48. Martin, William, 1992, p. 64.
49. Richardson, Paul A. and Sharp, Tim, 2010. p. 2.
50. Pritchard, William H., 1984; 1993, p. 257.
51. Pratt Green, Fred, 1989, p. xxi.
52. Bridges, Robert, 1935, p. 65.
53. Chadwick, Henry, ed., 1991; 1992, pp. 207, 208.
54. Begbie, Jeremy, 2008, p. 65.
55. p. xi.
56. Routley, Erik, 1960, p. 22.
57. Webster, Donald, 1992, p. 2.
58. Baker, Frank, ed., 1962, p. 117.
59. St John, Patricia, 1993, p. 99.
60. Sampson, George, 1947, p. 199.
61. Hustad, Donald, 1981, p. 243.

CHAPTER 6. CONTENT AND FORM

* Watson, J. R. 2004, p. 31.
1. Betjeman, John, 1960, p. 17.
2. Ackroyd, Peter, 1984, p. 51.
3. Stanford, Peter, 2007, p. 169.
4. Larkin, Philip, 1983, p. 69.
5. Larkin, Philip, 1983, p. 80.
6. Housman, Henry, 1896, p. 238.
7. Housman, Henry, 1896, p. 235.
8. Housman, Henry, 1896, p. 258.
9. Graham, Ysenda M., 2001; 2007, pp. 50, 51.
10. Sayers, Dorothy L., 1946, pp. 36, 39.
11. 'Souls of men, why will ye scatter', 1862.
12. Watson, Richard and Trickett, Kenneth, 1988, p. 159.
13. Reynolds, W. J., 1976, p. 109.
14. From Frances Ridley Havergal's 'Take my life, and let it be/Consecrated, Lord, to thee'.
15. Drain, Susan, 1989, p. 55.
16. Manning, Bernard L., 1942, p. 140.
17. Lofthouse, W. F., 1965, p. 132.
18. Routley, Erik, 1951, p. 106.
19. Gilbert, Thomas, 1935; revised edn 1948, p. 21.
20. Manning, Bernard L., 1942, p. 143.
21. Matthews, A. G., 1953, p. xxv.
22. Bett, Henry, 1913; 1945, p. 16.
23. Green, Peter, 1959, p. 8.
24. Dillistone, F. W., 1980, p. 121.
25. Lockhart, J. G., 1949, p. 228.
26. Lockhart, J. G., 1949, p. 290.

ENDNOTES

27 Motion, Andrew, 2006, p. 285.
28 Routley, Erik, 1966, p. 19.
29 Watts, Isaac, 1707–09, Preface.
30 Snow, C. P., 1975; 1991, p. 161.
31 Bett, Henry, 1945, p. 60.
32 Order of Holy Communion: Prayer for the Church Militant.
33 Battiscombe, Georgina, 1963, p. 111.
34 Battiscombe, Georgina, 1963, p. 111.
35 Pratt Green, Fred, 1982, p. 83.
36 Dudley-Smith, Timothy, 2003, p, 279.
37 Larkin, Philip, 2010; 2011, p. 232.
38 Hildebrandt, Franz and Beckerlegge, Oliver, 1983, p. 51.
39 Watts, Isaac, 1948, p. 36.
40 Tindall, Adrienne, 1997, p. 316.
41 Watson, J. R., 1988, p. 126.
42 Whistler, Theresa, 1993, pp. 69, 239.
43 Cecil, Lord David, 1973, p. 3.
44 Whistler, Theresa, 1993, p. 158.
45 Osborne, Charles, 1980; 1995, p. 29.
46 Brain, Russell, 1957, p. 64.
47 Francis, Robert, 1972, p. 54.
48 Day-Lewis, C., 1965, p. 149.
49 Osborne, Charles, 1980; 1995, pp. 336f.
50 Barker, Juliet, 2002, p. 185.
51 Lewis, C. S., 1954, p. 95.
52 Lewis, C. S., 1947, p. 116.
53 *Poems of Grace: Texts of The Hymnal, 1982*, 1998.
54 Eliot, T. S., 1933; 1965, p. 107 n.
55 Betjeman, John, 1995, p. 145.
56 Bett, Henry, 1932, p. 83.
57 *Report to the General Assembly*, 2001.
58 Lovelace, Austin, 1965; 1982, p. 7.
59 Lewis, C. S., 1946, p. 16.
60 Barker, Juliet, 2002, p. 168.
61 Boswell, James, 1791; 1968, Vol. II, p. 346.
62 Motion, Andrew, 1993, p. 278.
63 Clark, Kenneth, 1981, p. 22.
64 Sondheim, Stephen, 2011, p. xviii.

CHAPTER 7. MEANING AND LANGUAGE

* Hardy, Thomas, 1874; 1995, p. 20.
1 Matthews, W. R., 1969, p. 120.
2 Day-Lewis, C., 1951; Preface 1969 ed.
3 Parini, Jay, 1998, pp. 302, 219.
4 Cohen, Morton N.,1995, p. 409.
5 Holmes, Richard, (*Early Visions*) 1998, p. 141.
6 Morgan, Charles, 1944, pp. 222, 3.
7 Richardson, Joanna, 1986, p. 240.
8 Alexander, Eleanor, 1913, p. 71.
9 Julian, John, 1907, p. 668.
10 Chadwick, Owen, 1990, p. 94.
11 Housman, Henry, 1896, p. 229.
12 Dearmer, Percy, 1933, p. xx.
13 Daniell, David, 1994, p. 95.
14 Dudley-Smith, Timothy, 2003, pp. 276, 457.
15 Dudley-Smith, Timothy, 2003, pp. 118, 359.
16 Pritchard, W. H., 1984; 1993, pp. 79, 117.
17 Montague, C. E., 1931, p. 199.
18 Thwaite, Anthony, 2001; 2002, p. 106.
19 Watson, J. R., 1983, p. 144.
20 Newton Flew, R., 1953.
21 Clark, Kenneth, 1969, p. 247.
22 Willey, Basil, 1956, p. 89.
23 Browning, Robert, 'Andrea del Sarto', 1855.
24 Lewis, C. S., 1964, p. 14.
25 Lewis, C. S., 1941, pp. 100, 103.
26 Watson, J. R., 2006, p. 15.
27 Knox, R. A., 1958, pp. 38, 55, 56.
28 Dudley-Smith, Timothy, 1984, pp. 173–94.
29 Dudley-Smith, Timothy, 1981, p. 135.
30 Sencourt, Robert, 1971, p. 172.
31 James, P. D., 1989, p. 4.
32 Wesley, Charles, 1750, part II, No. IX, v. 8.
33 Bett, Henry, 1932, p. 254.
34 Dearmer, Percy, 1933, p. 4.
35 Bateson, F. W., 1968, p. 145.
36 Jones, Kathleen, 1991; 1992, p. 44.
37 Clark, Kenneth, 1977, pp. 66f.
38 De-La-Noy, Michael, 1990, p. 12.
39 Whistler, Theresa, 1993, p. 203.
40 Eliot, T. S. 1933; 1965 ed., p. 118.
41 Marsh, Jan, 1994, p. 8.
42 Calder, Jenni, 1980; 1990, p. 315.
43 Stevenson, R. L., 1910, pp. 33f.
44 Bett, Henry, 1932, pp. 29f.
45 Ferris, Paul, 1977, p. 29.
46 Meyers, Jeffrey, 1996, p. 10.
47 Conrad, Joseph, 1919; 2005, p. 195.
48 Eliot, T. S., 1957, p. 169.
49 Knox, R. A., 1958, p. 201.
50 Benham W., ed., 1884, p. 120.
51 Lewis C. S., 1954, p. 506.
52 Tennyson, Hallam, 1897, Vol. II, p. 14.
53 Graves, Robert, 1967, p. 44.
54 'Where shall my wondering soul begin?'
55 'And can it be, that I should gain'.
56 'There is a fountain fill'd with blood'.
57 'All people that on earth do dwell'.
58 Houghton, Edward, 1991, p. 29.
59 Barker, Juliet, 2002, p. 170.

60 Housman, A. E., 1922, xxxvii
61 'Trebetherick'.
62 Bradley, Ian, 1997, p. 9.
63 Matthew 6.7.
64 Hammond, Cally, 2015, p. 79.
65 Dudley-Smith, Timothy, 2003, p. 227; cf. p. 266.
66 Manning, Bernard L., 1942, pp. 21f.
67 Myers, Jack and Simms, Michael, 1989, pp. 357–60.
68 Burnett, Archie, 2007, Vol. II., p. 17.

CHAPTER 8. RHYME AND METRE

* Larkin, Philip, 1983, p. 253.
1 Thwaite, Anthony, ed., 1994, p. 521.
2 Coward, Noël, 1965; 1983, p. vii.
3 Thwaite, Anthony, ed., 2001, p. 21.
4 Latham, E. C., ed., 1966; 1967, p. 249.
5 Blixen, Karen, 1937, p. 297.
6 Hardy, G. H., 1940, p. 53.
7 Pritchard, W. H., 1989, p. 719.
8 Lewis, C. S., Hooper, Walter, ed., 2000, p. 62.
9 Lewis, C. S., Hooper, Walter, ed., 2000, p. 574.
10 Ricks, Christopher, 2002, p. 273.
11 Opie, Peter and Opie, Iona, 1951, p. 44.
12 Sondheim, Stephen, 2010, p. xxv.
13 Vallins, G. H., 1957, pp. 80f.
14 Raverat, Gwen, 1962, p. 182.
15 MacDonald, George, 1893; 1911, p. 362.
16 Dick, Kay, ed., 1972, p. 90.
17 Sondheim, Stephen, 2010, p. xxvi.
18 Betjeman, John, 1994, p. 416.
19 Richards, Grant, 1941, p. 431.
20 Batchelor, John, 2012, p. 75.
21 Webb, Jimmy, 1998, p. 61.
22 Redfield, Bessie G., 1938.
23 Barker, Juliet, 2002, p. 185.
24 Lewis, C. S., Hooper, Walter, ed., 2000, p. 193.
25 Calder, Jenni, 1980; 1990, pp. 24–5.
26 Flecker, James Elroy, 1922; 1948, p. 121.
27 Frances, Robert, 1973, p. 54.
28 Dudley-Smith, Timothy, 2003, No. 280 'Before the world's foundation'.
29 Dudley-Smith, Timothy, 2011, p. 443.
30 Day, Barry, ed., 2007, p. 432.
31 Coward, Noël, 1965; 1983, p. 268.
32 Montgomery, James, 1825; 1846, p. xxii.
33 Caplan, David, 2014, p. 36.
34 Eliot, T. S. 1933; 1965, p. 155.
35 Coleridge, S. T., 1813; 1997, p. 220.
36 Coleridge, E. H., 1912, p. 401.
37 Leech, Geoffrey N., 1969, p. 11.
38 See Milgate, Wesley, 1982; 1985, p. 9.
39 Baker, Frank, 1962, p. xliv.
40 Carpenter, Humphrey, 1981; 1983, p. 419.
41 E.g. Baughen, Michael, ed., 1982, No. 89.
42 Nash, Ogden, 1983, p. 154.
43 Stevenson, R. L., 1885.
44 Wordsworth, William and Coleridge, S. T., 1798, 1800; 2003, p. 21.
45 Sacks, Oliver, 2007, p. xi.

CHAPTER 9. CREATIVITY AND CRITICISM

* Knox, R. A., 1950, p. 14.
1 Whistler, Theresa, 1993, pp. 224, 297.
2 Latham, E. C., ed., 1966; 1967, p. 247.
3 Levi, Peter, 1993, p. 99.
4 Jones, Kathleen, 1991; 1992, p. 65.
5 Larkin, Philip; Thwaite, Anthony, ed., 2010; 2011, p. 240.
6 Quoted in Holmes, Richard (*Darker Reflections*), 1998, p. 376.
7 Housman, Henry, 1896, p. 51.
8 Ogilvy, David, 1964, p. 20.
9 Larkin, Philip; Thwaite, Anthony, ed., 2010; 2011, p. 199.
10 Martin, Robert Bernard, 1980, p. 570. cf. Tennyson, Charles, 1976, p. 21.
11 Thomas, R. S., 1977, pp. 91, 165.
12 Bridge, Anthony, 1985, p. 65.
13 Koestler, Arthur, 1964; 1969, pp. 115, 116.
14 Tennyson, Hallam, 1897, Vol. II, p. 142.
15 Tomalin, Claire, 2006, p. 108.
16 Parini, Jay, 1998, p. 182.
17 Clark, Kenneth, 1973; 1976, p. 268.
18 Dudley-Smith, Timothy, 2012, pp. 31, 62.
19 Bradley, Ian, ed., 1990, p. 21.
20 Hindmarsh, D.Bruce, 1996, p. 280.
21 Day-Lewis, C., 1965, p. 147.
22 White, Michael. 2001, p. 9.
23 Carpenter, Humphrey, 1977, p. 178.
24 Housman, A. E., 1933, p. 49.
25 Wordsworth, William, 1850, book lx, 9, 10.
26 Levi, Peter, 1999, p. 228.
27 Escott, Harry, 1962, p. 176.
28 Carpenter, Humphrey, 1983, p. 330.
29 Sisman, Adam, 2006, p. 64.
30 Housman, Laurence, 1957, p. 253.
31 Housman, Laurence, 1957, p. 102.
32 Housman, Laurence, 1957, p. 102; cf. Burnett, Archie, 1997, p. 23.

[33] Hardcastle, C. D., 1899, Vol. II, part 1, p. 15.
[34] Wodehouse, P. G., Donaldson, Frances, ed., 1990, p. 204.
[35] Milgate, Wesley, 1982; 1985, p. 216.
[36] Larkin, Philip; Thwaite, Anthony, ed., 2010; 2011, p. 37.
[37] Lewis, C. S.; Hooper, Walter, ed., 2000, p. 888.
[38] Gittings, Robert, 1968, p. 275.
[39] Murray John G.; Murray, John R. ed., 1996, p. 22.
[40] Quoted in Le Faye, Deidre, 1989; 2004, p. 245.
[41] Wodehouse, P. G.; Donaldson, Frances, ed., 1990, p. 49.
[42] Escott, Harry, 1962, p. 137.
[43] Nicolson, Harold; Nicolson, Nigel, ed., 1967, p. 447.
[44] 1906 ed., p. xxx.
[45] Ricks, Christopher, 2002, p. 179.
[46] Bett, Henry, 1913; 1945, pp. 132, 133.
[47] Routley, Erik, 1951, p. 118.
[48] Bett, Henry, 1913; 1945, p. 82.
[49] Watson, J. R., 2002, p. 342.
[50] 'Lord of all life and power' in Dudley-Smith, Timothy, 2003, p. 247.
[51] Ricks, Christopher, 2002, p. 1.
[52] Ferris, Paul, 1977; 1978, p. 7.
[53] Holmes, Richard, (*Darker Reflections*), 1998, p. 402.
[54] Sisman, Adam, 2006, p. 165.
[55] Wesley: 'O thou who camest from above'; Watts: 'Come Holy Spirit, heav'nly dove'.
[56] Raine, Craig, 2006, pp. 138, 139.
[57] Meynell, Everard, 1926, p. 126.
[58] Stott, J. R. W., 1982, p. 238.
[59] Barfield, Owen, 1928, p. 40.
[60] Lewis, C. S., 1947, pp. 88f.
[61] Lewis, C. S., 1943, p. 54.
[62] Clark, Kenneth, 1981, p. 62.
[63] Willey, Basil, 1956, p. 76.
[64] Day-Lewis, C., 1965, p. 132.
[65] Benson, A. C., 1912, p. 275.
[66] Raverat, Gwen, 1962, p. 132.
[67] Boswell, James, 1791; folio edn, Vol. I, 1968, pp. 316, 341.
[68] Gordon, Grant, ed., 2009, p. 12.
[69] Barker, Juliet, 2002, p. 22.
[70] Tindall, Adrienne, 1997, p. 248.
[71] Betjeman, John, 1954.
[72] Macaulay, Rose, 1961, p. 67.
[73] Larkin, Philip; Anthony Thwaite, ed., 2010; 2011, p. 395.
[74] Martin, Robert Bernard, 1980, pp. 407, 393.
[75] Burnett, Archie, 2007, Vol. I., p. 490.
[76] Burnett, Archie, 2007, Vol. I., pp. 503, 504.
[77] Lowther Clarke, W. K., 1960, p. 46.
[78] Bett, Henry, 1913; 1945, p. 10.
[79] Beeson, Trevor, 2002, p. 109.

CHAPTER 10. WHAT OF THE FUTURE?

[*] Lough, A. G., 1962, p. 74.
[1] Mark 13.32.
[2] Matthew 24.44.
[3] Routley, Erik, 1977; 1997, p. 120.
[4] Edwards, David, 1984, Vol. III, p. 366.
[5] Tennyson, Hallam, 1897, Vol. II, p. 401.
[6] Carpenter, S. C. 1949, p. 10.
[7] McGrath, Alister and McGrath, Joanna Collicutt, 2007, p. vii.
[8] Field, Frank, 2008.
[9] Wright, Tom, 2014, p. 23.
[10] *Eureka*, December 2009.
[11] See, e.g., Doran, Carl and Troeger, Thomas H., 1986.
[12] Routley, Erik, 1964; 1966, p. 172.
[13] Dakers, Lionel, 1977, p. 119.
[14] Kendrick, Graham, 2004.
[15] Lee, Hermione, 2013, p. 16.
[16] Waugh, Evelyn, 1959, p. 253.
[17] Morris, Colin, January 1992.
[18] Noll, Mark A, 2000, p. 19.
[19] Bettenson, Henry, ed., 1943, p. 4.
[20] Quoted in Housman, Henry, 1896, p. 196.
[21] Kidner, Derek, 1975, p. 349.
[22] Barker, Juliet, 2002, p. 50.
[23] Montgomery, James, 1825; 1846, p. viii.
[24] Davie, Donald, ed., 1981, p. xxiv.
[25] Manning, Bernard L., 1942, p. 109.
[26] Newton, John, 1779, p. vii.
[27] Sutcliffe, Peter, 1978, p. 122.
[28] Packer, J. I., 1999.
[29] Davie, Donald, 1952; 1992, p. 63.
[30] Watson, J. R., 2004, p. 127.
[31] Hustad, Donald P., 1998, p. 58.
[32] Page, Nick, 2004, p. 25.
[33] Leaver, Robin and Litton, James H., eds, 1985, p. 223.
[34] Tasker, R. V. G., 1960, p. 125.
[35] Hastings, Adrian, 1986; 1991, pp. 385, 386; and McKay, Roy, 1972, p. 35.
[36] McKellar, Hugh D., 1992, p. 47.

BIBLIOGRAPHY

Page numbers in the endnotes refer to any later edition listed below. London is the place of publication unless otherwise shown.

Ackroyd, Peter, *T. S. Eliot*, 1984.
Adey, Lionel, *Class and Idol in the English Hymn*, Vancouver, 1988.
Alexander, C. F., *Hymns for Little Children*, 1848.
Alexander, C. F., *Poems*, William Alexander, ed., 1896.
Alexander, Eleanor, *Primate Alexander*, 1913.
Alexander, William, ed., *Cecil Frances Alexander: Poems*, 1896.
Amis, Kingsley, ed., *The New Oxford Book of Light Verse*, Oxford, 1978.
Archbishops' Commission on Church Music, 1992.
Austen, Jane, *Northanger Abbey*, 1818.
Babington Smith, C.—*see* Macaulay, Rose.
Baker, Frank, ed., *Representative Verse of Charles Wesley*, 1962.
Barfield, Owen, *Poetic Diction*, 1928.
Barker, Juliet, *Wordsworth: A Life in Letters*, 2002.
Barry, F. R., *Mervyn Haigh*, 1964.
Batchelor, John, *Tennyson*, 2012.
Bateson, F. W., 'The Poetry of Emphasis', Christopher Ricks, ed., *A. E. Housman: A Collection of Critical Essays*, New Jersey, 1968.
Battiscombe, Georgina, *John Keble: A Study in Limitations*, 1963.
Baughen, Michael A., ed., *Youth Praise I*, 1966.
Baughen, Michael A., ed., *Youth Praise II*, 1969.
Baughen, Michael A., ed., *Psalm Praise*, 1973.
Baughen, Michael A., ed., *Hymns for Today's Church*, 1982; 2nd edn 1987.
Bayly, Albert, *Rejoice O People*, 1950.
BBC Songs of Praise, Oxford, 1997.
Beeson, Trevor, *The Bishops*, 2002.
Begbie, Jeremy, *Resounding Truth*, 2008.
Benham, W., ed., *Letters of William Cowper*, 1884.
Benson, A. C., *Edward White Benson: Archbishop of Canterbury*, 1899.
Benson, A. C., *Hymns and Carols*, Windsor & London, 1907.
Benson, A. C., *The Leaves of the Tree*, 1912.
Benson, E. F., *As We Were*, 1932.
Berridge, John, 'The Rev. John Berridge and his Hymn-Book', *Proceedings of the Wesley Historical Society*, Vol. II., 1918.
Betjeman, John, 'John Betjeman Replies', *The Spectator*, 8 October 1954.
Betjeman, John, *Summoned by Bells*, 1960.
Betjeman, John, *Letters*, Candida Lycett Green, ed., 1994; 2nd edn 1995.
Bett, Henry, *The Hymns of Methodism*, 1913; 3rd enlarged edn 1945.
Bett, Henry, *Some Secrets of Style*, 1932.
Bettelheim, Bruno, *The Uses of Enchantment*, New York, 1976; Harmondsworth, 1991.
Bettenson, Henry, ed., *Documents of the Christian Church*, Oxford, 1943.

Blixen, Karen, *Out of Africa*, 1937.
Boswell, James, *The Life of Samuel Johnson*, 1791; folio edn 1968.
Bradley, Ian, ed., *O Love that Wilt Not Let Me Go*, 1990.
Bradley, Ian, ed., *Abide with Me: The World of Victorian Hymns*, 1997.
Brain, Russell, *Tea with Walter de la Mare*, 1957.
Bridge, Anthony, *One Man's Advent*, 1985.
Bridges, Robert, *Yattendon Hymnal*, 1899.
Bridges, Robert, 'A Practical Discourse on some Principles of Hymn Singing'; *Collected Essays, Papers &c. of Robert Bridges*, Oxford, 1935.
Brittain, Frederick, *It's a Don's Life*, 1972.
Brooks, Cleanth, 'Alfred Edward Housman', Christopher Ricks, ed., *A. E. Housman: A Collection of Critical Essays*, Englewood Cliffs, 1968.
Browning, Martin, 'Meditation from South of the Border on First Encountering the Scottish Psalter in Use', *Bulletin of the Hymn Society of Great Britain and Ireland*, Vol. 14, No. 7, July 1995.
Browning, Robert, *Men and Women*, 1855.
Burnett, Archie, ed., *The Poems of A. E. Housman*, Oxford, 1997.
Burnett, Archie, ed., *The Letters of A. E. Housman*, Oxford, 2007.
Burton, Robert, *The Anatomy of Melancholy*, 1621.
Calder, Jenni, *RLS: A Life Study*, 1980; Glasgow, 1990.
Caplan, David, *Rhyme's Challenge: Hip Hop, Poetry and Contemporary Rhyming Culture*, New York, 2014.
Carpenter, Humphrey, *J. R. R. Tolkien: A Biography*, 1977.
Carpenter, Humphrey, *W. H. Auden*, 1981; 2nd edn 1983.
Carpenter, S. C., *Winnington Ingram*, 1949.
Carter, Sydney, *Green Print for Song*, 1963.
Castle, Brian, *Sing a New Song to the Lord*, 1994.
Catholic Hymn Book, The, compiled and edited at the London Oratory; Leominster, 1998.
Cecil, Lord David, ed., *The Oxford Book of Christian Verse*, Oxford, 1940.
Cecil, Lord David, 'Walter de la Mare'; Presidential Address to the English Association, 1973, Oxford, 1973.
Chadwick, Henry, 'Why Music in Church?', Lecture to the Church Music Society, 1981.
Chadwick, Henry, ed., *Saint Augustine: Confessions*, Oxford, 1991; 2nd edn 1992.
Chadwick, Owen, *The Spirit of the Oxford Movement*, Cambridge, 1990.
Church Hymnary Trust (ed.), *Church Hymnary 4, Full Music Edition*, 2005.
Church Society, *Anglican Hymn Book*, 1965.
Churchill, W. S., *The Gathering Storm*, London, 1948; folio edn 2000.
Citron, Stephen, *The Wordsmiths: Oscar Hammerstein 2nd and Alan J. Lerner*, 1996.
Clark, Kenneth, *Civilization: A Personal View*, 1969; 2nd edn 1972.
Clark, Kenneth, *The Romantic Rebellion: Romantic versus Classic Art*, 1973; 2nd edn 1976.
Clark, Kenneth, *The Other Half*, 1977.
Clark, Kenneth, *Moments of Vision*, 1981.
Cohen, Morton N., *Lewis Carroll: A Biography*, London & New York, 1995.
Coleridge, E. H., *The Poems of Samuel Taylor Coleridge*, Oxford, 1912.
Coleridge, S. T., *Biographia Literaria*, 1813; Nigel Leask, ed., 1997.
Common Praise: a new edition of Hymns Ancient and Modern, Norwich, 2000.
Congregational Union of England and Wales, *Congregational Praise*, 1951.
Conrad, Joseph, *Tales of Unrest*, 1898; included in *Almayer's Folly*, folio edn 2002.
Conrad, Joseph, *The Mirror of the Sea*, 1919; folio edn 2005.
Cooke, Victoria, *Understanding Songs in Renewal*, Cambridge, 2001.

Cosnett, Elizabeth, 'Language in Hymns: One Woman's Experience', *Bulletin of the Hymn Society of Great Britain and Ireland*, Vol. 12, No. 9, January 1990.
Coward, Noël, *The Lyrics of Noël Coward*, 1965; 2nd edn 1983.
Cowper, William, and Newton, John, *Olney Hymns*, 1779.
Cowper, William, *The Task: A Poem in Six Books*, 1785.
Cowper, William, *Letters of William Cowper*, W. Benham, ed., 1884.
Creighton, Louise, *The Life and Letters of Mandell Creighton*, Vol. II, 1904.
Dakers, Lionel, 'The Contemporary Scene, 1976–96', Erik Routley, ed., *A Short History of English Church Music*, 1977; Carol Stream, 1997.
Daniell, David, *William Tyndale: A Biography*, New Haven and London, 1994.
Davie, Donald, *The Eighteenth-Century Hymn in England*, Cambridge, 1933.
Davie, Donald, ed., *The New Oxford Book of Christian Verse*, Oxford, 1981.
Davie, Donald, *Purity of Diction in English Verse*, 1952; 2nd edn 1992.
Day, Barry, ed., *The Letters of Noël Coward*, New York, 2007.
Day, Thomas, *Why Catholics Can't Sing: The Culture of Catholicism and the Triumph of Bad Taste*, New York, 1990.
Day-Lewis, C., *Selected Poems*, Harmondsworth, 1951; 3rd edn 1969.
Day-Lewis, C., *The Lyric Impulse*, 1965.
Dearmer, Percy, ed., *The English Hymnal*, 1906.
Dearmer, Percy, *Songs of Praise Discussed*, Oxford, 1933.
Dearmer, Percy, Shaw, Martin, and Vaughan Williams, Ralph, eds, *Songs of Praise*, 1925.
De la Mare, Walter, 'The Listeners', 1912.
De-la-Noy, Michael, *Michael Ramsey: A Portrait*, 1990.
Dick, Kay, ed., *Writers at Work: Interviews from the* Paris Review, Harmondsworth, 1972.
Dillistone, F. W., *Into all the World: A Biography of Max Warren*, 1980.
Doran, Carol and Troeger, Thomas H., *New Hymns for the Lectionary*, New York, 1986.
Drain, Susan, *The Anglican Church in Nineteenth-Century Britain: Hymns Ancient and Modern*, Lampeter, 1989.
Dryden, John, *Alexander's Feast*, 1697.
Dudley-Smith, Timothy, *A Collection of Hymns, 1961–1981*, Norwich, 1981.
Dudley-Smith, Timothy, *Lift Every Heart*, London and Carol Stream, 1984.
Dudley-Smith, Timothy, *A House of Praise*, Oxford and Carol Stream, 2003.
Dudley-Smith, Timothy, 'What can a Hymn Writer Learn from a Lyricist?', *Bulletin of the Hymn Society of Great Britain and Ireland*, Vol. 19, No. 11, July 2011.
Dudley-Smith, Timothy, *Beyond our Dreaming*, Oxford and Carol Stream, 2012.
Duncan-Jones, Katherine, Introduction to *Shakespeare's Sonnets*, folio edn 1989.
Dykes Bowers, John, ed., *100 Hymns for Today. A Supplement to Hymns Ancient & Modern*, 1969.
Edwards, David L., *Christian England*, 1981; 2nd edn 1983; 3rd edn 1984.
Eliot, T. S., *The Use of Poetry and the Use of Criticism*, 1933; 2nd edn 1965.
Eliot, T. S., *On Poetry and Poets*, 1957.
Elvy, Peter, *The Future of Christian Broadcasting in Europe*, Great Wakering, 1991.
English Hymnal Company, *English Praise. A Supplement to the English Hymnal*, 1975.
Escott, Harry, ed., *Isaac Watts's Guide to Prayer, Abridged*, 1948.
Escott, Harry, ed., *Isaac Watts, Hymnographer: A Study of the Beginnings, Development, and Philosophy of the English Hymn*, 1962.
Ferris, Paul, *Dylan Thomas*, 1977; 2nd edn 1978.
Field, Frank, 'Back Page Interview', *Church Times*, 21 November 2008.
Flecker, James Elroy, *Hassan: A Play in Five Acts*, 1922; Harmondsworth, 1948.
Fletcher, Andrew, *Poetical Works*, 1732.
Fletcher, Winston, *Powers of Persuasion: The Inside Story of British Advertising*, Oxford, 2008.

Forbes, Wesley L., ed., *Handbook to the Baptist Hymnal*, Nashville, 1992.
Frances, Robert, *Robert Frost: A Time to Talk*, 1972.
Frost, David, 'The Language of the Liturgy', unpublished paper for the Liturgical Commission, n.d.
Gilbert, Thomas, *William Cowper and the Eighteenth Century*, 1935; revised edn 1948.
Gilbert, W. S., *The Bab Ballads*, 1869.
Gittings, Robert, *John Keats*, 1968.
Gordon, Grant, ed., *Wise Counsel: John Newton's Letters to John Ryland, Jr*, Edinburgh, 2009.
Graham, Ysenda Maxtone, *The Real Mrs Miniver*, 2001; 2nd edn 2007.
Graves, Robert, *Poetic Craft and Principle*, 1967.
Green, Fred Pratt—*see* Pratt Green, Fred.
Green, Peter, *Kenneth Grahame: A Biography*, 1959.
Hammond, Cally, *The Sound of the Liturgy*, 2015.
Hardcastle, C. D., 'Hymn 143 (Wesleyan Hymn Book) and its Would-be Improvers', *Proceedings of the Wesley Historical Society*, Vol. II, part I, 1899, p. 15.
Hardy, G. H., *A Mathematician's Apology*, Cambridge, 1940.
Hardy, Thomas, *Afternoon Services at Melstock*, 1850.
Hardy, Thomas, *Far from the Madding Crowd*, 1874; folio edn 1995.
Hardy, Thomas, *The Trumpet Major*, 1880; folio edn 1990.
Harvey, Paul, *The Oxford Companion to English Literature*, Oxford, 1932.
Hastings, Adrian, *A History of English Christianity, 1920–1990*, Philadelphia and London, 1986; 2nd edn 1991.
Heaton, Joseph, *Two Lectures on the Wesleyan Hymn-book*, 1862.
Herbert, George, *The Temple*, 1633.
Hildebrandt, Franz and Beckerlegge, Oliver, eds, *The Works of John Wesley*, Vol. 7, Oxford, 1983.
Hindmarsh, D. Bruce, *John Newton and the English Evangelical Tradition*, Cambridge UK and Grand Rapids, 1996.
Holmes, Richard, *Coleridge: Early Visions*, 1989; 2nd edn 1998.
Holmes, Richard: *Coleridge: Darker Reflections*, 1998.
Hooper, Walter, ed., *C. S. Lewis: Collected Letters*—*see* Lewis, C. S.
Hopkins, Hugh A. Evan, *Charles Simeon: Preacher Extraordinary*, Bramcote, 1979.
Horne, C. Sylvester, *A Popular History of the Free Churches*, 1903.
Horrobin, Peter and Leavers, Greg, eds, *Mission Praise*, 1981.
Horrobin, Peter and Leavers, Greg, eds, *Junior Praise 1*, 1990.
Houghton, Edward, 'Enjambment in John Wesley's Verse', *Bulletin of the Hymn Society of Great Britain and Ireland*, Vol. 13, No. 2, April 1991.
Housman, A. E., *A Shropshire Lad*, 1896.
Housman, A. E., 'Epitaph on an Army of Mercenaries', *Last Poems*, No. XXXVII, 1922.
Housman, A. E., *The Name and Nature of Poetry*, Cambridge, 1933.
Housman, Henry, *John Ellerton: Being a Collection of his Writings on Hymnology together with a Sketch of his Life and Works*, 1896.
Housman, Laurence, *A. E. H.: Some Poems, Some Letters and a Personal Memoir*, 1957.
Howarth, T. E. B., *Cambridge Between Two Wars*, 1978.
Humphries, C. F.—*see* Alexander, C. F.
Hustad, Donald, *Jubilate! Church Music in the Evangelical Tradition*, Carol Stream, 1981.
Hustad, Donald, *True Worship*, Wheaton, 1998.
In Tune with Heaven: Report of the Archbishops' Commission on Church Music, 1992.
James, P. D., *Bad Language in Church*, 1989.
Jenkyn, Richard, 'All Together Now', *The London Review of Books*, 11 December 1997.
Jones, Kathleen, *Learning Not to be First*, 1991; Oxford, 1992.

Julian, John, ed., *A Dictionary of Hymnology*, 1907.
Kaan, Fred, *Pilgrim Praise: Hymns*, 1972.
Keble, John, *The Christian Year*, 1827.
Keble, John, *The Psalter in English Verse*, 1839.
Kendrick, Graham, 'An Interview with Leah Perona-Wright', *Church Music Quarterly*, Spring 2004.
Keswick Convention, *Keswick Praise*, 1975.
Kidner, F. D. and committee, eds, *Christian Praise*, 1957.
Kidner, F. D., *Psalms 1–72*, 1973.
Kidner, F. D., *Psalms 73–150*, 1975.
Knowles, Elizabeth, ed., *The Oxford Dictionary of Quotations*, 6th edn, Oxford, 2004.
Knox, R. A. *A Spiritual Aeneid*, 1918; 2nd edn 1950.
Knox, R. A., *Literary Distractions*, 1958.
Koestler, Arthur, *The Act of Creation*, 1964; 2nd edn 1969.
Larkin, Philip, *High Windows*, 1974.
Larkin, Philip, *Required Writing*, 1983.
Larkin, Philip, *Further Requirements*, Anthony Thwaite, ed., 2001; revised edn 2002.
Larkin, Philip, *Letters to Monica*, Anthony Thwaite, ed., 2010; 2nd edn 2011.
Latham, E. C. ed., *Interviews with Robert Frost*, New York, 1966; London, 1967.
Le Faye, Deirdre, *Jane Austen: A Family Record*, Cambridge, 2004.
Leach, John, *Hymns and Spiritual Songs*, Nottingham, 1995.
Leaver, Robin, 'A Decade of Hymns: Reflections on the Tenth Anniversary of the Anglican Hymn Book', *Churchman*, April/June, 1975.
Leaver, Robin A. and Litton, James H., eds, *Duty and Delight: Routley Remembered*, Carol Stream and Norwich, UK, 1985.
Leckebusch, Martin E., *The Psalms*, Stowmarket, 2006.
Lee, Hermione, *Penelope Fitzgerald: A Life*, 2013.
Lee, Vernon, *The Handling of Words and Other Studies in Literary Psychology*, 1923; 2nd edn 1992.
Leech, Geoffrey N., *A Linguistic Guide to English Poetry*, 1969.
Levi, Peter, *Tennyson*, 1993.
Levi, Peter, *Virgil: His Life and Times*, 1999.
Lewis C. S., 'Review of *The Oxford Book of Christian Verse*', *The Review of English Studies*, Vol. 17, No. 65, January 1941.
Lewis, C. S., *A Preface to Paradise Lost*, Oxford, 1942.
Lewis, C. S., *The Screwtape Letters*, 1942.
Lewis, C. S., *Christian Behaviour*, 1943.
Lewis, C. S., *George MacDonald: An Anthology*, 1946.
Lewis, C. S., *Miracles*, 1947.
Lewis, C. S., 'On Church Music', *English Church Music*, XIX, No. 2, April 1949.
Lewis, C. S., *English Literature in the Sixteenth Century excluding Drama*, Oxford, 1954.
Lewis, C. S., *Letters to Malcolm: Chiefly on Prayer*, 1964.
Lewis, C. S., *Of This and Other Worlds*, Walter Hooper, ed., 1982.
Lewis, C. S., *Collected Letters*, Walter Hooper, ed., 2000; 2nd edn 2004; 3rd edn 2006.
Lewis, Warren, *Brothers and Friends*, Clyde Kilby and Marjorie Mead, eds, San Francisco, 1982.
Linklater, Eric, *The White Ship and Rabelais Replies*, 1944.
Lockhart, J. G., *Cosmo Gordon Lang*, 1949.
Lofthouse, W. F., 'What Makes a Good Hymn?', *The Congregational Quarterly*, Vol. XXXI, No. 4, October 1953.

Lofthouse, W. F., 'Charles Wesley', Rupert Davies and Gordon Rupp, eds, *A History of the Methodist Church in Great Britain*, Vol. 1, 1965.
Lough, A. G., *The Influence of John Mason Neale*, 1962.
Lovelace, Austin, *The Anatomy of Hymnody*, Chicago, 1965; 2nd edn 1982.
Lowther Clark, W. K., *A Hundred Years of Hymns Ancient & Modern*, 1960.
Lucarini, Dan, *Why I Left the Contemporary Music Movement*, Darlington, 2002.
Luff, Alan, ed., *Strengthen for Service: 100 Years of the English Hymnal, 1906–2006*, Norwich, 2005.
Lycett Green, Candida, ed., *John Betjeman: Letters—see* Betjeman, John.
Macaulay, Rose, *Letters to a Friend, 1950–52*, Constance Babington Smith, ed., 1961.
MacDonald, George, *Poetical Works*, Vol. II, 1893; 2nd edn 1911.
Manning, Bernard L., *Essays in Orthodox Dissent*, 1939.
Manning, Bernard L., *The Hymns of Wesley and Watts: Five Informal Papers*, 1942.
Marsh, J. B. T., *The Story of the Jubilee Singers, including their Songs*, 1898.
Marsh, Jan, *Christina Rossetti: A Literary Biography*, 1994.
Martin, Robert Bernard, *Tennyson: The Unquiet Heart*, New York, Oxford, and London, 1980.
Martin, William, *The Billy Graham Story: A Prophet with Honour*, 1992.
Matthew, D., ed., *The Westminster Hymnal: New and Revised Edition Authorized by the Hierarchy of England and Wales for Use in All Churches and Oratories*, 1940.
Matthews, A. G., 'General Introduction', in K. L. Parry, ed., *Companion to Congregational Praise*, 1953.
Matthews, W. R., *Memories and Meanings*, 1969.
Mayhew, Kevin, *20th Century Folk Hymnal, Vols 1–4*, 1974–79.
McGrath, Alister, *C. S. Lewis: A Life*, 2013.
McGrath, Alister and McGrath, Joanna Collicutt, *The Dawkins Delusion*, 2007.
McKay, Roy, *John Leonard Wilson: Confessor of the Faith*, 1972.
McKellar, Hugh D., 'In my Memory Locked: or Change and Decay', *The Hymn [The journal of the Hymn Society in the United States and Canada]*, Vol. 45, No. 1, January 1992, p. 47.
The Methodist Church, *Singing the Faith*, 2011.
Meyers, Jeffrey, *Robert Frost: A Biography*, Boston, 1996.
Meynell, Everard, *The Life of Francis Thompson*, 1926.
Milgate, Wesley, *Songs of the People of God*, London and Sydney, 1982; revised edn 1985.
Milton, John, *Areopagitica*, 1644.
Milton, John, *Il Penseroso*, 1645.
Monk, Wiliam Henry, ed., *Hymns Ancient and Modern*, 1868, 1889.
Montague, C. E., *A Writer's Notes on his Trade*, 1930; 2nd edn 1931.
Montgomery, James, *The Christian Psalmist; or, Hymns Selected and Original, with an Introductory Essay*, Glasgow, 1825; 9th edn 1846.
Moore, Henry, *The Life of the Rev. John Wesley and the Rev. Charles Wesley*, New York, 1825.
Morgan, Charles, *The House of Macmillan (1843–1943)*, 1944.
Morris, Colin, 'Songs of Praise Anniversary', *Bulletin of the Hymn Society in Great Britain and Ireland*, Vol. 13, No. 5, January 1992.
Motion, Andrew, *Philip Larkin: A Writer's Life*, 1993.
Motion, Andrew, *In the Blood: A Memoir of my Childhood*, 2006.
Murray, Ian, *D. Martyn Lloyd-Jones: The Fight of Faith, 1939–1981*, Edinburgh, 1990.
Murray, John G. *A Gentleman Publisher's Commonplace Book*, John R. Murray, ed., 1996.
Myers, Jack and Simms, Michael, *The Longman Dictionary of Poetic Terms*, London and New York, 1989.
Nash, Ogden, *I Wouldn't Have Missed It*, 1983.
Newsome, David, *On the Edge of Paradise*, 1980.

Newsome, David, *The Convert Cardinals*, 1993.
Newton, John, *Letters*—*see* Gordon, Grant.
Newton, John, 'Preface', John Newton and William Cowper, *Olney Hymns*, 1779.
Newton Flew, R., *The Hymns of Charles Wesley: A Study of their Structure*, 1953.
Nicolson, Harold, *Diaries and Letters, 1939–1945*, Nigel Nicolson, ed., 1967.
Noll, Mark A., 'Evangelicalism at its Best', Mark A. Noll and Ronald F. Thiemann, eds, *Where shall my Wondering Soul Begin?*, Grand Rapids, 2000.
Ogilvy, David, *Confessions of an Advertising Man*, 1964.
Opie, Iona and Opie, Peter, eds, *The Oxford Dictionary of Nursery Rhymes*, Oxford, 1951.
Orton, Job, *Hymns Founded on Various Texts in the Holy Scriptures*, Philip Doddridge, ed., Salop, 1755.
Osborne, Charles, *W. H. Auden: The Life of a Poet*, 1980; 2nd edn 1995.
Oxford Dictionary of National Biography, Oxford, 2013.
Oxford Dictionary of Modern Quotations, Tony Augarde, ed., Oxford, 1991.
Packer, J. I., 'Living Truth for a Dying World', *Articulate*, Vol. 2, 1999.
Page, Nick, *And Now Let's Move into a Time of Nonsense: Why Worship Songs are Failing the Church*, Milton Keynes, 2004.
Paget, Violet—see Lee, Vernon (her pen name).
Parini, Jay, *Robert Frost: A Life*, 1998.
Parry, K. L., ed., *Companion to Congregational Praise*, 1953.
Patrick, Millar, *Four Centuries of Scottish Psalmody*, Oxford, 1949.
Peacock, David, *Lets Praise: The Worship Songbook for a New Generation*, 1988.
Peacock, David and Tredinnick, Noël, eds, *Carol Praise*, 2006.
Phillips, Catherine, *Robert Bridges: A Biography*, Oxford, 1992.
Poe, Edgar Allan, 'The Raven', 1845.
Poems of Grace; Texts of The Hymnal, 1982, New York, 1998.
Praise!, 2000.
Pratt Green, Fred, *The Hymns and Ballads of Fred Pratt Green*, Carol Stream and London, 1982.
Pratt Green, Fred, *Later Hymns and Ballads and Fifty Poems*, Carol Stream and London, 1989.
Preston, David, ed., *The Book of Praises*, Liverpool, 1986.
Pritchard, William H., 'Larkin's Presence', D. Salwark, ed., *Philip Larkin: The Man and his Work*, Basingstoke, 1989.
Pritchard, William H., *Frost: A Literary Life Reconsidered*, Oxford, 1984; 2nd edn, Amherst, 1993.
Prothero, R. E., *The Psalms in Human Life*, 1903.
Psalms and Hymns Trust, *Praise for Today*, 1974.
Psalms and Hymns Trust, *Baptist Praise and Worship*, 1991.
Purcell, William, *Onward, Christian Soldier: A Life of Sabine Baring-Gould*, 1957.
Quiller-Couch, Arthur, *On the Art of Writing*, Cambridge, 1925.
Quiller-Couch, Arthur, ed., *The Oxford Book of English Verse, 1250–1918*, 1963.
Raine, Craig, *T. S. Eliot*, Oxford, 2006.
Rattenbury, J. E., *The Evangelical Doctrines of Charles Wesley's Hymns*, 1941.
Raverat, Gwen, *Period Piece: A Cambridge Childhood*, 1962.
Redfield, Bessie G., *Aid to Rhyme*, New York, 1938.
Report of the Archbishops' Commission on Church Music: In Tune with Heaven, 1992.
Report to the General Assembly of the Church of Scotland, Edinburgh, 2001.
Reynolds, William J., *Companion to Baptist Hymnal*, Nashville, Tennessee, 1976.
Reynolds, William J., 'Baptist Hymnody in America', Wesley L. Forbis, ed., *Handbook to the Baptist Hymnal*, Nashville, 1992.
Richards, Grant, *Housman, 1897–1936*, Oxford, 1941.
Richardson, Joanna, *The Brownings*, 1988; folio edn 1988.

Richardson, Paul A. and Sharp, Tim, *Jubilate, Amen!*, New York, 2010.
Ricks, Christopher, *Allusion to the Poets*, Oxford, 2002.
Rivers, Isabel and Wykes, David L., eds, *Dissenting Praise*, Oxford, 2011.
Robertson, Charles, ed., *Singing the Faith*, Norwich, 1990.
Routley, Erik, *I'll Praise my Maker*, 1951.
Routley, Erik, *Hymns and Human Life*, 1952.
Routley, Erik, 'What Remains for the Moder Hymn-Writer to Do?', *Congregational Quarterly*, October 1954.
Routley, Erik, *Music, Sacred and Profane*, 1960.
Routley, Erik, *Hymns Today and Tomorrow*, Nashville, 1966.
Routley, Erik, *A Short History of English Church Music*, 1977; Carol Stream, 1997.
Routley, Erik, *Christian Hymns Observed*, Princeton, 1982.
Royal School of Church Music and Hymns Ancient & Modern, *Sing Praise*, Norwich, 2010.
Ruffer, Tim, Harrison, Anne, Barnard, John, and Giles, Gordon (eds), *Ancient and Modern Full Music Edition: Hymns and Songs for Refreshing Worship*, 2013.
Sacks, Oliver, *Musicophilia: Tales of Music and the Brain*, 2007.
Sampson, George, *Seven Essays*, Cambridge, 1947.
Sanders, Andrew, ed., *Great Victorian Lives*, 2007.
Sayers, Dorothy L., *The Man Born to be King*, 1946.
Scholes, Percy A. and Ward, John Owen, eds, *The Oxford Companion to Music*, 10th edn, Oxford, 1970.
Scripture Union, *Jesus Praise*, 1981.
Scruton, Roger, *The Aesthetics of Music*, Oxford, 1997.
Sencourt, Robert, *T. S. Eliot: A Memoir*, 1971.
Sharpe, Eric, '1970–1980: The Explosive Years for Hymnody', *Bulletin of the Hymn Society of Great Britain and Ireland*, Vol. 10, No. 1, January 1982.
Shelley, P. B., *A Defence of Poetry*, 1821; 2nd edn 1840.
Shute, Nevil, *Slide Rule*, 1954.
Sidney, Sir Philip, *A Defence of Poetry*, 1595.
Simeon, Charles, *Horae Homileticae*, 1832.
Sisman, Adam, *The Friendship: Wordsworth and Coleridge*, 2006.
Smyth, Charles, *Simeon and Church Order*, Cambridge, 1940.
Snow, C. P., *Trollope: An Illustrated Biography*, London, 1975; New York, 1991.
Sondheim, Stephen, *Finishing the Hat: Collected Lyrics (1954–1981)*, New York and London, 2010.
Sondheim, Stephen, *Look, I Made a Hat: Collected Lyrics (1981–2011)*, New York, 2011.
Songs of Fellowship, Eastbourne, 1991.
St John, Patricia, *Patricia St John Tells her Own Story*, Carlisle, 1993.
Stanford, Peter, *C. Day-Lewis: A Life*, 2007.
Stevenson, R. L., *A Child's Garden of Verses*, 1885.
Stevenson, R. L., *Essays in the Art of Writing*, 1910.
Stott, J. R. W., *The Canticles and Selected Psalms*, 1966.
Stott, J. R. W., *The Whole Christian*, Lee Moy Ng, ed., 1980.
Stott, J. R. W., *I Believe in Preaching*, 1982.
Struther, Jan, *Mrs Miniver*, 1940.
Swinburne, Algernon Charles, 'A Forsaken Garden', 1876.
Sutcliffe, Peter, *The Oxford University Press: An Informal History*, Oxford, 1978.
Tasker, R. V. G., *The Gospel according to St John*, 1960.
Temple, William, *Readings in St John's Gospel*, 1949.
Tennyson, Alfred Lord, *Poems*, 1833.

Tennyson, Alfred Lord, 'The Princess', 1847.
Tennyson, Alfred Lord, 'The Charge of the Light Brigade', 1856.
Tennyson, Alfred Lord, *The Promise of May*, 1882.
Tennyson, Alfred Lord, 'Crossing the Bar', 1889.
Tennyson, Charles, *Farringford: The Home of Alfred Lord Tennyson*, Lincoln, 1976.
Tennyson, Hallam, *Alfred Lord Tennyson: A Memoir*, Vols I & II, 1897.
Thomas, R. S., *Autobiographies*, 1977.
Thwaite, Ann, *A. A. Milne*, 1990.
Thwaite, Anthony, ed., *Selected Letters of Philip Larkin, 1940–1985*, 1994.
Thwaite, Anthony, ed. Philip Larkin, *Further Requirements*, 2001; enlarged edn 2002.
Thwaite Anthony, ed. Philip Larkin, *Letters to Monica*, 2010; 2nd edn 2011.
Tindall, Adrienne, *Encounter with Erik Routley*, Vernon Hills, 1997.
Tomalin, Claire, *Thomas Hardy*, 2006.
Tozer, A. W., *Born after Midnight*, Camp Hill, 1959.
United Reformed Church, *Companion to Rejoice and Sing*, 1999.
Vallins, G. H., *The Wesleys and the English Language*, 1957.
Wallace, Valerie, *Mrs Alexander, 1818–1875*, Dublin, 1995.
Ward, Pete, *Selling Worship: How What We Sing Changed the Church*, Bletchley, 2005.
Watson, J. R., *The Victorian Hymn*, Durham 1981.
Watson, J. R., 'The Day Thou Gavest', *Bulletin of the Hymn Society of Great Britain and Ireland*, Vol. 10, No. 6, September 1983.
Watson, J. R., 'The Alphas and Omegas of Hymn Writing', *Bulletin of the Hymn Society of Great Britain and Ireland*, Vol. 15, No. 6, April 1988.
Watson, J. R., *The English Hymn: A Critical and Historical Study*, Oxford, 1997.
Watson, J. R., *An Annotated Anthology of Hymns*, Oxford, 2002.
Watson, J. R., 'Hymns and Literature; Form and Interpretation', *Bulletin of the Hymn Society of Great Britain and Ireland*, Vol. 17, No. 5, January 2004.
Watson, J. R., 'Ancient or Modern, *Ancient and Modern*: The Victorian Hymn in the Nineteenth Century', *The Yearbook of English Studies*, Vol. 36, 2006.
Watson, J. R. and Hornby, Emma (eds), *The Canterbury Dictionary of Hymnology*, at: https://hymnology.hymnsam.co.uk, 2013.
Watson, Richard and Trickett, Kenneth, *Companion to Hymns & Psalms*, Peterborough, 1988.
Watts, Isaac, *Hymns and Spiritual Songs*, 1707–1709.
Watts, Isaac, *The Psalms of David Imitated in the Language of the New Testament, and Apply'd to the Christian State and Worship*, 1772.
Watts, Isaac, *A Guide to Prayer*, abridged and edited by Harry Escott, 1948.
Waugh, Evelyn, *Ronald Knox*, 1959.
Webb, Jimmy, *Tunesmiths: Inside the Art of Songwriting*, New York, 1998.
Weber, Derek, 'Making Graven Images', Peter Elvy, ed., *Opportunities and Limitations in Religious Broadcasting*, Edinburgh, 1991.
Webster, Donald, *The Hymn Explosion and its Aftermath*, Croydon, 1992.
Wellesley, Dorothy, ed., *Letters on Poetry from W. B. Yeats to Dorothy Wellesley*, 1940; 2nd edn 1964.
Wesley, Charles, *Hymns on God's Everlasting Love; To Which is Added the Cry of a Reprobate and the Horrible Decree*, Bristol, 1741.
Wesley, Charles, *Hymns on the Occasion of his being Prosecuted in Ireland as a Vagabond*, 1749.
Wesley, Charles, *Hymns Occasioned by the Earthquake, March 8, 1750*, part II, 1750.
Wesley, Charles, *Short Hymns on Select Passages of the Holy Scriptures*, 1762.
Wesley, Charles, *Preparation for Death, in Several Hymns*, 1772.
Wesley, John, ed., *Select Hymns with Tunes Annext*, 1761.

Wesley, John, ed., *A Collection of Hymns for the Use of the People called Methodists*, 1780.
Whistler, Theresa, *The Imagination of the Heart*, 1993.
White, Michael, *Tolkien: A Biography*, 2001.
Willey, Basil, *More Nineteenth-Century Studies*, 1956.
Williams, Rowan, Foreword, Alan Luff, ed., *Strengthen for Service: 100 Years of the English Hymnal, 1906–2006*, Norwich, 2005.
Wilson, A. N., *Betjeman: A Life*, London and New York, 2006.
Wilson-Dickson, Andrew, *The Story of Christian Music*, Oxford, 1992.
Wodehouse, P. G., *Yours, Plum: The Letters of P. G. Wodehouse*, Frances Donaldson, ed., 1990.
Wootton, Janet, ed., *This is our Song: Women's Hymn-Writing*, 2010.
Wordsworth, William, *The Prelude*, 1850.
Wordsworth, William and Coleridge, S. T., *Lyrical Ballads and Other Poems*, 1798; 2nd edn 1800; 3rd edn 2003.
Wren, Brian, *What Language Shall I Borrow?*, 1989.
Wright, Tom, *Finding God in the Psalms*, 2014.
Wyndham Lewis, D. B. and Lee, Charles, *The Stuffed Owl: An Anthology of Bad Verse*, 1930; enlarged edn 1963.

ACKNOWLEDGEMENTS FROM EARLIER WRITING

Grateful acknowledgement is made for permission to use material by the author, previously published by way of forewords, interviews, talks, articles and the like, from among the following. Unless shown otherwise, the place of publication is London.

Books

Lift Every Heart, Collins; Carol Stream: Hope Publishing Company, 1984.
A Flame of Love, SPCK, 1987.
Praying with the English Hymn Writers, SPCK, 1989.
Songs of Deliverance, Hodder & Stoughton; Carol Stream: Hope Publishing Company, 1988.
A Voice of Singing, Hodder & Stoughton; Carol Stream: Hope Publishing Company, 1993.
Great is the Glory, Carol Stream: Hope Publishing Company, 1997.
A House of Praise: Collected Hymns 1961–2001, Oxford: Oxford University Press; Carol Stream: Hope Publishing Company, 2003.
A Door for the Word, Oxford: Oxford University Press; Carol Stream: Hope Publishing Company, 2006.
Praise to the Name, Oxford: Oxford University Press; Carol Stream: Hope Publishing Company, 2009.
Beyond our Dreaming, Oxford: Oxford University Press; Carol Stream: Hope Publishing Company, 2012.
A House of Praise, part two: Collected Hymns 2002–2013, Oxford: Oxford University Press; Carol Stream: Hope Publishing Company, 2015.

Articles, Papers, Interviews, etc.

'Interview with Paul Westermeyer', *The Hymn*, journal of the Hymn Society in the United States and Canada, January 1985.
'What Makes a Good Hymn Text?', *The Hymn*, January 1985; republished with minor changes in the *Bulletin of the Hymn Society of Great Britain and Ireland*, May 1985.
'Charles Wesley; Hymn Writer for Today', *The Hymn*, October 1988; reprinted in *Christian History,* August 1991; *The John Milton Magazine*, September 1993.
'The Hymn Maker: Interview with David Waite', *Worship Together*, November/December 1996.
'The Poet as Hymn Writer', Leland Ryken, ed., *The Christian Imagination*, Colorado Springs, 2002; adapted from 'Hymns and Poetry—A Personal Reflection', *Lift Every Heart*, Collins; Carol Stream: Hope Publishing Company, 1984.
'Putting Words into People's Mouths: Interview with Anne Harrison', *Church Music Quarterly*, September 2006.
'Snakes and Ladders: A Hymn Writer's Reflections', Occasional Paper of the Hymn Society of Great Britain and Ireland, third series, No.1, January 2009.
'Hymns and Songs in Christian Worship: Past, Present and Future', lecture in Coventry Cathedral, 28 March 2009, under the auspices of the Pratt Green Trust to mark their 25th anniversary. Published in the *Bulletin of the Hymn Society of Great Britain and Ireland*, January 2010.
'A Ministry for the Word: Interview with Jeff Devine', *The Hymn*, Summer 2010.

'What can a Hymn Writer Learn from a Lyricist?', *Bulletin of the Hymn Society of Great Britain and Ireland*, July 2011.

'A Mirror to the Soul: Interview with Andrew Reid', *Church Music Quarterly*, March 2014.

'A Mirror to the Soul: Interview with Alan Smith', *Music and Liturgy*, June 2014.

'Faith, Hymns and Poetry', *Occasional Paper of the Hymn Society of Great Britain and Ireland, third series*, No. 8, July 2016.

INDEX

Abelard, Peter 11
Ackroyd, Peter 70
Addison, Joseph 28, 120, 131, 142
Adey, Lionel 51–2
Alexander, Cecil F. 2, 15, 63, 78, 82, 86, 94
Alexander, William 86
Alliteration 24, 50, 62, 96–8, 114
Allusion 58, 61, 74–5, 86–7, 130
Alternative Service Book, 1980 11
Ambrose, St 11
Amis, Kingsley 61
Amos, Book of 6, 65
Anstruther, Joyce (Jan Struther) 71
Appleford, Patrick 18
Archaisms 13, 47–8, 72
Arnold, Matthew 82
Assonance 97–8
Auden, W. H. xvii, 79, 80, 116, 118, 126, 128
Augustine, St 1, 2, 6, 11, 64–5, 147
Austen, Jane 21, 128

Bach, J. S. 118, 146
Bagehot, Walter 85
Baker, Frank xv, 118
Baker, Henry 28, 128
Barfield, Owen 47, 132
Baring-Gould, Sabine 45, 49, 125
Barnard, John 19
Battiscombe, Georgina 63
Baughen, Michael xviii, 18–19, 64
Baxter, Richard 5
Bayly, Arthur 18, 142
Beaumarchais, Pierre 90
Beaumont, Geoffrey 18
Bede, St 11
Beethoven, Ludwig van 124
Begbie, Jeremy 65
Bell, John 19, 143
Belloc, Hilaire 96
Benson, Arthur C. 43–4, 124, 133
Benson, Edward White 37, 42–3
Berlin, Irving 114
Bernard of Cluny 11
Berridge, John 20–1
Betjeman, John xiv, 5, 42, 69–70, 79, 82, 100, 111, 135
Bett, Henry xiv, 74, 76, 82, 93, 95, 129, 136–7
Bettelheim, Bruno 11
Bible
 songs in 21–2
 updated versions 12
biblical imagery 50, 73–5, 94, 133
Blake, William 77
Blixen, Karen 108, 145

Book of Common Prayer xvii, 7, 12, 27, 76, 77, 91
Borrowings 15, 20, 73, 129–32, 131
Boyce-Tillman, June 19
Bradley, Ian 41, 100–1, 125
Brady, Nicholas 29, 142
Bridges, Robert 6, 12–13, 46, 64, 91, 112, 127–8, 146
Brontë, Charlotte 128
Brooks, Phillips 112
Brown, Rosalind 19
Browning, Elizabeth Barrett 136
'Browning, Martin' 30
Browning, Robert 65, 86, 134
Bunyan, John 11, 131
Burbridge, Paul 59
Burton, Robert 132
Butler, H. Montagu xvi
Byrom, John 101–2
Byron, Lord George Gordon 74–5

Caird, George 19
Calvin, John 26
Carey, George 136
Carroll, Lewis 85
Carter, Sydney 18, 142
Castle, Brian 17, 62
Caswall, Edward 17, 82
Cecil, Lord David 51, 79
celebration: and singing 25, 142, 145
Chadwick, Henry xviii, 56, 59, 65, 86, 123
Chadwick, Owen 40, 86
charismatic worship 32–3
Chesterton, G. K. 38
chiasmus 103
Christmas hymns xv
Church Light Music Group 18
Churchill, Winston 58
Clark, Kenneth 83, 90–1, 94, 133
Clarkson, Margaret 18, 19, 48
Clephane, Elizabeth 75
Coggan, Donald 13, 44, 77
Coleridge, Hartley 117
Coleridge, Samuel Taylor 85–6, 116–17, 123, 131
comic verse 61
common metre 117
Common Worship 89
Conrad, Joseph xiv, 96
Constable, John 125
content: and form 69–83
controversy
 lack of 76–7
 theological 39–40
Corot, Camille 90
Cosin, John 123

Cosnett, Elizabeth 19, 49
courtesy rhymes 110–11
Coverdale, Miles 24
Coward, Noël 42, 107, 110, 115
Cowper, William 11, 24, 61, 74, 87, 91, 129
  assonance 98
  and borrowings 130
  inversion 98
  and language 93, 94, 96
Cranmer, Thomas 38
creativity 122–6
  and criticism 133, 137
  données 125–6
Creighton, Mandell 7–8
criticism 133–7
  and creativity 133, 137
  self-criticism 134–5, 136
Crossman, Samuel 2, 11, 102–3, 118
Cunningham, Alison 95
Cutts, Peter 18

Dakers, Lionel xx, 140–1
Dale, R. W. 4
Dart, R. Thurston 59
Darwin, Charles 3
Darwin, Henrietta 133–4
David, King 20
Davidson, Randall 75
Davie, Donald 147
Daw, Carl 19
Day-Lewis, C. 70, 80, 85, 125, 133
de la Mare, Walter xiv, 79–80, 95, 122–3
Dearmer, Percy 2, 15, 71, 87, 93, 112
denominationalism 40–2
Dickinson, Emily 80, 82
Dixon, Macneile 132
Doddridge, Philip 61, 63
Drain, Susan 72–3
Dryden, John 129–30
Duck, Ruth 19
Dunbar, William 80
Dwelly, F. W. 1
Dylan, Bob 17

Ecclesiastes, Book of 73
echoes 129–32
Elgar, Edward 43
Edwards, David 40, 141
Eliot, T. S. xiii, xiv, 22, 70, 82, 85, 93, 96, 95, 116, 132
Ellerton, John 1–2, 17, 26, 30, 38, 87, 90, 123, 130
  on content and form 70, 75–6
Elliott, Charlotte 112
endings 78–9, 80
enjambment 98–100
evangelism 75
Evans, David 34
experience: and truth 147–8
expressiveness 38
eye rhymes 110–11

Faber, F. W. 17, 72
false (near) rhymes 109–10, 111–12
Farrell, Bernadette 19
feminine rhymes 109, 110
Field, Frank 141–2
Fisk Jubilee Singers 40–1
Flecker, James Elroy 113–14
Fletcher, Andrew 4
Fletcher, G. B. A. 112
Flew, R. Newton 90
Foley, Brian 19
form: and content 69–83
Frost, Robert 63–4, 80, 114
  and creativity 122, 124–5
  on meaning and language 85, 89–90, 96
  on rhyme and metre 108, 111, 113

Gardner, Helen 73
Gaunt, Alan 18
Gelineau, Joseph 142
genuineness 72
Gilbert, W. S. 55, 113, 114, 132
Gill, Caroline xx
Glover, T. R. 4
Gore, Charles xiv
Gosse, Edmund 42–3
Graham, Billy 63
Grahame, James 75
Grahame, Kenneth 75
Graves, Robert 79, 97
Gray, Scotty xiv
Great Ormond Street Hospital, London 87–9
Greatorex, Walter xvi–xvii
Greeves, Arthur 113, 128

Hallam, Arthur 108
Hammerstein, Oscar II 55, 113
Hammond, Cally 101
Handel, G. F. 146
Hardy, G. H. 2, 63, 71, 76, 108
Hardy, Thomas 16, 27, 62, 85, 124
Hare, Augustus 6
Harwood, Basil 42
Heber, Reginald 14, 44, 97–8, 133
Hebrews, Letter to the 92
Hemingway, Ernest 136
Henry, Matthew 73
Henson, Herbert Hensley 75, 137
Herbert, George 2, 4, 11, 28, 146
Hindmarsh, Bruce 38, 125
Hopkins, John 28–9
Houghton, Frank 18, 19
Housman, A. E. xiv–xvi, 56–7, 61–2, 63, 96, 104
  and criticism 136
  poetic structure 100
  and revision 126–7
  rhymes 112
  A Shropshire Lad 56–7, 96, 127
Housman, Laurence 61, 127
Humphreys, C. F. (C. F. Alexander) 15
Hunnis, William 24

INDEX

Hustad, Donald 67, 148
hymn collection titles 24–5
hymn explosion 17–18, 143
hymnicide 50
hymns
  classification of 25
  definitions 1–2, 31
  familiarity of 10–12, 16
  future of 140–50
  given-ness of 17
  good 37–40
  heritage of 11–12
  new hymns, reasons for 10–22
  not so good 39–50
  publication process 19–20
  purpose of 1–8
  structure of 14, 15–16

identities 110
Idle, Christopher 19, 28, 60, 108, 143
imagery 38, 87, 91, 94, 130, 147–8
  biblical imagery 50, 73–5, 94, 133
imagination 60, 76, 86, 91, 95, 132
inclusivity 13, 38, 48–50, 127–8
inexact rhymes 109–10, 111–12
inspiration 123–6
internal rhymes 112
intimacy 91–2
inversion 98

James, P. D. 93
Jeremiah, Book of 33
Jesus, the Lord 6, 26, 50, 94, 140, 142
Jewel, John 145
Job, Book of 87
John of Damascus 11
John of Salisbury, Bishop of Chartres 33
Johnson, Samuel xiii, 4, 83, 93–4, 134
Jones, Richard 92
Jowett, Benjamin 37
Jubilate Group 19
Julian, John 30, 31, 46, 86
Julian of Norwich 94

Kaan, Fred 18, 62, 142
Keats, John 109, 128
Keble, John 2, 17, 30, 43, 63, 76–7, 82, 86, 99, 130
Kelly, Thomas 131
Ken, Thomas 132
Kendrick, Graham 18, 143
Kern, Jerome 55
Kethe, William 47–8, 98
Kidner, Derek xix, 8, 26–7, 73, 125, 145
Kings, First book of 133
Kipling, Rudyard 58, 77
Klee, Paul 80
Knox, Ronald 12, 61, 92, 96, 122, 144
Koestler, Arthur 124

Lacock, Geoffrey 19
Lambert, Constant 33

Lang, Cosmo Gordon 75
language
  archaic 13, 47–8
  changes in 12–15, 92–3
  inclusive 13, 48–50, 127–8
  and meaning 85–104
Larkin, Philip xiv, xx, 6, 56, 76, 78, 128
  on content and form 70, 83
  on creativity 123–4
  and criticism 136
  on meaning and language 90
  on rhyme and metre 107, 108
Lawrence, D. H. 57
Lazarus, Emma 94
Leach, John 33
Leacock, Stephen 61
Leckebusch, Martin 30
Lee, Vernon (Violet Paget) 60
Levi, Peter 126
Leviticus, Book of 73
Lewis, C. S. xiii, xiv, xviii, 10, 15, 38, 51, 128
  on form and content 80–1, 83
  on Greek oral tradition 55
  on imagination 60
  on meaning and language 91, 97
  and metaphors 132–3
  on rhyme and metre 108, 113
Lewis, Warren 37–8, 46
Liddon, Henry 141
Linklater, Eric 60
Littledale, R. F. 130
Llewellyn, William xvi, xx
Lloyd-Jones, Martyn 56
Lofthouse, W. F. 52, 74
'London Pride' 115
long metre 117
Lonsdale, Lord 99
Lovelace, Austin 83
Luff, Alan 18
Luther, Martin 28, 135, 145
Lyte, Henry 16, 103, 145

Macaulay, Rose 28, 135–6
McCheyne, Robert Murray 140
MacDonald, George 111
McGrath, Alister 141
MacGregor, Neil 92
Mackail, J. W. 136
Macmillan, Alexander xiii
Macmillan, Harold 86
majesty 91–2
Manning, Bernard xiv, 5, 14, 39, 51, 58, 74, 103, 147
Marriott, John 92
Martyr, Peter 145
Marvell, Andrew 107, 132
Masefield, John 64
Mason, John 2
Matheson, George 125
Mayhew, Kevin 18
meaning: and language 85–104

Mendelssohn, Felix 146
metaphors 132–3
metre
  definition of 117
  and rhyme 107–20
metrical psalms 28–31
Micklem, Nathaniel 62
Milgate, Wesley 58
Milne, A. A. 61
Milton, John 57, 93, 95, 97, 128, 129, 146
Moffat, James 12
Montague, C. E. 90
Montgomery, James xiv, 11, 20, 28, 29, 39, 61, 116, 130, 147
Moody, D. L. 140
Moore, George 56
Morris, Colin 144–5
Mothering Sunday 89
Motion, Andrew 76
Mowbray, David 19
Moxon, Edward xiv
multiple rhymes 112
music: words and 55–67

Nash, Ogden 118
Neale, J. M. 17, 32, 41, 47, 140
near (false) rhymes 109–10, 111–12
Newman, John Henry 17, 40, 43, 86
Newman, Richard 24
Newsome, David 43
Newton, John 11, 24, 38, 94, 125, 134, 147
Nicholson, Sydney 65–6
Nicolson, Harold 129

Ogilvie, David 123–4
onomatopoeia 94–6
openings 77–8
Opie, Iona and Peter 109
oral tradition: poetry 55–6
Orpen, William 75

Packer, J. I. 148
Paget, Violet (Vernon Lee) 60
partisanship, ecclesiastical 40–2
Patrick, John 29
Payne, Roger 108
perfect (true) rhymes 109, 111
Perry, Michael 19
piety: and poetry 146–7
plagiarism 129–32
Pliny the Younger 145
Plumptre, Edward 42, 45–6, 96, 136
Poe, Edgar Allen 100
Poems of Grace 81
Poincaré, Henri 124
Pott, Francis 49
Pratt, Andrew xx
Pratt Green, Fred xiii–xiv, xix, 18, 50–1, 64, 77, 100, 148
Preston, David 30
printing conventions 81–2

proper names: musical value of 57–8
psalms 25–31
punctuation 82

Quiller-Couch, Arthur 56, 147
Quinn, James 19

Ramsey, Michael 94
Rattenbury, J. E. 58
Raven, Charles 1
Raverat, Gwen 3, 110, 133–4
Rawley, Francis 72
Rennew, Anne 24
repetition 100–3
revision 126–8
Reynolds, W. J. 40
rhyme: and metre 107–20
rhyming dictionaries 113
Richards, Grant 112, 136
Romaine, William 17
Rossetti, Christina 63, 95, 123
Rossetti, Dante Gabriel 93–4
Routley, Erik xiv, 3, 18, 50, 118, 129, 135, 140–1
  on content and form 74, 76
  and criticism 135
  on endings 78–9
  on future of hymnody 143
  on music and faith 65
  on words and music 56, 57, 61
Royde-Smith, Naomi 79
Ruffer, Tim xx
Runcie, Robert 148
Ruskin, John 46
Ryland, John 134

Sacks, Oliver 119–20
Sackville-West, Vita 129
St John, Patricia 66–7
St John's Gospel 6
St Luke's Gospel 13
St Mark's Gospel 11
St Matthew's Gospel 11
St Paul 11, 20, 24–6, 34, 38, 73–4, 87
St Peter, First letter of 87
Saintsbury, George 132
Saward, Michael 19
Sayers, Dorothy L. 71
Scott, Walter 57, 129
screens, texts on 82–3
Scruton, Roger 33
Seddon, James 19
self-criticism 134–5, 136
sense: and sound 94–6
Shakespeare, William 110, 117
  and borrowings 131, 132
  language 13, 49, 92, 93, 94, 97
  sonnets 2, 57
Sharpe, Eric 17
Shea, George Beverly 63
Shelley, P. B. 2, 4, 71
Shorney, George xviii–xix, 10

INDEX

short metre 117
Shute, Nevil 60–1
Sidney, Philip 39
Simeon, Charles 5, 21, 38
simplicity 75–6
sincerity 70–3
singability 38
singing: and celebration 25, 142, 145
Sitwell, Edith 94
Smyth, Charles xv
Snow, C. P. 76
Sondheim, Stephen 83, 109, 110, 111, 114–15
songs: in Bible 21–2
sound: and sense 94–6
spiritual songs 25, 31
spirituality 38
Staff, Kathy 3–4
Stennett, Samuel 130
Sternhold, Thomas 28–9
Stevenson, Robert Louis xvi, 95, 113, 119
Stone, Samuel J. 44–5, 110, 131
Stott, John 27–8, 59, 132
Struther, Jan (Joyce Anstruther, Torrens, Placzek) 18, 71, 142

Tasker, R. V. G. 148–9
Tate, Nahum 29, 64, 142
Taylor, Cyril 62–3
Taylor, Herbert xvi
temperance 2–3
Temple, Sebastian 108
Temple, William 6, 38
Tennyson, Alfred xiv, 57, 20, 37, 64, 94–5, 141
  and creativity 123–4
  and criticism 136
  on language 97
  on plagiarism 129
  and revision 126
  and rhyme 110, 112–13
Tennyson, Hallam 37, 124
Thirty-nine Articles of Religion 7
Thomas, Dylan 96, 130–1
Thomas, R. S. 124
Thompson, Francis 132
Tindall, Adrienne 135
Tolkien, J. R. R. 125
Tolstoy, L. N. 39
Toplady, A. M. 13, 76, 131
Torrens, Joyce (Jan Struther) 71
Townend, Stuart 28
Tozer, A. W. 32
Trajan, Emperor Marcus 145
Tredinnick, Noël 19
triple rhymes 112
Tristram, H. B. 77
Troeger, Thomas 19, 142–3
Trollope, Anthony 76
true (perfect) rhymes 109, 111
truth 4–5, 74, 75, 85, 131
  and experience 147–9
  worship 'in spirit and in truth' 6, 7, 38

Tucker, Francis Bland 19
Tucker, Peter xix
Turl, Emma 19
Turner, W. J. 57
Tyndale, William 47, 87

Valéry, Paul 126
Vaughan Williams, Ralph 57, 65, 71, 146

Walker, Christopher 28
Ward, Pete 32–3, 34
Warren, Herbert 37
Warren, Max 75
Watson, J. R. xiv, 2, 5, 13, 31, 42, 148
  on content and form 69
  on endings 79
  on meaning and language 90
  on textual similarities 130
  on words, sound of 57
Watts, Isaac 1, 2, 5–6, 11, 29, 61, 80, 99, 128–9, 137, 148
  and borrowing 130, 131
  on content and form 76
  on emendation 134
  endings 78
  hymn collection titles 24
  on meaning and language 91–2, 94
  and metre 117–18
  poetic structure 100
  and revision 126
  rhyme 110
  and self-criticism 134–5
Waugh, Evelyn 144
Webb, Jimmy 55, 113
Weber, Derek 60
Wesley, Charles xv, xx, 11, 12, 13, 16–17, 21, 24, 39–40, 44, 60–1, 77–8, 100, 136, 146–7, 149
  'And can it be' 86–7
  assonance 98
  biblical imagery 73–4
  and borrowing 131
  chiasmus 103
  and Dryden 129–30
  endings 78, 79
  enjambment 99
  'Forth in thy name' 51–2
  hymn collection titles 24
  'Jesu, lover of my soul' 56, 103, 127
  and language 91, 93
  and metre 116, 118
  on music 66
  poetic structure 99
  poetry and piety 147
  proper names, use of 58
  and rhyme 81, 109–10, 116
  and self-criticism 134
Wesley, John 7, 11–12, 13–14, 25, 73, 77, 80, 136, 148
  editorial work 77, 136–7
  on emendation 134
  enjambment 99

Wesley, John (*cont.*)
　hymn collection titles 24
　on poetry and piety 146–7
　and repetition 101
Wesley, Samuel 146
West, Jonathan xix
Weymouth, Richard 12
White, Michael 125
Whitefield, George 13, 40
Whittier, John Greenleaf 57, 63, 133
Wilbur, Richard 101
Wild Goose team, Iona 19
Wilks, Samuel xv
Willey, Basil 91, 133
Williams, Rowan xv, 47, 74
Wilson, David 19, 118
Wilson, John 66, 135
Wilson, Leonard 149
Winkworth, Catherine 146
Wiseman, Nicholas 41
Withers, Percy 57
Wodehouse, P. G. 98, 127

Wogan, Terry 60
Wooton, Janet 19
words
　and images 60
　and music 55–67
Wordsworth, Christopher 17, 44, 133
Wordsworth, Dorothy 135
Wordsworth, William xiv, 29, 80, 83, 113, 134, 147
　and borrowing 131
　and creativity 126
　enjambment 99
　on metre 119
worship songs 31–4, 107–8, 110, 143–4
worship wars 34
Wren, Brian 18
Wright, Tom 26, 142

Yattendon Hymnal 46, 112
Yeats, W. B. 56, 86, 125–6

Zeffirelli, Franco 60